European Traditions
in the Twentieth Century

European

Traditions

in the Twentieth Century

William W. MacDonald

John M. Carroll

FORUM PRESS

For Maryellen and Ryan

Contents

Preface

This book contains twelve original essays on the main political, economic, social, cultural, and military themes in twentieth century European history. The authors, although concerned with sophisticated, scholarly material, have made a real effort to write clearly and understandably for the undergraduate student so that his reading in European history will be both meaningful and enjoyable. Designed to complement a standard twentieth century European history text, this book presents interpretive material, new viewpoints as well as traditional ones, and can, therefore, assist in stimulating class discussion. The authors have not hesitated to express opinions or to pass judgments, and thus they present twentieth century European history as an exciting, thought-provoking study rather than a mere collection of facts.

European Traditions in the Twentieth Century is divided into three interrelated parts with a general introduction. The general introduction surveys Europe on the eve of World War I, critically analyzing Europe's apparent though fleeting dominance in the world. William W. MacDonald's thesis is that it was the very superficiality of Europe's ephemeral position of dominance that contributed to the "end of the European age" in world history. Almost all Europeans interpreted Europe's role as world leader in 1914 as a natural right; few Europeans saw that the very forces that created European supremacy, forces like nationalism, militarism, and imperialism, would be the same forces that would shatter Europe's grand illusion that Europe, European society, and European culture would continue to play the dominant role they played in the world since the Renaissance. Part I, the "World War I and Its Impact on Europe" section, deals with the cataclysmic effects of the Great War on European society. It covers such diverse topics as the origins and consequences of the war, the Versailles settlement and its aftermath, and the Russian Revolution and its effects on both the Soviet Union and Western Europe. Part II, the "Europe Between the World Wars" section, analyzes the triumphs and failures of European democracies during the 1920s and 1930s, the bizarre Fascist movements of Adolf Hitler and Benito Mussolini, the complex and contradictory European diplomacy that contributed to the origins of World War II, and the course and consequences of that war on Europe and the world. Part III, the "European Society After World War II" section, focuses on Europe's remarkable economic, political, and social recovery after the war, the European search for security in the nuclear age, and, finally, the collapse of the European colonial empires and the results of that collapse on Europe and the world. The book concludes with an intriguing and, we think, a prophetic analysis of today's Europe, in which a concerted effort has been made to give a thoroughgoing exposition of contemporary Europe's dilemmas, problems, successes, failures, and future.

We would like to acknowledge the numerous scholars who contributed to the completion of this book. Many friends offered suggestions, many colleagues read parts of the book in manuscript; to all our friends and colleagues, we thank you. We wish to thank Ms. Frances Shelton for preparing the essays for publication. We wish also to thank the various museums, picture agencies, archives, and individuals who helped us locate and obtain illustrations. We also wish to express our gratitude to the staff of Forum Press, especially to Vandora Elfrink for her editorial assistance, to Pauline Spencer, who directed the project during production and to Erby M. Young, who initiated the project and continued his strong interest in publishing new materials in history. We wish, finally, to express our appreciation to the historians who contributed essays to this book. They were helpful, met deadlines and accepted our editorial revisions with remarkable courtesy.

John M. Carroll
William W. MacDonald

Leon Trotsky, Russian revolutionary leader. (*Courtesy of the National Archives*)

INTRODUCTION

Europe's Grand Illusion in 1914

William W. MacDonald

The prevailing mood among Europe's educated classes prior to World War I was one of unbounded optimism and pride. In 1914, indeed, Europe was enjoying a power and a prestige that was unparalleled in her history. Never before had a culture, broadly defined as Western civilization, affected the world so widely, so intimately, so dynamically. As the great German historian Leopold von Ranke observed in 1879, nothing could stop Europe from impressing itself upon mankind. Irresistibly, Ranke wrote, and "armed with weapons and science, the spirit of the West subdues the world." This concept had been echoed previously by the German philosopher Georg Hegel, who commented that the "Europeans had sailed around the world and for them it was a sphere. Whatever has not yet fallen under their sway is either not worth the trouble or is destined to fall under it." By 1914 Hegel's prophecy had been fulfilled, and there was much truth to the maxim that when Europe sneezed the rest of the world caught a cold. There were, however, few if any men wise enough to foresee that by 1914 the European supremacy was, in reality, a grand illusion.

These European attitudes of optimism and arrogance were well-founded in certain indisputable facts. The accomplishments of Europe's scientific, economic, political, and intellectual life since the 100 years that had elapsed since the French Revolution were triumphs that produced confidence and optimism throughout Europe. Political freedom and industrial power had combined within Europe to create a political system that appeared to set the standard throughout the world. By any measurable yardstick, the European century that began in 1815 (the ending of the Napoleonic age) and ended in 1914 (the beginning of the twentieth century) was the most expansive, teeming, and varied of any equal period in European history. European man, it appeared, had conquered his violent past, was beginning to control his own fate, was fulfilling the optimistic prophecy of the eighteenth century Enlightenment, that is, human progress and the perfectibility of mankind.

During the preceding 100 years, Europe had more than doubled its population, from 200 million in 1800 to 450 million in 1914. And most of those millions enjoyed standards of living and comfort never before available to so many peoples. Europe's mechanized industries, particularly those in Western Europe, poured out products in steadily increasing volume, at lower cost, which consistently increased the per capita income of its workers. European education had brought literacy to millions; railroads and the new modes of communication made all Europeans neighbors. Slavery and the notorious slave trade had been extinguished nearly everywhere, and, with the notable exception of Russia, torture and judicial and administrative injustices were being abolished; laws had been passed with increasing regularity for the protection of children, workers, and animals. Women, often the beasts of European society, had been emancipated from many of their ancient disabilities, even acquiring the right to vote in several Western European states. Medicine and public health, moreover, had been vastly improved; hospitals were no longer chambers of horror; infant mortality had been cut to a fraction of its previous toll; the span of human life was steadily extended. In domestic politics, most importantly, as the success of Bismarck's social welfare program in Germany demonstrated, the utility of political art was measured not by government repression but by government assistance. Finally, in the realm of ideas and culture, Europeans led the way and the world followed. The "isms" of progress, from liberalism to positivism to socialism to radicalism, elicited positive response from across the seas, while European cultural and intellectual life, headed by the famous and glorious names of Freud, Einstein, Renoir, Mahler, Brahms, and hundreds of others, was the envy of the world. It is little wonder that Europeans thought of themselves as the civilized world.

The "civilized" Europeans who reflected on their happy lot were keenly aware that their society played a special role in the world, a role clearly out of all proportion to its size. Geographically, a mere peninsula of Asia, Europe is only a third the size of Africa and little more than a fourth as large as Asia. But while the major part of the world remained fixed in its traditions and customs, observed the French poet Paul Valéry, the little European cape on the Asiatic continent set itself clearly apart from the rest of the world. And wherever the European spirit prevails, wrote Valéry

> one sees the maximum of needs, the maximum of work, the maximum of capital, the maximum of production, the maximum of ambition, the maximum of power, the maximum of modification of external nature, and the maximum of communications and exchanges.

Economically, Europe was the hub of an elaborate and intricate global network of production, distribution, and consumption. In 1914, despite the recent economic surge of the United States and Japan as industrial powers, Europe still retained an impressive lead in the world's economic life. Europe produced approximately 55 percent of the world's coal and 60 percent of the world's shipping. London had evolved into the financial capital of the world, handling, for example, 70 percent of American companies' foreign accounts. The rest of the world had been drawn irresistibly into a single world economy with Europe as its economic keystone. The great English economist John Maynard Keynes harked back nostalgically in the 1920s to the pre-World War I European economy, recalling that a Londoner, a Parisian, a Berliner

> could order by telephone, sipping his morning tea in bed, the various products of the whole earth, in such quantity as he might see fit, and reasonably expect their early delivery upon his doorstep; he could at the same moment and by the same means adventure his wealth in the natural resources and new enterprises of any quarter of the world, and share, without exertion or even trouble, in their prospective fruits and advantages; or he could decide to couple the security of his fortunes with the good faith of the townspeople of any substantial municipality in any continent that his fancy or information might recommend.
>
> He could secure forthwith, if he wished it, cheap and comfortable means of transit to any country or climate without passport of other formality, could despatch his servant to the neighborhood office of a bank for such supply of the precious metals as might seem convenient, and could proceed abroad to foreign quarters, without knowledge of their religion, language, or customs, bearing coined wealth upon his person, and would consider himself greatly aggrieved and much surprised at the least interference. But, most important of all, he regarded this state of affairs as normal, certain, and permanent, and any deviation from it as aberrant, scandalous, and avoidable.

This personal, individual sense of security created not only a personal, individual arrogance but also a collective arrogance which often took the form of an aggressive nationalism. Each of the European nations, but particularly those in Western Europe, exhibited their national pride and sense of security in its own way. England, possessing the greatest navy, the greatest empire, and the most money, was solid and steady, the great arbiter of international disputes. Germany, which had just recently completed her unification under the leadership of Prince Bismarck, possessed the largest, most feared army in the world, a strong navy, the most dynamic and expansive economy in Europe, and the most admired scholarship and culture in Western civilization—everyone, it appeared, seemed to genuflect before the German power. In France, this was the period of the *belle* epoch, the banquet years, the good life, when Europeans spoke of being as content as God in France. The Austro-Hungarians took pride in the realization that their capital, Vienna, was the most beautiful, captivating, exciting city in the world, while Italians rejoiced that Rome, even after two thousand years, remained, as ever, the "eternal city." Even that mysterious, enigmatic, brooding, sleeping giant, Russia, appeared to be making her way, however slow and tortuous, along the road toward economic, political, and human progress.

Europe, then, was the intellectual, cultural, and economic center of the world and justly proud of it. But, more importantly, she was also the military and political center of world power and she was aggressively expanding. European imperialism—the acquisition of colonial empires—was certainly not unique to the twentieth century, for Europeans had been establishing colonies as early as the fifteenth century, bringing them into the orbit of Western civilization and spreading the culture of European society to such distant places as Australia, South America, Canada, and the United States. But the European colonizing activities of the previous four hundred years pales before the great age of imperialism (1870-1914), when the European powers seized immense tracts of land throughout the underdeveloped lands of Asia and Africa, as well as the islands of the Pacific and the Near East. European powers created vast empires, and they accomplished this gigantic feat essentially without recourse to war.

The origins and motivations for the "new imperialism" of the late nineteenth and early twentieth century have confounded and confused historians for the past 100 years; there is, of course, no consensus of opinion. To some scholars, imperialism was an "atavism," the result of culturally inherited political and social attitudes which continued to exist and prosper from the previous age when European expansion had a justifiable existence and purpose. To other historians, the new imperialism was the result of a profound mission of Europeans to Christianize and civilize the world of heathens and barbarians: in the words of the Marquess of Salisbury, "I do not exactly know the cause of this sudden revolution. But there it is. It is a great force—a great civilizing, Christianizing force."

5

To still other observers, the expansion of Europe in the age of imperialism was an essentially nationalistic phenomenon which enjoyed wide support in Europe, created strategic bases for the European powers throughout the world, and created the famous "white man's burden" mentality in Western civilization for more than a century. To still others, finally, particularly Marxist and economic determinist historians, imperialism was the result of economic drives, the result of financial weaknesses inherent within the European capitalist system which forced European financial leaders to expand overseas to invest their surplus goods and surplus capital. According to this theory, made famous by the British economist J. A. Hobson and the great Russian revolutionary leader Nikolai Lenin, imperialism was the last stage of capitalist development, which not only revealed but also would destroy the contradictions within the European capitalist world. These theorists suggested that the consistent maldistribution of wealth in Europe left European workers with such low wages that capitalists could only escape periodic depressions by searching and conquering newer and richer markets throughout the world.

Whether late nineteenth and early twentieth century imperialism was the result of God, Gold, or Glory, and the debate on its origins is still raging, several factors, nonetheless, are now clearly evident. First, the scramble for colonial domination created European tensions abroad in the areas of conflict, particularly in Africa and the Near East, and exacerbated tensions within Europe itself. European political, economic, military, and nationalistic rivalries, indeed, can be traced directly to imperialist conflicts, most notably between Germany and France and between Germany and Great Britain. Germany's desire to find her "place in the sun" and her opponents' desire to hold on to their established "places in the sun" led to a series of crises in Europe. The German-British naval race, the Moroccan crises of 1905 and 1911, and numerous other conflicts shook the fragile balance of power in Europe prior to World War I, and most certainly contributed, in an admittedly unmeasurable way, to the coming of the Great War of 1914. Second, despite these tensions and crises, there is little doubt that imperialism, at least from the

European point of view, was a remarkable success. Between 1870-1914 the Europeans parceled out among themselves almost all of Africa, either as colonies or as "protectorates," most of the Near East, primarily through economic and diplomatic pressures, and staked out "spheres of influence" in most of Asia. By 1914, England possessed an empire 140 times the size of Britain; France 20 times its own size; Belgium 80 times; Holland 60 times. Germany and Italy, latecomers to the imperialist tradition, nevertheless gobbled up essentially unprofitable lands in Africa, to reaffirm, as the Italians believed, their "sacred egotism." Finally, European imperialism created several contradictions within European society, particularly the Western democratic European nations. Colonial imperialist rule was, by definition, an anomaly in a democracy, a contradiction that many Europeans rationalized in Rudyard Kipling's famous phrase: "the white man's burden." Conquering and ruling millions and millions of nonwhites was a heady business, an ego-building process, and it certainly encouraged ugly sentiments of nationalistic and racial superiority already latent in European politics and society. In reality, "the white man's burden" essentially meant to most Europeans "the white man's superiority," a racial theory which, when brought to its logical conclusion, would have ominous results in twentieth century European history.

All these factors, therefore, economic domination, intellectual and cultural leadership, political and military supremacy, and world hegemony, appeared to produce in Europeans an unbounded optimism in themselves and in their European heritage. These factors seemed to produce an equilibrium so secure, so stable, so *evident* as almost to give the atmosphere of permanence. The primacy of Europe and Europeans was a fact taken for granted by Europeans, who naturally assumed that their small continent would continue to enjoy in the twentieth century the same supremacy they had exerted in the world since the Renaissance, some four hundred years ago. Very few Europeans were aware that the end of the European age was already on the horizon; very few Europeans were conscious of the historical fate that was about to overtake them. Instead, almost all Europeans believed it was the natural right of Europe and Europeans to dominate the world. In this sense, then, the period just prior to World War I, the period say between 1900 to 1914, can thus best be seen and interpreted as Europe's grand illusion, for there were dozens of factors present in European society in 1914 that would help ignite a world war, a devastating war that would shatter the European supremacy and bring about the political collapse of European society.

In retrospect, it is now apparent that the European age, at least as Europeans had known it, was over and that the world would no longer continue to pay economic, political, and cultural tribute to European society. There were, in fact, several ominous signs of decay, of fall and decline, already apparent prior to the Great War of 1914. The inadequacy of Europe's territorial base was already clear. Its scale was too small, its national and international markets were too restricted, its industries were too old, too dated, too cumbersome. The European economies had been slowly put·together, a piece here, a piece there, a piece added here and there as the needs dictated. Out of this process had emerged a highly complex and extremely delicate structure that was vitally dependent upon overseas sources of food stuffs and raw materials, sources which if they were denied to the Europeans would throw the European economies into large-scale depressions and major alterations. At the same time, Europe's supremacy in the world had been challenged by force of arms and been found wanting. In 1898 the Spanish fought the United States and were soundly routed in the Spanish-American War, much to the amazement of the German kaiser, William II, who had predicted that the hidalgo would punch Uncle Sam black and blue. Similarly, the Russians had been humiliated by the Japanese in the Russo-Japanese War of 1904, an event that shook both Russia, leading to the political revolution of 1905, and the rest of Europe, which assumed that white Europeans could never lose to inferior yellow people like the Japanese. The very forces, indeed, that seemed to make for European strength, European supremacy, were, in reality, the very forces that would lead to European weaknesses and European decline. The so-called "isms" of progress, like nationalism, imperialism, militarism, and racism, as then interpreted by Europeans, were really "isms" of decay that would catapult Europe into two world wars and lead to the collapse of European society and culture.

The single most important issue in pre-World War I Europe was the fact that like the Greece of Pericles' time and like the Italy of the Renaissance period, Europe was characterized by political disunity. Like the ancient Greeks, who gave the world the city-state, which promoted great cultural and intellectual creativity but also provoked bitter rivalries that would eventually destroy Greek civilization, the Europeans gave the world the nation-state, which while promoting cultural, industrial, and intellectual creativity, also provoked bitter rivalries. The Europeans considered these rivalries, say between France and Germany or between Russia and Austria-Hungary, as essentially healthy competition that contributed to Europe's supremacy in the world; they ignored its potential dangers and totally failed to comprehend the catastrophes to which such rivalries could lead. And, most importantly, if the so-called healthy rivalries threatened to degenerate into debilitating wars, there was no positive means for Europeans to resolve the potential conflict except through a show of force, the rattling of sabers, which, in turn, never solved the problem but merely postponed the clash of arms.

During the nineteenth century, there were essentially two methods employed by European states to keep the peace. The first was the balance of power. But the balance of power in 1815 did not mean as it meant in 1914—a balanced alignment of two hostile coalitions; it meant instead that no European state could obtain aggrandizement against another European state without the consent of the rest of the major European nations. The second method of maintaining peace was "federative polity." Federative polity was a system by which European states discussed and acted in unison in an institution, like the twentieth century League of Nations or the United Nations, which theoretically possessed collective sovereignty or power over and above that of the individual sovereign state. The complete realization of the full claims of sovereignty leaves only anarchy between competing states; the complete realization of federative polity leaves no sovereign organization anywhere.

The political structure of Europe in mid-nineteenth century European society can best be described as federative polity, which emerged from the numerous conferences, the "Congresses," that settled European disputes by diplomacy and negotiations. During the period, indeed, between the Congress of Vienna in 1815 and the completion of the unification of Germany in 1871, there existed in Europe the "Concert of Europe," a valid if somewhat vague federative polity premise that European disputes should be negotiated by European diplomacy for the general good of European society as a whole. The Concert of Europe was a belief, an idea, that there existed a harmony between European states and that this harmony would tend to keep the peace. The Concert of Europe was a concept which held that there was a society of European states, a community of European interests, which bound all European states to join together to achieve European peace and stability. The Concert of Europe was essentially the instrument by which the great powers of Europe gave their consent to the actions of individual European states. This Concert of Europe worked remarkably well for almost half a century, for between 1815 and 1859 no great territorial changes took place in Europe which were not ratified or legalized by a European conference.

Between 1859 and 1871, from the beginning of the unification of Italy to the end of the unification of Germany, however, the federative polity Concert of Europe came crashing down, and out of the ruins emerged the new national states of Italy and Germany and the international anarchy of the armed peace of 1871-1914. It was the collapse of the Concert of Europe that elicited the observations from Bismarck, Mazzini, and others that "Europe was no more," that they "no longer saw Europe—old Europe dead," that a "new historical age is upon us; it is a terrifying age."

The Concert of Europe was greatly weakened by the Crimean War of 1854, the unification of Italy wars of 1859-1860, and the Austro-Prussian War of 1886. But the final blow, the fatal blow, to the Concert of Europe was the unification of Germany, which occurred at France's expense. If the Concert of Europe was working, was a viable concept in 1871, a conference of European nations would have met to resolve the territorial disputes between France and Germany resulting from the French defeat in the Franco-Prussian War of 1870—and that is what French leaders proposed at the time. But England refused to agree to such a conference and publicly applauded France's defeat, her traditional enemy, for it weakened England's chief rival in the imperialistic race of empire-building, particularly in Africa. The Austrians also opposed the calling of a European congress and instead took secret delight that France, which had aided Italy in helping to drive Austria out of Italy during the unification of Italy, was now being severely punished for such a transgression. The Russians, too, rejected the summoning of a conference and, instead, took advantage of the confusion the war created to denounce the Treaty of Paris of 1856, which had forbidden Russian naval vessels on the Black Sea, and to occupy militarily that body of water. The Italians also rejected the idea of a European conference of states and, instead, took advantage of the war to seize Rome and the Papal Estates from the Pope, who had been under French protection up to the beginning of the Franco-Prussian War in 1870.

What did Bismarck, Mazzini, and other European observers mean when they commented that Europe was dead, that the idea of Europe was no more, that a new and terrifying age was upon Europe? They meant that the system designed by the Congress of Vienna, the Concert of Europe, was dead, gone, finished. The society of European states, the harmony of European interests, the community of European nations was dead. European states had ceased to exist as a European social polity and by the end of the unification periods of Italy and Germany, the Concert of Europe had ceased to function. There existed at the end of the Franco-Prussian War in 1871 a seriously, ominously divided Europe, for each European state possessed its own *national* aims and goals, as opposed to *European* aims and goals, and the remainder of European states in reality opposed the individual, national goals of the European nation-states. The dream of a federated Europe had dissolved into the reality of a nationally desperate Europe. There no longer existed European cooperation; there no longer existed the European harmony of interests. Each European state, motivated by purely national ends, was poised to acquire what it could acquire without regard to the general welfare of Europe as a whole. Europe had entered into a system of international anarchy. The European armies, for example, which in 1860 had been the chief bulwark against domestic rebellions, were now in 1871 the chief bulwark against the threat of other European states. The accomplishments of Bismarck's policy of "Blood and Iron," of *realpolitik,* the belief that force and only force can achieve success in both domestic and foreign relations, was not lost on his adversaries. Within a decade of the unification of Germany, all the major continental states of Europe had introduced universal military conscription and refashioned their armies on the German model.

The unification of Germany, then, not only delivered the final blow to the Concert of Europe and established a frightening system of international anarchy in European foreign relations, but it also inaugurated a period of intense fear and insecurity in Europe, because if there was no federated way of resolving disputes, no congresses, for example, then each European state was alone in the world, a separate entity in the jungle of tangled European rivalries and hostilities. The result of such insecurity and fear, the effect of such terrifying isolation, was the emergence of the complex and explosive alliance systems that dominated European history from the unification of Germany in 1871 to the outbreak of world war in 1914. The architect of the alliance systems was Otto von Bismarck, Germany's famous Iron Chancellor. Bismarck was a brilliant diplomat, the most important figure in European history during the latter half of the nineteenth century, a man of many shades and nuances, a man of great vision who correctly understood that in the world of foreign politics there were never any rigid antagonisms, that any nation's current ally could be a potential adversary or that any nation's current enemy could be a potential ally. Bismarck believed, after Germany had achieved her unification and emerged as a dominant power in European politics, that the rest of Europe would not tolerate further German expansion or aggression. He believed, therefore, that Germany must then become the international arbiter of European disputes and that Germany must have seriously limited goals. Bismarck was also aware, however, that France was not reconciled to her military defeat and to the loss of Alsace-Lorraine from the Franco-Prussian War; but France alone could never challenge Germany successfully in war because of the superiority of Germany's army, population, and economy. The only way France could challenge Germany would be if France acquired an ally from one of Europe's major states. The diplomatic isolation of France, therefore, became the cardinal goal of Bismarck's foreign policy, and he achieved this goal through numerous and complex (and occasionally contradictory) alliances with the major continental European states. The most successful and lasting alliance system Bismarck fashioned was the Triple Alliance of Germany, Austria-Hungary, and Italy, signed in 1882 and still in effect in 1914. But all of Bismarck's brilliant foreign policy achievements were dissolved when the German kaiser, William II, dismissed him in disgrace in 1890. Bismarck's successors refused to renegotiate an alliance agreement with Russia on the false assumption that democratic France and autocratic Russia (rigid antagonists) could never reconcile their domestic hostilities to agree to an international foreign policy pact. The result of Germany's failure to agree to the so-called reinsurance treaty with Russia in 1890 was that Russia and France, then both isolated and fearful, agreed to a firm economic and military alliance in 1894. The unthinkable had happened—France, revisionist France, had acquired a major ally within Europe and now posed a serious challenge to Germany and to European peace. At the same time, moreover, Germany, under the arrogant, abrasive, and impetuous leadership of the kaiser, consistently challenged England's interests. Germany engaged England in a naval race, challenging England's naval supremacy; she announced the building of a railroad from Berlin to Baghdad, challenging England's interests in Persia and the Suez Canal; Germany demanded a significant "place in the sun," challenging England's enormous colonial empire. The result of a decade of German-English enmity was a revolution in European foreign policy, for England reversed her policy of opposition toward her traditional foreign policy enemies, the French and Russians, and instead signed a series of agreements with France and Russia that established the Triple Entente in 1907.

The insecurity of international anarchy had produced the alliance systems, and slowly but surely these alliances had grown into two hostile alignments, the Triple Alliance on the one side and the Triple Entente on the other. Europe in 1914 was ominously divided into two conflicting, antagonistic coalitions. Indeed, a veritable cold war existed between the alliances, and every international incident tended to become a test of strength between the two hostile systems. A given incident, such as the Moroccan crisis of 1905, or the Balkan crisis of 1908, or the final crisis of the assassination of the heir to the Austrian throne in 1914 could never be judged or settled on its own merits. No matter how the incident was resolved, one of the alliance systems was judged, was interpreted, as having won or lost in prestige and influence. The various countries involved in the alliance systems not only supported their policies with a show of force, but they also supported their allies' policies, even though they had nothing tangible to gain, simply because it was, in the terrifying age of international anarchy of the alliance systems, the only way to maintain the alliances and avoid being isolated and encircled by predator nations.

The economic rivalries, the imperialistic rivalries, the nationalistic rivalries, the militaristic rivalries, moreover, compounded and heightened the alliance rivalries and made Europe an armed camp in 1914. Europe was, in fact, a powder keg ready to explode and all that was needed to plunge Europe into a civil war was an incident that would once more test to the breaking point the fragile balance of power of the alliance systems. Such an incident occurred on a quiet, sunny Sunday morning on June 28, 1914, when Franz Ferdinand, the hapless heir to the Austrian throne, was murdered by members of the fanatical organization of Slavic nationalists, an event that inaugurated World War I. It is ironic that the alliances, which were designed to keep the fragile European peace, almost automatically turned a local, isolated event like the assassination into a general European war and then a world war.

While he was observing the events that catapulted Europe into World War I, the English foreign minister, Lord Grey, commented that "the lamps are going out in Europe" and they would not be put on again during his lifetime. Lord Grey was an astute observer and a deadly prophet, for the coming of war had a cataclysmic, earth-shattering influence on Europe and world history. The war destroyed European men, European treasures, and European empires and distorted the men, the treasures, and the empires that survived. It demolished institutions and ideas that in 1914 seemed imposing, like the Austro-Hungarian Empire, the German Empire, the Russian Empire, anarchism and international socialism. It gave birth to new and unexpected forces, most notably the rise of fascism in Europe in the bizarre movements of Mussolini and Hitler. The war fundamentally altered the character of European society and the pattern of European politics, making it impossible for Europe to rebuild on the past, and created situations in which Europe could not maintain domestic and international stability. It decimated a generation of future leaders and dealt an unmeasurable psychological blow to the millions who survived the war. The effect World War I had on the *timing* of history was profound, for it reduced great European powers, unprepared in psychology or policy, to permanent weakness, and other nations, like the United States and the Soviet Union, also unprepared in psychology or policy, into positions of world leadership. It ended Europe's age of liberalism, of progress, of peace, and of stability and inaugurated a period of war, of revolution, of upheaval, of chaos that is still with Europe today. Most important of all, however, World War I smashed Europe's dominant position in the world, ended the European age, and shattered Europe's grand illusion that Europe, European society, and European culture would continue to play the dominant role they had played in the world since the Renaissance.

Suggested Readings

The best introductions to twentieth century Europe are H. Stuart Hughes, *Contemporary Europe, A History* (1976 ed.); Robert O. Paxton, *Europe in the Twentieth Century* (1975); and Kent Forster, *Recent Europe, A Twentieth Century History* (1965). The European climate of opinion is explored well in G. Masur, *The Prophets of Yesterday* (1961); H. Stuart Hughes, *Consciousness and Society* (1958); and C. J. H. Hayes, *A Generation of Materialism, 1871-1900* (1941). For European technology and economy, see W. W. Rostow, *The Stages of Economic Growth* (1960) and D. S. Landes, *The Unbound Prometheus: Technological Change and Industrial Development in Western Europe from 1750 to the Present* (1969). For European nationalism, see Hans Kohn, *The Idea of Nationalism* (1961 ed.) and B. C. Shafer, *Faces of Nationalism: New Realities and Old Myths* (1961). The phenomenon of European imperialism is examined in E. M. Winslow, *The Pattern of Imperialism* (1948), Joseph Schumpeter, *Imperialism and Social Classes* (1955 ed.), M. E. Townsend, *European Colonial Expansion Since 1870* (1941); the classic economic interpretations of imperialism are in J. A. Hobson, *Imperialism, A Study* (1902) and in V. I. Lenin, *Imperialism: The Highest State of Capitalism* (1917). R. C. Binkley, *Realism and Nationalism, 1852-1871* (1941), has an excellent introduction to Europe's crisis of "federative polity," while Hajo Holborn, *The Political Collapse of Europe* (1952), examines the results of World War I on Europe and the world. The best diplomatic histories of Europe are found in R. J. Sontag, *European Diplomatic History, 1871-1918* (1935); W. L. Langer, *The Diplomacy of Imperialism* (1951 ed.); A. J. P. Taylor, *The Struggle for the Mastery of Europe, 1848-1918;* Erich Brandenburg, *From Bismarck to the World War* (1927); and Laurence Lafore, *The Long Fuse* (1965). The best single volume on all aspects of European society in the decade before 1914 is Oran J. Hale, *The Great Illusion, 1900-1914* (1971).

World War I and Its Impact on Europe

When a member of the Black Hand, a fanatical Slavic nationalist organization, assassinated the heir to the Austrian throne on June 28, 1914, he set in motion monumental events that are still affecting the world today. World War I is the most significant event in the twentieth century, comparable to the French Revolution and the Protestant Reformation in its impact and consequences on European history. The war destroyed European men, European treasures, and European empires, and distorted the men, treasures, and empires that survived. It demolished old institutions, gave birth to new and unexpected forces and movements, and fundamentally altered the character of European society and the pattern of European politics. Most important of all, World War I shattered Europe's age of liberalism, progress, peace and stability, and inaugurated a period of war, revolution, and chaos that is still prevalent in Europe today. There is little doubt, as one historian has observed, that for contemporary man, "the First World War was the decisive experience."

In the first essay in this section, Professor Charles Bussey critically examines the origins and consequences of World War I. He describes the underlying forces that led to war, imperialism, alliance systems, nationalistic "Pan" movements, and economic rivalries, and the critical days of July 1914, when European diplomats turned a "local" issue into a general European war. In the second essay, John M. Carroll analyzes the peace settlement that ended the First World War. In 1919, world leaders assembled in Paris with a golden opportunity to revitalize Europe and to reconstruct a new world order which would provide social justice, prosperity, and lasting peace to all nations. Carroll examines the major policies of the United States, England, France, and Italy, demonstrating that though differences existed between these nations, the peace that was established worked remarkably well during the 1920s. It faltered only during the 1930s, when economic depression, political abandonment of the League of Nations, and the revisionist powers of Germany, Italy, and Russia combined to shatter the hopes of the peace delegates of 1919. In the final essay in this section, G. D. Balsama examines the origins and consequences of the Russian Revolution, a monumental event that is still shaping the history of Europe and the world. He describes the origins of the revolution, the various reasons for Lenin's triumph, and the impact of the Bolsheviks in both Russia and Europe.

CHAPTER 1

The Origins and Consequences of World War I

Charles Bussey

Scholars have investigated and debated the causes of World War I for the past sixty-five years without anything like a consensus being reached. Perhaps writers have been overly concerned with an unanswerable question: Which nation should bear the guilt for starting the war? Normally historians have distinguished between underlying and immediate causation. A list of the former would include such things as imperialism, militarism, nationalism gone wrong, and the unwieldy alliance system which had developed in Europe since the 1870s. Immediate causes are considered to have been the assassination of the heir to the Austro-Hungarian throne by a Serbian nationalist and a subsequent failure of leadership. This essay will take into account both long- and short-term issues and will argue that a combination of attitudes and events blew a Balkan conflict into a global war and disoriented European civilization. The causes of the war, in other words, were cumulative.

As a result of the events of 1914-19, the old world of Europe in effect collapsed to be replaced by a new order, which varied from country to country. For example: communism replaced tsarism in Russia; Germany moved from the autocracy of William II to the weak democracy of the Weimar Republic; the Austro-Hungarian Empire was replaced by several smaller and weaker nations; and in some countries, like England, there was change of a more evolutionary sort. In Britain, the change was of the kind which moved that country from the rather staid age of Victoria to the twentieth century with its challenge to nearly all established authority. Taken in its totality, World War I and its aftermath represents a great watershed in Western civilization comparable to the Reformation and the French Revolution.

The underlying causes of World War I were interrelated and fed upon each other. A good starting point is imperialism, the control of one people by another by whatever means necessary. Although imperialism was as old as history, by around 1750 it seemed to peak and was dormant rather than dynamic. But in the 1870s a "new" imperialism which was concentrated primarily in Africa and Asia began to emerge and to be practiced by European nations into the twentieth century. Although that imperialism was exploitative and certainly economic in nature, perhaps the most important factor stimulating post-1870 imperialism was the quest by European nations for national power and world prestige.

The desire to enhance national status in the eyes of the world, as well as to increase the market for industrial products, led to clashes between several European nations during the late nineteenth and the early twentieth century. For example, France infuriated newly-united Italy in 1881 by occupying Tunis in North Africa. And imperial rivalry on that same continent nearly brought Britain and France to war in 1898. Both nations wished to control the Upper Nile in the Sudan, and conflict was avoided only because France evacuated Fashoda in November. Anglo-German tensions, however, were probably the most serious. While problems between those two nations were evident particularly in South Africa between 1895 and 1900, there was a complex rivalry between the two from 1870 to 1914. The phenomenal growth of Germany's industrial output between 1870 and 1910 (by the latter year Germany was producing 13,698,000 metric tons of steel annually to England's 6,374,000) was a constant irritation to the export-conscious British. The competition for sales dramatized other conflicts. As the Germans moved into direct imperial competition with the British, the friction remained constant. R. R. Palmer has pointed out that "when the British wished to expand, whether it was in Africa or the Pacific, there . . . were the Germans, asking for compensation."

Another factor which strained relations among European nations was the arms race which helped to promote the belief that war was the ultimate solution to national problems. Author Golo Mann wrote in 1964:

> War, as a concept and an institution, is an important factor contributing to war itself. Why should not something assume real shape from time to time which in one's thoughts one considers quite normal, which forms the high point in the life of nations, which is the standard by which the affairs of state—in their ranks, values, and morals—tend to be measured.

Such a description fits perfectly the prevailing attitude among European powers in the pre-World War I period. That technological innovations, which made weapons increasingly destructive, did not reorient thought processes is regrettable but true. National expenditures on military preparedness escalated dramatically between 1870 and 1914. Per capita spending for the military during those years was as follows: Great Britain moved from $3.54 to $8.23; Germany from $1.25 to $8.19; France from $2.92 to $7.07; Austria-Hungary from $1.08 to $3.10; and Russia from $1.28 to $3.44. Such increases reflected among other things the growth in the size of armies and navies. The German army, for example, increased from 430,000 men in 1875 to 761,000 in 1914. In the 1870s, all nations in Europe, except Britain, had followed Germany's lead under Otto von Bismarck in making military service compulsory. Thus, the size of a nation's army at any given time did not reflect the number of men who had, in fact, been trained. Great Britain increased her naval personnel from 53,600 in 1880 to 151,000 by 1914. Especially touchy for the British, because of her geographic circumstance, was the fact that from 1890 on Germany increased her naval capacity to rival Britain's. This policy, contrary to Bismarck's plans and implemented by Kaiser William II only after he dismissed Bismarck, led to increased Anglo-German tensions. The introduction in 1906 of a new superbattleship, the Dreadnought, intensified friction as German production was such that Britain was unable to maintain her traditional two to one naval superiority.

Moreover, as armed forces increased, so did the influence of the military over the civilian elements in government. The military glorified war in the romantic tradition and inclined toward a belief in the inevitability of war. (That such a mood gripped Europe by 1914 can be seen by the way five million young men marched off to war in August of that year with innocent enthusiasm. The soldiers brought to life in Jules Romain's novel *Verdun* personify such ebullience: "They were setting off for a noisy, bustling, rough sort of holiday, a real schoolboy expedition.") The military establishment in each nation had conceived of specific military plans to be followed in the event of war. These plans (Plan 17 in France, Plan A or B in Russia, and the Schlieffen Plan in Germany) were secret—even in some cases from the foreign ministers—and when the spark ignited in 1914, there seemed to be no choice but to follow those prearranged military schedules.

Nationalism, which had been a healthy attribute of European state development during most of the nineteenth century, became more extreme after 1870. Individual liberty, the dream of the classical liberals, was subordinated to the will of the state as the twentieth century approached. A strong sense of ethnocentrism began to dominate, to be the true faith, of each nation. As Thomas H. Greer has pointed out, "the people of each nation believed in their own superiority, sovereignty, and peculiar mission in the world. . . . Each nation viewed itself as the chosen instrument of God. . . ." That collective feeling fed both imperialism and militarism. In an atmosphere of excessive nationalism, it was easy to view militarism and the preparation for war as sound moral training and to justify imperialism as ordained by God.

The creation of a cheap, mass circulation press by the end of the nineteenth century also played a role in accentuating nationalism and preparing the public for war. Historian Sidney B. Fay has argued with justification that "too often newspapers in all lands were inclined to influence nationalistic feelings, misrepresent the situation in foreign countries, and suppress factors in favor of peace." For example, the London *Daily Mail* published in 1909 the statement that "Germany is deliberately preparing to destroy the British Empire." That provocation elicited from the German kaiser the response that "people [in England] seem to think that I am standing here with my battle ax behind my back ready to fall upon them at any moment." Such an episode, if an isolated example, might be laughed off. It was neither!

Within the framework of this developing international anarchy, the system of alliances (public and private) was introduced. Originally designed and controlled by Germany's Bismarck in the 1870s and 1880s, the alliance systems gradually expanded and became difficult to control. Perhaps Bismarck's gravest diplomatic nightmare was that Germany would one day be caught between an allied France to the west and Russia to the east. Also possible, and equally dangerous from Bismarck's perspective, was an alliance between France and Austria-Hungary. Therefore, the Iron Chancellor aimed his diplomacy at precluding such action by the French, who were certain to seek revenge for the crushing defeat France had suffered at the hands of Prussia in 1871. In 1879, Bismarck achieved a treaty with Austria-Hungary, and in 1881 he revived the Three Emperors' League which included Russia. A year later Italy joined with Germany and Austria-Hungary to create the Triple Alliance. By shrewd diplomatic action France was thus isolated and would remain so as long as Bismarck retained power.

In opposition to the Triple Alliance, the Triple Entente gradually came into being over a period of thirteen years—the Franco-Russian Alliance in 1894, the Anglo-French Entente in 1904, and the Anglo-Russian Entente in 1907. While there were no formal military commitments involved in the Triple Entente, there was a "close understanding," and staff officers from that trio's military establishments began to hold informal discussions. Members of the Triple Entente drew closer after 1907 as trouble developed in the Balkans, an explosive area in Europe.

Although the factors discussed thus far were essential in

establishing a climate for war, and for ensuring that war would be international, World War I "grew out of a single international event which was the conflict between the Habsburg Monarchy [Austria-Hungary] and the kingdom of Serbia." Thus, the Balkan region and its relationship to the rest of Europe merits a thorough discussion.

Serious problems had existed in the Balkan region for over a century, and as Europe entered the twentieth century, the conflicts there revolved around incompatible national aims. Russia felt a kinship with her fellow Slavs (the predominant ethnic group in the Balkans) and sought control of the Dardanelles and Bosporus straits, connecting the Black Sea and the Aegean Sea. With control of those two straits, Russia would be assured of a warm-water outlet for its sea-going traffic and might be able to promote the liberation of the Slavic population. By invading and crushing Turkish forces in 1878—Turkey at that time controlled much of the Balkan region—Russia almost achieved its aim. But the rest of Europe intervened at the Berlin Conference—called to establish peace—and as a result of pressure by Britain, Austria-Hungary, and Germany, Russia came away with little more than an indemnity and a few harbors. The Turkish sultan, though, did recognize the independence of Serbia, Montenegro, and Rumania. However, to Russia's dismay, Austria-Hungary was allowed to administer the Balkan provinces of Bosnia and Herzegovina. Thus Russia and Austria-Hungary were in direct competition for power in the Balkans, while Germany had designs on that region as well. In many ways though, "the most serious and irrepressible conflict [there] . . . was between the Slavic nationalists and the polyglot empire of Austria-Hungary."

Serbia, independent since 1878, was intensely nationalistic and ambitious in its desire to create a south Slavic political unit. Consequently, Austria-Hungary's October 1908, annexation of Bosnia and Herzegovina (primarily Serb in population) created a frenzy of rage in Serbia. Immediately, Serbian nationalists began to intensify their efforts of subversion and agitation in hopes of liberating their ethnic kinsmen from Austrian control. Quite naturally the Austro-Hungarian leaders were disturbed. Their apprehension was based in part on the fear of the upheaval a Serbian success might set off among the multiplicity of ethnic populations in the Austro-Hungarian Empire. Russia encouraged the Serbs, and the Germans were also keenly interested in the situation since a fragmented Austria-Hungary would weaken the Triple Alliance. The remainder of the great powers, given the complex alliance system which had been constructed to secure order, watched with intense interest the developments in the Balkans.

Although many people in 1914 believed that war would come, practically everyone believed that it would be limited and localized in scope. General Alfred von Schlieffen, German chief of staff, had written in 1909 that a long war was "impossible in an age when the existence of the nation is founded upon the uninterrupted continuation of trade and industry." A French economist, Paul Leroy-Beaulieu, used mathematics to prove that "no war in Europe could escalate or last longer than six months." Such attitudes were universal in 1914, for since 1815 few wars had laster longer than a few weeks, and great progress had been made in human understanding—at least that was the prevailing view.

The Balkans proved to be the region where the final crisis developed, and a key figure in that crisis which precipitated the Great War was Dragutin Dimitrijević. Chief of Intelligence in the Serbian Army, Dimitrijević also was active in a secret society—Union of Death or more commonly, the Black Hand—which dreamed of a greater Serbia to include Macedonia, Bosnia, and Herzegovina. That organization, with its secrecy, loyalty oaths, rituals, terrorism, and emphasis on violence, was similar to various anarchist groups of earlier years and the American Ku Klux Klan.

By late 1913 or early 1914, in spite of propaganda and subversion, Dimitrijević was fearful that his dreams for a greater Serbia were on the verge of failure. The Austro-Hungarian Emperor, Franz Joseph, was eighty-four and in poor health. Heir to the throne Archduke Franz Ferdinand had indicated that once he assumed power, he would grant concessions to the Slavic population in Bosnia and Herzegovina. While the shape of such concessions was purely conjectural (perhaps an American- or Swiss-type federalism), if they produced happy Serbians in Bosnia, Dimitrijević's dream of absolute liberation would be ended.

Consequently, Dimitrijević determined that the Archduke must die. He learned that Franz Ferdinand would be touring Bosnia in June 1914, and would visit Sarajevo, the Bosnian capital. With motive and opportunity in force, the Black Hand secured the means to eliminate Franz Ferdinand. Dimitrijević recruited and trained an assassination squad of three young Serbians in the use of firearms and bombs and got them into Sarajevo in early June 1914.

In May, the Serbian prime minister learned of the Black Hand's plot. Instead of warning the Austro-Hungarian government of the specifics, and because (realistically) he felt he could not fire Dimitrijević and suppress the Black Hand, he chose a terrible alternative. He ordered the Serbian envoy in Vienna to approach the Austrian official who handled Bosnian matters and suggest a cancellation of the Archduke's visit. At the meeting nothing specific was mentioned—the suggestion was based on mere general discontent among Bosnia's Serbs. The Austrian minister was not impressed and dismissed the Serbian envoy with the words: "Let us hope nothing happens."

On June 28, 1914, Franz Ferdinand and his wife (Sophie) were assassinated. The chain of events which led to the assassination were almost ludicrous. The conspirators were placed strategically along the route which the open touring cars of Franz Ferdinand's motorcade would take to the city hall, a museum, and the governor's residence. Shortly after the motorcade moved out at 10:00 A.M., one of the assassins threw a bomb at the Archduke, but the driver saw it, accelerated, and the bomb went off behind the Archduke's car. Several spectators were injured and the driver of the second car suffered a head wound and was taken to the hospital. Once at the city hall, following his formal reception, Franz Ferdinand overruled objections and visited the wounded driver at the hospital. It was decided, however, to change routes and to travel Sarajevo's main street (Appel Quay) rather than down Franz Joseph Street. In the meantime, another recruited killer (Gavrilo Princip) left Appel Quay and strolled down Franz Joseph Street. By a stroke of misfortune, in the heat of the moment, no one informed the Archduke's chauffeur of the change in routes, so he proceeded to turn off Appel Quay onto Franz Joseph. Immediately, the general in charge of security ordered the driver to stop and informed him of the change in plans. Applying the brakes, the chauffeur stopped and backed up; just at that point Princip appeared and from a distance of not more than five feet fired two fatal shots.

The conspirators were captured, their Serbian ethnicity was determined, and the Serbian government was blamed. Although no facts were available to substantiate the charge, Austria-Hungary determined to punish Serbia realizing that such action might bring Russia into the controversy. Austria-Hungary therefore contacted Berlin early in July to see what Kaiser William's response would be to Russian aid to Serbia. At that point, acting impetuously, William II issued his famous "blank check" suggesting that Germany would support Austria-Hungary in whatever course she chose to pursue. The kaiser appears to have thought that his ally would act quickly, that there was a good case against Serbia, that Russia was not ready to fight, and that any conflict which developed would be localized.

With the kaiser's assurance in hand, the Austrians drew up an ultimatum which was presented to the Serbian government on July 23, at 6:00 P.M. Serbia was given forty-eight hours to respond to the harsh demands made by the Austro-Hungarian government. Shortly (two minutes to be precise) before the forty-eight hour period ended, the Serbs presented their answer in a conciliatory document. The Serbs argued, however, that they could not allow Austro-Hungarian agencies to come into Serbia for an investigation (one of the demands) since that would violate Serbia's constitution.

Approximately thirty minutes after receiving Serbia's response, Austria-Hungary broke off diplomatic relations with Serbia and mobilized her army. Germany, on July 27, tried to get her ally to negotiate—William II, upon reading Serbia's reply to Austria's ultimatum, had called it "a brilliant performance. . . . All reason for war is gone."—but Austria was determined to solve her Balkan problem.

The Russian army then began to mobilize. Germany demanded that Russian mobilization cease or at least be limited. But the Russian military had no plans for limited mobilization—a war against Austria-Hungary and not Germany was inconceivable. The Russians thought that given the vastness of their country, their poor railroad system, and their less efficient military they must get the jump on Germany. Hearing nothing positive from Russia, Germany declared war against Russia on August 1, 1914, and implemented the Schlieffen Plan. That contingency plan, drawn by General von Schlieffen in 1905, was based on the efficient movement of the German army and the slowness of the Russians to get into position. The German army would sweep through neutral Belgium in a surprise attack on France from that direction, defeat the French in a matter of a few weeks, and continuing its sweep in wheel fashion be back in position to defend Germany's eastern borders against the lumbering Russian army.

By midnight of August 4, as a result of Germany's invasion of Belgium, Great Britain had been drawn into the war, and the Austro-Serbian incident quickly developed into "a truly global conflict." Military plans which had been carefully drawn over the years—ironically, none of the timetables actually worked—went into operation, and the morally bankrupt leadership of the time did nothing creative. In at least a partial sense, novelist Franz Kafka's 1916 remark that "this war above all else was caused by a tremendous lack of imagination" was correct.

World War I, to which "the recruits of 1914 rushed . . . as if it were a feast or frolic," in Gordon Craig's words, turned into a nightmare very quickly. By the winter of 1914, the war which everyone had assumed would be over by Christmas, appeared endless. It settled into a war of attrition with the two sides locked in tactical immobility as they faced each other across "no man's land" in their rat-infested trenches. Science and technology had enhanced the potential for destruction; but at times it was a combination of two previously established articles of war used together for the first time which speeded the slaughter. For example, both sides discovered that the combination of barbed wire covering the open field between trenches and well-placed machine guns led to massive loss of life when the command to charge was given.

Innovations in the Great War included the tank, introduced by Great Britain in September 1916, but not effective until 1918; the Germans brought out poison gas in
April 1915, and the flame thrower in February 1916. Additionally, the kaiser's navy made effective use of the submarine for the first time. The airplane's potential in war
was recognized by 1918 and had become especially effective at demoralizing civilian populations through urban
bombing. World War I initiated the concept of total war
which touched every phase of belligerent nations' civilian
life.

Life in the trenches was horrible beyond description,
though poets and novelists came close to capturing the
feelings of the men trapped there. British poet Siegfried
Sassoon, himself in the trenches, wrote that "war is hell,
and those who institute it are criminals." A character in
German novelist Erich M. Remarque's *All Quiet on the
Western Front* described it this way: "The front is a cage
in which we must await fearfully whatever may happen.
We lie here under the network of arching shells and live
in a suspense of uncertainty. Over us Chance hovers."

That terrible conflict, which cost nine million military
lives, more than twenty million civilian lives, and trillions
of dollars, had unforeseen and far-reaching consequences.
By the time the shooting stopped in late 1918, changes had
taken place and others initiated which would forever
change European society. Morals and manners changed,
and in the eyes of many, "the old creeds and slogans . . .
had become mockeries . . . ." Gone forever was the concep-
tion of and faith in inevitable progress. The optimistic
humanism, which saw education and reason leading to a
better world, emerged from the war in a vastly weakened
position, and postwar reforms were quietly abandoned.

German philosopher Oswald Spengler's pessimistic *Decline of the West* (1918) was a best-seller in the 1920s.
Spengler argued that World War I was "the beginning of
the final act." But it was not just the defeated nations
which were demoralized as a result of the war. Dadaism,
the deliberate irrationality and negation of the laws of
beauty and organization, made an impact in Britain and
France; and the movement itself was an effective criticism
of prewar values in the postwar period. American-British

poet T. S. Eliot captured the spiritual emptiness of Western civilization in 1925 in a poem "The Hollow Men":

> This is the way the world ends
> This is the way the world ends
> This is the way the world ends
> Not with a bang but a whimper.

In addition to the loss of men, treasure, and ideals, four empires fell: the Russian, German, Austro-Hungarian, and Turkish. Institutions such as monarchy and aristocracy were discredited and replaced by unrealistic and vague concepts of democracy and self-determination of peoples. The Russian Revolution was precipitated and communism unleased as a world force. The liberal-democratic governments in Italy and Germany proved inadequate to meet postwar problems and gave way to fascism. But in terms of consequences for the future, as momentous as any of the changes was the shift in the balance of power away from Europe to the United States, which had entered the war in 1917 on the Allied side. The decline of Europe propelled the United States into a position of world responsibility for which she was unprepared.

Suggested Readings

The corpus of primary and secondary sources related to the origins and consequences of World War I has reached the point so as to overwhelm even the specialist. For the interested student, however, the following suggestions are representative of the best which scholarship has to offer.

A good starting point would be the classic works of Sidney B. Fay, Bernadotte E. Schmitt, and Pierre Renouvin. Fay's *The Origins of the World War* (1928) was an extraordinary study by an American only ten years after the war ended. Fay tended, perhaps, to overemphasize the question of "war guilt" and undercut the thesis that Germany alone should bear the blame for causing the war. In that same year, Renouvin published *The Immediate Origins of the War* (1928) and was very unsympathetic to Germany. Echoing Renouvin's thesis, though more convincing, was Schmitt's *The Coming of the War, 1914* (1930). Between 1952 and 1957, Luigi Albertini published his multivolume *The Origins of the War of 1914* (1952-57). Albertini's work, though often clumsy and heavy-handed, contains invaluable information and insight. The best short and perhaps most literate volume on European diplomacy is Raymond J. Sontag, *European Diplomatic History, 1871-1932* (1933). Though forty-six years old, Sontag's study is not out of date. A German scholar, Fritz Fischer, revived flagging interest in the question of "war guilt" with his *Germany's Aims in the First World War* (1967). Fischer's work tended to emphasize Germany's role in bringing about the war. American Laurence Lafore in *The Long Fuse, An Interpretation of the Origins of World War I* (1965) focused his attention on the situation in the Balkans. Lafore argued that historians had spent too much time debating "war guilt," that without the assassination at Sarajevo there would have been no war, and that in terms of consequences, World War I ranks with the Reformation and the French Revolution. René Albrecht-Carrie, *The Meaning of the First World War* (1965) deals almost exclusively with consequences. Joachin Remak, *The Origins of World War I, 1871-1914* (1967) is brief, though nearly overorganized, and clearly put. No bibliography touching any area or aspect of World War I would be complete without mentioning E. M. Remarque, *All Quiet on the Western Front* (1928). This novel by a German author describing the lot of the common soldier has become a classic against which all subsequent war novels must be measured.

Orlando, Lloyd-George, Clemenceau, and Wilson at the Paris Peace Conference, 1919. *(Courtesy of the National Archives)*

CHAPTER 2

The Versailles Settlement and Its Aftermath

John M. Carroll

In November 1918, the costliest and most destructive war in history up to that time came to an end. Early the following year, delegates from thirty-two nations met in Paris to make peace, readjust territorial boundaries, provide for future international security, and reconstruct the war-torn continent of Europe. The Treaty of Versailles was the most important of five treaties that were eventually ratified. It is not an exaggeration to say that the peace conference in the Paris suburb of Versailles was one of the pivotal events in twentieth century European and world history. Millions of people from all parts of the globe believed that the world leaders assembled in Paris had an opportunity to revitalize Europe and construct a new world order which could provide social justice, prosperity, and lasting peace for all nations. Although this hope might seem visionary today, it was widely shared in 1919 by statesmen, intellectuals, and common men alike. The Treaty of Versailles did not create an international system which embodied the idealistic concepts which many thought attainable at the end of the war. In fact, the peace settlement lasted barely twenty years and helped to generate a new conflict in 1939 that was even more costly and destructive than World War I.

By examining the Versailles conference, one can better understand what forces, personalities, and events made it so difficult to construct a just and lasting peace in 1919 and how the legacy of Versailles contributed to the renewal of war in Europe within a generation.

The Versailles conference convened in January 1919, amidst great disorder and confusion. Germany's sudden collapse and the ensuing armistice the previous November allowed the victorious powers little time to prepare for the most important international conclave since the defeat of Napoleon. It was imperative to conclude peace quickly, however, because Europe teetered on the brink of social, economic, and political disaster. Four empires (Germany, Austria-Hungary, Russia, and Turkey) had crumbled during the course of the war, and disease and famine afflicted large sections of Europe and Asia. The resulting chaos made Europe vulnerable to Russian bolshevism, which appeared to be sweeping westward, endangering the very existence of the established capitalist system. To make matters worse, the victors, with the exception of Japan and the United States, had been weakened by the war and faced serious social and economic problems both at home and in their empires. The Allied and Associate powers assembled in Paris to restore order to European society before it was too late. But the conditions in early 1919 were not conducive to an orderly and systematic realignment of the balance of power in Europe and throughout the world. These disturbing and threatening events weighed heavily on the minds of the peacemakers and contributed to the confusion and disharmony which permeated the Versailles conference.

Although the major victorious powers (Britain, France, Italy, and the United States) had agreed to conduct peace negotiations on the basis of President Woodrow Wilson's Fourteen Points, there was little unity among the four nations. The Allies and the United States had the common goal of defeating the Central Powers but did not share the same vision of how to reshape the postwar world. Midway through the conference, Italy withdrew from the negotiations in protest over the application of Wilson's point on self-determination to the Fiume question. Although the Italian delegates returned to sign the final treaty, Italy played only a minor role at the conference and quickly joined the ranks of those powers dedicated to revising the treaty. The main task of drafting the settlement was left to Britain, France, and the United States which were represented by Prime Minister David Lloyd George, Premier Georges Clemenceau and Wilson respectively—the so-called Big Three. Each of these men had distinctly different views on what constituted a just and lasting settlement to the complex problems resulting from the war.

France, under the leadership of Clemenceau, had the most clearly defined objectives of any nation at the peace conference. Having witnessed two German invasions of France in his lifetime, Clemenceau was determined to ensure French security by rendering Germany politically and economically impotent. Although France was one of the victors, she had suffered enormous damage during the war and still considered Germany a threat to her survival. The French population and industrial potential had been declining for several decades vis-a-vis Germany's and Clemenceau saw the Allied victory as an opportunity to extinguish the German menace once and for all. He proposed severe economic, military, and territorial penalties for Germany which might retard Germany's recovery for at least a generation. After that time, Clemenceau hoped that the newly established nations of Central Europe situated between Germany and Russia would be strong enough to neutralize the two eastern powers and tip the balance of power in favor of France. Clemenceau came to the peace conference in both an idealistic and cynical mood. He idealized France and distrusted everything else. In the words of the British economist and peace delegate John M. Keynes, Clemenceau "had one illusion—France; and one disillusion—mankind, including Frenchmen, and his colleagues not least." Committed to a policy of revenge against Germany, the French premier advocated a harsh peace and was a constant source of irritation to those leaders who urged moderation and restraint in shaping the postwar settlement.

Lloyd George's objectives at the conference were the most ambiguous of the Big Three. The shrewd Welshman was intent on protecting British interests. He wanted to maintain British mastery of the world's sea lanes and expand its colonial empire at the expense of Germany. These priorities brought Lloyd George into conflict with Wilson's points on freedom of the seas and self-determination. To the extent that it promoted British interests, Lloyd George supported the French demand for an exacting settlement with Germany. But the prime minister distrusted France and suspected her of attempting to construct a peace accord which would assure French hegemony in Europe. Lloyd George believed that both Germany and Russia were destined to recover from the war; that they could not be permanently constrained by the terms of peace. He preferred a settlement which would eventually restore a balance of power in Europe rather than one designed to promote French dominance on the continent. Britain, furthermore, did not want to cripple Germany to the extent that the latter could not revive and serve as a market for British exports. It was on the question of economic penalties against Germany, most notably reparations and territorial adjustments, that Lloyd George was caught in a dilemma. During the election campaign of 1918, he had encouraged his constituents to believe that Britain would squeeze Germany until "its pips squeaked." When the conference began, the prime minister was torn between supporting a harsh peace which he had promised the British people and a more moderate settlement which he believed was more in line with British long-term interests. Lloyd George vacillated between the two approaches at Versailles, but inched toward Wilson's position at the end of the conference.

President Wilson was the foremost advocate of a mild and nonpunitive settlement. He believed that Germany had caused the war but counseled for a peace with no indemnities or territorial annexations. His Fourteen Points called for the restructuring of European and world society along the lines of liberal democratic principles. Wilson proposed that the balance of power system be abolished and that a new order which emphasized international cooperation, economic and political freedom, and social justice take its place. The president, to be sure, was an idealist, but he was more realistic than many historians have been willing to admit. He realized that the European system of international politics had been discredited by the war and that bolshevism loomed as an attractive alternative if a new and appealing world order was not quickly constructed. Like many of the leaders at Versailles, Wilson was as much concerned with the specter of bolshevism which hovered in Eastern Europe as he was with the negotiations in Paris. He also understood that to the extent that his program could foster European confidence in republican principles, improve economic conditions, and reduce the threat of war, the United States would benefit. Although America had no specific territorial or economic objectives at the peace conference, it did want to establish a global order in which its political and economic system could flourish. Beyond this, Wilson firmly believed that his Fourteen Point program was just and that it was his mission to help construct a more peaceful, prosperous, and democratic world society. After his tumultuous welcome in Europe, Wilson was confident that he spoke for the great majority of people throughout the world. It is not clear whether or not he realized how much he would be forced to compromise in order to incorporate even a portion of his program into the final peace treaty.

On the eve of the peace conference, Wilson appeared to be in a strong position to carry through his program. The people of Europe viewed him as a savior who had come from the new world to redeem the old. In the opinion of Keynes, Wilson "enjoyed a prestige and a moral influence throughout the world unequaled in history. Never," the British economist continued, "had a philosopher held such weapons wherewith to bind the princes of this world." But few people in the various countries realized at the time that Wilson's vaguely stated Fourteen Points would require sacrifices which they were not prepared to accept. His colleagues at the conference greeted him with mixed feelings. The Allied leaders were mindful of Wilson's popularity and the important role which America, with its vast financial resources and moral authority, could play in making peace. But they also distrusted the president and resented his pompous sermons about saving the world. Clemenceau epitomized this feeling when he reportedly said: "God gave us the Ten Commandments, and we broke them. Wilson gave us the Fourteen Points. We shall see." When the conference opened, nearly every

Allied nation had already opposed or expressed reservations on one or more of the Fourteen Points. It was a bad omen for Wilson when it was quickly decided to set aside Point One on open covenants, openly arrived at, and to conduct important business in secret sessions attended only by the Big Four (later the Big Three) and their top aides. This decision speeded up the pace of the conference but undermined Wilson's position of standing firmly behind his Fourteen Points.

One of the most controversial of Wilson's Fourteen Points, which actually totaled some twenty-seven including additions and clarifications, was his support of self-determination for the peoples of the world. Taken at face value, this point meant that each national group should have the right to its own autonomous territory and self-government. In his pre-conference addresses, Wilson specifically applied the concept of self-determination to the people of the defeated nations and the colonies. He did not indicate whether or not he hoped to employ the doctrine in dealing with the territorial problems of the victorious nations. Should it not, for example, apply to the Irish question in the case of the British or to the American Philippine colony? It was unclear, moreover, what constituted a national group or people. At best, Wilson's doctrine of self-determination was ambiguous. This vagueness combined with the president's idealistic rhetoric in support of his Fourteen Points led to misunderstandings and caused many of his former supporters to charge Wilson with hypocrisy when self-determination was used selectively in shaping the peace settlement. In retrospect, it seems clear that Wilson's advocacy of self-determination was as much a response to Soviet communism as it was a manifestation of his idealism. After withdrawing from the war, the Russian Bolsheviks published a number of secret treaties which revealed the sordid war aims of the Allies. To combat the threat of bolshevism, Wilson, and to a lesser extent Lloyd George, felt obliged to counteract Soviet propaganda on this issue with the pledge of self-determination. In so doing, they raised expectations concerning territorial adjustments which they could not fulfill in Paris.

The territorial adjustments called for in the five treaties

of Paris were extensive. Germany lost fifty thousand square miles and nearly six million in population. This included Alsace-Lorraine in the west and a large area in the east that went primarily to the new state of Poland. Under two separate treaties with Austria and Hungary, the peace commissioners dismembered the once combined proud empire. Out of it the new nation of Czechoslovakia was created and Yugoslavia, Italy, Poland, and Rumania all received additional land. The remaining Central Powers, Bulgaria and Turkey, also sustained significant territorial losses. In redrawing the map of Europe, Wilson, often with the aid of Lloyd George, attempted to apply the doctrine of self-determination and foster democratic government.

The use and misuse of this principle both strengthened and weakened the final peace settlement. Given the difficult minority problems which existed in prewar Central Europe, the new territorial adjustment represented the best ethnic boundaries ever achieved in that region. To a great extent, national groups which had chafed under alien rule for centuries attained autonomy and established democratic governments. The Anglo-American stand on self-determination, moreover, prevented Clemenceau from separating Germany's Rhineland provinces from the rest of the Reich and averted other injustices in the disposition of the Saar and Upper Silesia. But the new territorial boundaries created as many problems as they solved: East Prussia was divided from the rest of Germany by a Polish corridor; the predominantly German city of Danzig was placed under international control; German minorities were entrapped within the new central European states—most notably in Czechoslovakia; Italy protested Wilson's decision on the Fiume question and withdrew from the conference. In addition, most of the new or revitalized states of Central Europe were economically weak and offered little prospect of either containing bolshevism or counterbalancing a resurgent Germany. Although the European territorial settlement was equitable in many respects, it also sowed the seeds of discord and revenge in Italy and the defeated nations. Outside of Europe, the principle of self-determination was not applied to any significant degree. The mandate system for former German and Turkish colonies was but a poorly disguised power-grab by the Allies to expand their empires. Perhaps the most flagrant violation of self-determination was the cession of Shantung, a Chinese province formerly belonging to Germany, to Japan as its reward for supporting the Allied cause. As a result of these actions, Wilson was discredited in the eyes of many of his followers and his new world order came under attack by a group of revisionist nations which were bent on overturning the territorial adjustments.

While the geographic settlement was controversial and created much bitterness, the section of the treaty that has been most criticized concerned reparations. Thomas W. Lamont, an American economic adviser at Versailles, wrote in 1921 that "reparations caused more trouble, contention, hard feeling, and delay at the Paris Conference than any other point of the Treaty of Versailles." Before the end of the war, Wilson made it clear in an official note that Germany should be responsible only for the "civilian damages" it had caused as opposed to total war costs or all damage and injury sustained by the Allies. Since Germany had occupied Belgium and parts of France for most of the war, the destruction of civilian property alone was extensive. American experts estimated that the reparations bill under their formula, which also included civilian damage done by German submarines, would be at least $15 billion. This was an enormous sum. The Allied leaders, however, had pledged to their citizens that Germany could and should pay much more. At the conference, British and French delegates discussed reparations figures which ranged from $50 to $400 billion. In explaining these astronomical sums, Winston Churchill noted that "it is too soon to expect the peoples who have suffered so much to regain their sanity. . . . We have to give satisfaction to the view of the multitude who have endured such frightful injuries." While the British saw a huge reparations bill as an expedient measure to satisfy public opinion, the French viewed it as a method to submerge Germany for a generation or more. It didn't matter to them whether or not Germany could eventually pay so long as the German economy and people were severely weakened. The Americans stood alone in urging moderation and restraint with regard to reparations.

Wilson, who believed that a harsh reparations settlement might lead to another war, successfully opposed an Allied attempt to include all war costs under reparations. But the president suffered a series of setbacks at the conference which negated this victory and helped to make the reparations section one of the most severe in the treaty. The United States hoped that by insisting on a "lump sum" payment and establishing a time limit beyond which Germany would not be expected to pay, it could effectively reduce Allied demands. In both instances, the Americans were rebuffed. It was agreed that no set amount for reparations would be stated in the treaty and that Germany must continue paying until its obligation was met in full. After the treaty was ratified, this led to the allegation that Germany was forced to sign a blank check. The American delegation suffered a more serious defeat on the question of military pensions. Allied leaders proposed that pensions and separation allowances be included under civilian damages, a dubious category which might raise reparations by $15-$25 billion. Although American experts advised the president that all logic was against such a decision, Wilson exclaimed: "Logic! Logic! I don't give a damn for logic. I am going to include pensions." By giving in on this issue, Wilson seemingly violated one of his own pledges to Germany and in the process appeared to have contributed to a larger reparations bill, a debt which was set at $33 billion in 1921.[1]

The reason for Wilson's willingness to compromise on reparations was linked to his concern for other issues before the peace conference. While the reparations negotiations were in progress, Clemenceau was pressing his case for the separation of the Rhineland from Germany and objecting to the president's proposal that the League of Nations Covenant be included in the treaty. In order to secure a favorable resolution of these and other problems, Wilson made concessions on reparations. He was hopeful, however, that the American-sponsored Reparation Commission, which would be chaired by the United States

---

1. Since reparations were supposedly determined on the basis of Germany's capacity to pay, military pensions were only a minor factor in setting the reparations bill in 1921.

provided it ratified the treaty, might redress the reparations settlement. The commission, which was charged with setting a final reparations figure, could reduce German obligations at a future time when some of the hatred and bitterness associated with the war had receded. When the United States rejected the treaty, however, the Reparation Commission was dominated by the French who followed a hard-line reparations policy. In addition to the inclusion of military pensions and the so-called blank check provision, the Allies included two other requirements in the reparations settlement which stirred controversy and heightened tensions during the next decade. Section 231 required that Germany admit its responsibility for "a war imposed on them [the victors] by the aggression of Germany and her Allies"—the infamous war guilt clause. The treaty also stipulated that the Allies would temporarily occupy the Rhineland to ensure reparations payments and that the region would be permanently demilitarized. The end result was that the reparations settlement was much harsher than the Germans had been led to expect on the basis of the Fourteen Points and Wilson's pre-Armistice note. Throughout the twenties and early thirties, German nationalists reiterated the alleged injustices of the reparations section of the treaty. They skillfully utilized the slogans "blank check" and "unilateral war guilt," neither of which appeared in the treaty, to evoke popular resentment against the Versailles settlement. This, combined with Keynes' *Economic Consequences of the Peace* (1919) which singled out the folly and injustice of reparations, made the reparations section the most criticized in the whole treaty. As Paul Birdsall has pointed out "the Reparation settlement was the chief stumbling block, partly because of impossible financial demands, even more because it combined an egregious breach of faith with an impolitic accusation of moral turpitude. In both financial and political results it proved disastrous."

Although Wilson recognized the deficiencies in the reparations settlement and in other sections of the treaty, he believed that his proposed League of Nations could ameliorate many of these problems. The League set the Treaty of Versailles apart from any other peace treaty in history. It was a supranational organization designed to supplant the prewar balance of power system and provide international security. Like the present-day United Nations, the League consisted of two important bodies: 1) a permanent and influential council of five leading nations; 2) a general assembly of all member nations which served as a forum for the discussion of international issues. By providing the League with moral, economic, and potential military power, Wilson hoped that the world organization could retard the growth of national rivalries, settle international disputes amicably, and prevent war. The president was so confident that the League could preserve future peace that he personally drafted its covenant and worked tirelessly to gain Allied approval of the international body. He insisted that the covenant be made part of the treaty in order to enhance the prospect of United States membership and ensure British and French cooperation with League peacekeeping efforts. Because of his faith in the League of Nations, Wilson was willing to compromise on other issues to increase its chances of success. He believed that in the future the League would become the most important element in the entire peace settlement.

Articles 10 and 16 were the most unique and controversial parts of the League Covenant. The former authorized the League to guarantee its members' independence and territorial integrity against outside aggression and the latter provided that economic sanctions should be imposed on any aggressor nation. Article 10 implied that the League could summon armies from all member states to counteract an unprovoked attack against any one of them. This kind of collective action would represent a new departure in international politics. Never before had nations of the world been willing to entrust such extensive powers in the hands of an international organization. Wilson believed that the establishment of the League of Nations would mark a turning point in world history because war as an instrument of diplomacy would become obsolete. He maintained that the very idea of League members mobilizing against an aggressor would be enough to prevent general war in the future. In addition, Wilson hoped that the League would lead to greater understanding among nations, facilitate disarmament, and help to resolve world social and economic problems.

Everyone did not share Wilson's view that the League of Nations would usher in a millenium in international affairs. At the peace conference, Clemenceau was unimpressed by Wilson's arguments in favor of the untested world body. The French premier maintained that many sections of the covenant, including Article 10, were too vague to ensure lasting peace. He was much too cynical to entrust French security to a world organization which might or might not rally to France's defense in case of another German attack. If Clemenceau had had his way, he would have struck the League Covenant from the treaty and restored the prewar balance of power system. But the idea of a league of nations was popular in Europe and the French leader grudgingly gave his approval to Wilson's world body. In exchange for his acceptance of the League, Clemenceau won a number of concessions on other issues which affected French interests. He also obtained from Wilson and Lloyd George, who supported the League of Nations concept, a pledge to engage in two separate defense treaties with France to allay French fears of future German aggression. Although the treaties were never ratified by either the United States or Britain, the proposed agreements helped to overcome French opposition to the League of Nations at the conference. The inclusion of the League Covenant in the Versailles Treaty without major revision was Wilson's greatest achievement in Paris. The president was convinced that the establishment of the League justified the modifications which he had been forced to make in his Fourteen Point program.

By early May 1919, the treaty, which had been drafted piecemeal, was put together and rushed to the printer. When it was returned in published form, many delegates were shocked by its contents. Herbert Hoover, an American economic adviser, later recalled his reaction:

> Although I had known the gist of many of the segments, I had not before had an opportunity to envision it as a whole. Aside from the League Covenant, many provisions had been settled without considering their effect on others. . . . I believed the Treaty contained the seeds of another war. It seemed to me that the economic sections alone would pull down the whole continent and, in the end, injure the United States.

Other delegates such as John M. Keynes and Jan Smuts of South Africa shared Hoover's views. Despite warnings from their aides, the Big Three presented the draft treaty to the Germans in a tense ceremony at Versailles on May 7. Confined behind a protective fence, the German delegation was given one copy of the treaty and told that Germany must accept the settlement without substantial revision—a virtual ultimatum. On June 28, the German government, having little other choice, ratified the treaty in essentially the same form as it had been received. The heavy-handed negotiations with the Germans proved to be a major tactical error by the Big Three. During the 1920s and 30s, many Germans had little respect for a treaty which they considered to be a *Diktat* or for the Weimar Republic whose officials had signed the hated document. Unwittingly, the victors heightened the resentment toward the peace settlement in Germany and helped to undermine the republican leaders who represented one of the most moderate forces in German politics.

The peace settlement, to be sure, had glaring weaknesses. Reparations and other economic restrictions combined with the territorial adjustments impoverished sections of Central Europe and disrupted commercial activity in that area. With the exception of the temporary relief provided by the American Relief Administration, nothing was done to rehabilitate Europe economically. The Russian problem, which weighed heavily on the minds of the Big Three, was not formally addressed at the conference. Europe's largest and most populous nation was not even invited to Versailles. Japan, another major world power, played only a peripheral role in the settlement, and Far Eastern questions, with the exception of German possessions in that area, were ignored. The treaties of Paris simply did not constitute the kind of world settlement which was implied in Wilson's Fourteen Points. It should be pointed out, however, that even if the peace settlement had been less harsh and the Fourteen Points applied more rigorously on a global scale, the revisionist powers, Germany, Italy, and Japan, would not have been satisfied. All of them made their most strenuous objections to proposed adjustments that were based firmly on the Fourteen Points—i.e., in regard to Poland, Fiume, and Shantung. In the case of Germany, she did not accept defeat and would have opposed any settlement, no matter how lenient, which diminished German territory or influence. To that extent, the peacemakers had faced an impossible task. When the Big Three left Paris in mid-1919, they were convinced they had set Europe on the road to recovery, preserved Allied-American unity, and made the best settlement possible under difficult circumstances.

Soon after the end of the conference, a severe negative reaction set in against the Treaty of Versailles. Upon his return to the United States, Wilson found the Republican opposition mobilizing various interest groups against the peace settlement. The Senate, which was required to ratify the treaty, focused most of its attention on the League of Nations issue. Republican leaders, motivated by political expediency and constitutional scruples, opposed American membership in the League under Wilson's formula. Henry Cabot Lodge, chairman of the Senate Foreign Relations Committee, proposed a series of reservations to the treaty which he demanded that Wilson accept in order to guarantee ratification. His most strenuous objection was to Article 10 which Lodge believed violated the United States Constitution and might involve the nation in unnecessary wars. Wilson countered that Article 10 was the heart of the covenant and could not be altered under any circumstances. Throughout the fall and winter of 1919-20, both leaders refused to compromise. The Senate held two separate votes on the treaty and in both cases rejected it. And when in the next presidential election the Wilsonian candidate, James Cox, was soundly defeated, it was generally believed that the American people had decisively spoken out against the League of Nations and the Treaty of Versailles.

During the height of the debate over the treaty in America, a small book was published in London which triggered an outburst of reaction against the peace settlement in Britain and in other parts of the world. John M. Keynes' *Economic Consequences of the Peace* was a devastating attack on the peace settlement and the peacemakers alike. The former adviser to the British peace delegation analyzed the economic sections of the treaty and predicted a grim future for Europe unless some of the provisions were revised. He gave special attention to the Allied reparations demands which he characterized as absurdly high and unjust. Beyond this, Keynes painted a most unflattering portrait of the Big Three. Clemenceau and to a lesser degree Lloyd George appeared as cynical power brokers fighting over booty and scraps of territory. Keynes depicted Wilson as an inept old Presbyterian who was bamboozled by the unscrupulous statesmen of Europe. The book created an immediate sensation and had a profound impact on European diplomacy for a generation. Keynes' polemic was followed by a number of revisionist volumes which questioned the assumptions upon which the treaty had been based. All of this contributed to a "guilt complex" which took root in the Big Three countries in varying degrees. The aggrieved powers, meanwhile, were encouraged by the growing malaise which afflicted the nations that stood behind the peace settlement.

Despite the defection of the United States and the wave of criticism directed at the treaty, the peace settlement held up during the 1920s. It was revised in part and functioned imperfectly at times, but it did work. The League of Nations never became the world-governing body that Wilson had envisioned and it was often bypassed in favor of big power diplomacy. Article 10, as Clemenceau predicted, was too vague to provide collective security. But the League did settle disputes between smaller nations, rehabilitate impoverished countries, facilitate arms control, and ameliorate a number of world health and social problems. By the end of the 1920s, all major nations, with the exception of Soviet Russia and America, were members and the League attained a position of respect in international affairs. The reparations settlement was revised twice during the postwar decade. As a result of the Dawes Plan (1924) and the Young Plan (1930), German obligations were reduced from \$33 to \$8 billion, reparations control agencies were removed from Germany, and occupation forces were withdrawn from the Rhineland five years ahead of schedule. It is important to note, moreover, that between 1924 and 1930 Germany paid every single installment on its reparations debt. During the 1920s, the territorial adjustments remained basically unchanged. In fact, Germany made additional pledges guaranteeing the existing boundaries in Western Europe under the Locarno Pacts of 1925. Despite the dire warning of Keynes and others, Europe was reasonably secure and prosperous under the provisions of the Versailles Treaty in 1930.

During the next decade, however, the Versailles settlement collapsed under the weight of the Great Depression which had begun in 1929. Dispirited by the economic catastrophe and the increasing boldness of the revisionist powers, Britain and France declined to invoke the full power of the League to counteract aggression in Asia and Africa. After its ineffectual response to the Manchurian crisis of 1931 and the Italian invasion of Ethiopia in 1935, the League of Nations was discredited in the eyes of the world and declined in international importance. The reparations system also broke down in the early 1930s. Pressured by the increasing danger of a general financial collapse and German demands for cancellation, the Allies suspended reparations payments in 1932. The issue was never revived and Germany's postwar obligation was in effect ended. Encouraged by the impotence of the League and the lack of determination shown by the Allies to enforce the provisions of the treaty, Hitler embarked on a program to overturn the territorial adjustments in the mid-thirties. With stunning suddenness, the German chancellor successfully remilitarized the Rhineland (1936), united Austria with the Reich (1938), and occupied the Sudetenland, and most of the rest of Czechoslovakia (1938-39). When Hitler issued his final demand on Danzig and the Polish Corridor in 1939, most of the postwar territorial settlement in Europe lay in ruins and the Versailles Treaty was a mere skeleton.

For nearly a half century, historians and politicians have debated the causes of the failure of the Versailles settlement. Some, like Winston Churchill, concluded that the peace conference was a "turbulent collision of embarrassed demagogues" who produced a treaty that was fundamentally unsound, unworkable, and bound to fail. Others, such as Lloyd George, maintained that the treaty was "the most abused and least perused document in history." In referring to the territorial provisions, Lloyd George contended that they held up for twenty years and "when they cracked finally it was not from inherent weak-

ness or injustice but from external assault." Both views
have some merit. The treaty was constructed in the smol-
dering ashes of the greatest war in history until that time
by leaders who shared no common perspective on how to
shape a new world order. Many provisions of the treaty
were ill conceived and important problems were completely ignored. But the settlement did work tolerably well
in the 1920s despite the constant criticism of writers like
Keynes and the best efforts of the revisionist powers to
undermine it. In retrospect, it appears that the Treaty of
Versailles was not as good as its most ardent supporters
believed or as bad as its worst enemies charged. A fair
assessment would be that the impact of the Great Depression rather than the intrinsic weaknesses of the treaty contributed most to the collapse of the Versailles settlement
by 1939.

Suggested Readings

For a general introduction to the Versailles conference,
see Ferdinand Czernin, *Versailles 1919* (1965) and Harold
Nicolson, *Peacemaking, 1919* (1933). Thomas A. Bailey,
Woodrow Wilson and the Lost Peace (1944) and N. Gordon
Levin, *Woodrow Wilson and World Politics* (1968) give
different views of Wilson at the conference. For the British
and French positions, see Seth Tillman, *Anglo-American
Relations at the Paris Peace Conference of 1919* (1961) and
Andre Tardieu, *The Truth About the Treaty* (1921). On
Italy and Germany, see René Albrecht-Carrié, *Italy at the
Paris Peace Conference* (1938) and Alma Luckau, *The German Delegation at the Paris Peace Conference* (1941). The
importance of bolshevism and the Russian Revolution is
discussed at length in Arno J. Mayer, *Politics of Peacemaking: Versailles, 1918-1919* (1967). An examination of
self-determination can be found in the previously cited
books by Bailey, Levin, and Mayer. For an introduction to
the subject of reparations, see the spirited accounts by
John M. Keynes, *The Economic Consequences of the Peace*
(1919) and Etienné Mantoux, *The Carthaginian Peace: Or
the Economic Consequences of Mr. Keynes* (1946). On the
League of Nations, see F. P. Walters, *A History of the
League of Nations* (2 vols., 1952). Thomas A. Bailey,

Woodrow Wilson and the Great Betrayal (1945) gives a good account of the treaty's defeat in the United States. For a favorable evaluation of the peace settlement, see Paul Birdsall, *Versailles Twenty Years After* (1941). Sally Marks, *The Illusion of Peace* (1976) is critical of the Versailles Treaty and its implementation. For a more balanced account of the post-Versailles world, see Raymond J. Sontag, *A Broken World: 1919-1939* (1971).

The persistent influence of the Russian Revolution in Europe. Paris, 1978. Sign on left reads "All Communists with all unemployed." *(Philip Chiviges Naylor)*

CHAPTER 3

The Russian Revolution and Its Impact on Europe

George D. Balsama

At the outbreak of World War I, the people of most belligerent countries rose up in support of their governments.
Internal political squabblings were adjourned, at least
temporarily, as the English, French, and Germans expressed a willingness to accept the heroic self-sacrifice
necessary for the defense of the "fatherland."

Imperial Russia, however, enjoyed no such phenomenon in the autumn of 1914. Governed since 1894 by
Nicholas II, a quixotic, fumbling autocrat and his supersti-
tious, paranoid wife, Alexandra, it lacked both the capacity and desire to foster national survival by effecting an
indispensable union of the Russian people.

Oppressed by long hours, low salaries, and dismal conditions, city workers did not distinguish themselves with
outpourings of patriotism when they went to do battle
with German invaders. Likewise, the great unwashed,
illiterate mass of peasants, for centuries burdened by
crushing taxation, hardly accepted conscription with enthusiasm. Furthermore, national minorities, such as the
Poles, Ukrainians, and Jews, who traditionally had been
officially persecuted and brutalized, would give no support whatever to the czarist autocracy in World War I.

Only the Russian middle classes seemed ready to protect the country from the horrors of enemy attack. Yet even solid business and professional men quickly became infuriated with the corruption and inefficiency of their tottering, reactionary government. Devastating military reverses, crippling labor, food and fuel shortages, acute transportation breakdowns, and the czar's suppression of the national parliament (Duma) converted many moderates and liberals into revolutionaries. In March 1917, they joined hungry, suffering workers and peasants in a successful attempt to destroy the imperial regime and replace it with a republican political system. Thus three days before the beginning of spring, the long-awaited revolution was a *fait accompli*. It now merely remained to be seen which groups of Russians would fill the power vacuum created by the abrupt and unceremonious abdication of Nicholas II.

Of the various political organizations in Russia at the time, three in particular stood out as reasonably capable and most anxious to preside over a new form of government, demonstrably superior to the ramshackle monarchy. The least radical was the Constitutional Democratic party (the K.D.'s or "Cadets"). Dominating the loyal opposition movement to the czar since its founding in 1903, the liberal K. D. party initially sought to restructure the Russian body politic along English lines. Accordingly, it had advocated the forcible extraction of a constitution from Nicholas II in order that a parliamentary government might be introduced into Russia. Once the March revolution swept the Russian empire away, however, the Cadets demanded the establishment of a complete democracy, although they stopped short of championing the cause of desperate workers and peasants.

K. D. hesitation to embrace socialism sharply differentiated it from the Social Revolutionary party (SR). Basically agrarian populists, the SRs inveighed against the plight of the peasantry and the abuses of proprietorship. Land was central to their political program; and they saw little evil in employing terrorism and assassination to promote its transfer to peasant hands. Yet even these rural socialists did not consider themselves so far to the left that they could not cooperate with the Cadets if such might facilitate the appeasement of their land hunger.

In any case, SR socialism was strictly Russian in orientation, and Social Revolutionary leaders kept their movement away from all international entanglements. Conversely, however, its mystical faith in the people of Russia notwithstanding, the SR party was not nationalistic to the extent that it favored state worship. Rather, it bridled at comprehensive government power and emphatically proclaimed the virtues inherent in decentralization of authority.

Far more disciplined than the large, at times unwieldy, Social Revolutionary party were the Social Democrats. Internationalist and elitist, the Social Democrat party believed that world revolution would be effected by a small dedicated band of professionals, rank and file obedience to whom was to be uncompromising.

Early in the existence of the Social Democrat party, when a minority of members protested against its excessive centralization, the organization split irrevocably into two factions, Mensheviks and Bolsheviks. Destined to pass into oblivion, the Mensheviks (or minority men) lacked the leadership to implement their desire for an open party that would cooperate with Social Revolutionaries and Cadets.

The Bolsheviks (or majority men), on the other hand, who consistently distinguished themselves by cohesiveness, tenacity, and unity of purpose, would attain their goals thanks in great measure to a leader of exceptional brilliance, Vladimir Ilyich Ulyanov. Known as Lenin, this Bolshevik firebrand proclaimed that true socialism (as only he could interpret it) should not be compromised or diluted in any way. Cooperation with business and professional men, natural enemies of the oppressed masses, was therefore unconscionable.

Furthermore, Lenin believed, the Social Revolutionaries were fatuous and confused, nothing more than objects of scorn and ridicule. He derisively asked: How could these puerile peasants possibly believe Russia can escape the development of a capitalist class? How could they assume that mindless assassination can lead to human betterment when a murdered bad government official will invariably be replaced by a worse oppressor? With the zeal of a religious fanatic, Lenin argued that unskilled city workers were the only true revolutionary class and that the only legitimate form of government was one which guaranteed sovereignty to them. The Bolsheviks, he therefore concluded, must impose their will upon Russia through a dictatorship of the proletariat.

In March 1917, the Bolsheviks, Mensheviks, Social Revolutionaries, and Cadets all vied for control over the Provisional Government, to which ruling power passed after the abdication of Nicholas II. And to the chagrin of hardcore revolutionary megalomaniacs, the organizational superiority of the K. D. party enabled the middle classes initially to dominate the new regime. Indeed, the latter's executive council included but one radical, Alexander Kerensky, an ambivalent Social Revolutionary, who became minister of justice.

In classic liberal style, the Provisional Government officially proclaimed civil liberties, equality before the law, and autonomy for national minorities. It also concocted a social program highlighted by a decree legalizing the transfer of imperial and ecclesiastical land to the peasantry. Unfortunately, however, the implementation of these reforms had to await the election of a national constituent assembly.

Meanwhile, the socialists had organized the Petrograd Soviet (Council of Workers' and Soldiers' Deputies), which would conflict sharply with the Provisional Government. While the Liberals pledged to continue the war against Germany and her allies, Soviet leaders demanded the conclusion of a non-annexationist peace. Fearing, moreover, that the military high command might attempt a counterrevolution, the Petrograd Soviet issued Order No. 1, depriving generals of all authority except for strategic operations, and entrusting control of the army to democratically elected committees.

Shortly thereafter, Lenin and other Bolshevik leaders arrived in Petrograd. Further accentuating the rift between the Provisional Government and the Petrograd Soviet, he demanded that all power be given to the Soviets, the war be stopped immediately, peasants be authorized to seize land without waiting for approval by the Constituent Assembly, and industry be subjected to worker control. Ably endorsing Lenin's "peace and bread" program was Leon Trotsky (Bronstein), an independent socialist, soon to join the Bolsheviks, to whom he would render invaluable service through his military expertise.

With the utter failure of a Russian offensive against Austro-German forces in July, the Bolsheviks attempted to seize power; but the Provisional Government quelled the rebellion, imprisoned Trotsky, and caused Lenin to flee for his life. Then, in a last ditch effort at popularity, it allowed Kerensky to become prime minister. Unfortunately for Russian democracy however, General Kornilov, a new military commander, attacked Petrograd in order to supplant Kerensky, whom he mistakenly thought a dangerous radical. The prime minister in turn released Trotsky, as well as other rabble-rousers, from prison and appealed to all socialists to help him overcome the counterrevolution.

Kornilov was defeated in September, but the Provisional Government now lay under a Red shadow. The following month the Bolsheviks secured a majority in the Petrograd Soviet, to which they elected Trotsky chairman; and on November 6, Lenin launched his revolution.

Although its success was not a foregone conclusion and government resistance proved sufficiently threatening as to cause Lenin, an avowed atheist, to make the sign of the cross and turn to God in a moment of crisis, the Bolsheviks still seized power with remarkable ease. Led by the military revolutionary committee, soldiers from the Petrograd garrison, sailors from Kronshtadt, and the workers' Red Guards, the Bolsheviks captured most government offices, stormed the royal palace, and arrested the members of the Provisional Government. Kerensky luckily escaped, and, after a fumbling attempt to counterattack, went into hiding and ultimately exile.

On November 7, a new government was organized under Lenin. Taking the name Council of People's Commissars, it included Trotsky, who was put in charge of foreign affairs, and Iosif Vissarionovich Dzhugashvili, later called Stalin, who assumed responsibility for national minorities. Thus began the history of Soviet Russia, which may be conveniently divided into three periods: (1) the period of militant communism (1917-21), (2) the period of the New Economic Policy (1921-27), (3) the period of the New Socialist Offensive (1927–).

Attempting to translate his slogans into laws and government policies, Lenin immediately ordered the partition of large estates and the distribution of their component parts to the peasantry. In February 1918, the Red state took nominal title to all land, which remained in the hands of those willing to cultivate it. Meanwhile, other official decrees nationalized all banks and ecclesiastical properties, repudiated the national debt, authorized workers to assume control over factories, abolished religious instruction in schools, and recognized only civil marriages.

Determined to honor the demands of minorities, Lenin also proclaimed the Declaration of the Rights of the Peoples of Russia, by the terms of which certain national groups, persecuted during the czarist autocracy, were promised self-determination and the removal of civil and religious disabilities. Similar declarations, issued subsequently, abolished class privileges and granted equal rights for women.

Regrettably, all these reforms and advantages had their price: Bolshevik tyranny. At the beginning of January 1918, the SR party scored an overwhelming victory in a national election, in which thirty-six million citizens cast votes to determine the composition of the first Russian Constituent Assembly. Lenin, however, who refused to "compromise with the malignant bourgeoisie," ordered the assembly's dissolution. Immediately thereafter he proclaimed the dictatorship of the proletariat, to be exercised by the Bolsheviks, who, in March 1918, renamed themselves the Communist party.

At the same time German armies, which were now threatening Petrograd (renamed Leningrad), forced the Bolshevik government to sign the humiliating Treaty of Brest-Litovsk. By its terms, Russia lost Poland, the Ukraine, and all the borderlands occupied by non-Russian nationalities.

Less than a week later, Moscow became the new capital of the Communist state, a development which might have been foreseen owing to Leningrad's geographical vulnerability both to the Germans and borderland counterrevolutionary movements. Potentially lethal to the new regime, the latter included not only czarists, liberals, and moderate socialists, but also the British and French, who stigmatized the Bolsheviks as lackeys of the German High Command and therefore encouraged all anti-Communist activities.

Opposition to the dictatorship of Lenin indeed proved strong enough to plunge Russia into civil war, the first victories of which went to the counterrevolutionaries, collectively known as the "Whites." Gradually, however, a new "Red" Army was organized under the leadership of Trotsky, who recruited his men by conscription and subjected them to the strictest discipline.

In the summer of 1918, the Communist government, with real control over only 25 percent of the Russian population, took the offensive. A reign of terror was initiated to crush all opposition in areas dominated by the Red Army. Hunted down by the new political police, called successively the Cheka, OGPU, NKVD, and MVD, the anarchists, Social Revolutionaries, and Mensheviks were slaughtered as ruthlessly as were Cadets, czarists, and the royal family itself. Millions of others, earmarked for liquidation, fled the country with only the shirts on their backs.

Meanwhile, although White opposition to Lenin's regime was widespread, it suffered from disunity, bad organization, and a confusion in aims. Furthermore, the half-hearted assistance the Whites received from England and France (joined later by Japan and the United States) merely encouraged them to continue struggling against the Bolsheviks without substantially enhancing their prospects for victory.

Conversely, the Red Army, profiting from a unified command, interior lines of communication, and the support historically given "defenders of Russia," could, by straining every effort, secure a dominant military advantage. With Trotsky at the controls, it expanded to three million after a year of warfare, and despite mass desertions and repeated bloodbaths in areas under its yoke, the Red Army sytematically converted possible defeat into certain victory. By 1922, the Whites and their foreign allies had been either smashed or forced to withdraw from Russia, the borders of which were now reestablished, under Communist control, at the prewar locations in every direction except that of Europe.

Once the Red tide had crested in the Russian Civil War, Lenin proclaimed world revolution and urged the Communists of other countries to seize power as soon as possible. In March 1919, he hosted a conference of representatives from the international Communist movement, in the course of which the Comintern was founded. A laboratory for revolution and an "apparatus" for the extension of Lenin's influence into foreign states, the Comintern immediately sponsored Communist uprisings in Berlin, Munich, and Budapest.

Unfortunately for the Bolshevik dictator, however, all three subversive movements suffered premature deaths. Meanwhile, Russia became embroiled with Poland in a frontier war, which proved both costly and indecisive. Six bloody months of Russo-Polish conflict combined with the effects of the devastating Civil War and a concomitant Allied blockade to impose unbearable hardships on the Russian people. Magnifying the latter was the disruptive economic policy of the Red government, which led inevitably to sharp declines in industrial and agricultural production, widespread disorganization of transport, and acute shortages of food and fuel.

In 1920, peasant insurrections broke out across the map of Russia while thousands of factory workers from Leningrad struck and rioted. Finally, a mutinous uprising of the sailors at Kronshtadt that was suppressed only with great difficulty and wholesale butchery during the next year signaled the near collapse of the Russian economy.

Lenin now had no choice but to admit that the process of "militant communism" was moving perhaps too rapidly and therefore should be temporarily suspended in favor of a government-sponsored convalescence. Some compromise with capitalism, he could hardly deny, seemed to be dictated by the ravages of the preceding eight years.

Consequently, from 1921 to 1927, the Communist party adopted the New Economic Policy. Under NEP, as it was usually called, the state controlled the "commanding heights" of the economy through its ownership of the basic productive industries. Yet although large manufactures and transport indeed remained nationalized while foreign trade continued to be a government monopoly, a substantial amount of private trading for private profit was also officially condoned.

To placate the peasantry, an emergency food levy, which had been imposed during the Civil War, was replaced by a limited grain tax. Thus Russian farmers retained part of their surplus crops, which they in turn were allowed to sell. The Communist regime also permitted the reconstruction of small individual farms, lease of land, and use of hired labor. Private commercial establishments were even allowed to exist in urban areas. Ultimately, the currency would be stabilized and the entire financial system recast on a semicapitalist basis. Already in 1922, the state bank received the right to print paper money, backed either by goods or foreign bonds.

Spreading outside the economic sphere, the revisionist spirit of NEP led to an abatement of government censorship, repression, and persecution. Along with this relaxation of Lenin's dictatorial rule came a greater official interest in cultural affairs, one important manifestation of which was the establishment of an ambitious educational program for the elimination of illiteracy.

Under NEP the worst damages resulting from war and revolution were repaired. Regrettably, however, although the national economy recovered at a rapid pace, economic progress was still more apparent than real. In 1927, Russia managed to produce barely as much grain, cotton, coal, oil, and cattle as she did on the eve of World War I. And in view of the economic growth rate before 1914, Russia probably would have been producing far more had the Bolshevik revolution never succeeded.

In any case, prior to the inception of NEP and the resultant relaxation of Communist militance, Lenin had experienced only frustration in numerous aggressive attempts to extend his system into other parts of Europe. He therefore decided to modify his foreign policy and deal with non-Communist states, at least temporarily, in a less hostile, more diplomatic way. Realizing that after the cessation of World War I, Germany as well as Russia had been condemned to a pariah status in Europe, the Bolshevik dictator gave his assent to a Russo-German rapprochement, and in April 1922, signed the Treaty of Rapallo.

Ostensibly negotiated for the purposes of formalizing German diplomatic recognition of the new Russian government and vastly expanding trade between the two countries, the Treaty of Rapallo also contained secret clauses. Among the latter was an arrangement whereby Germany would be allowed to train a secret military force on Russian soil in return for which German generals, the best in Europe, would help increase the Red Army's efficiency and discipline. Three years later economic cooperation between the Russians and Germans was further enhanced by the enactment of a new trade treaty, subject to periodic renewal. This in turn was quickly followed by a Russo-German nonaggression pact, in which each state promised to remain neutral if a third power attacked one or the other.

Meanwhile, on December 30, 1922, the Union of Soviet Socialist Republics was organized, bringing together, in one federation, Russia, the Ukraine, White Russia, and Transcaucasia. In one of its first official acts the USSR formally censured the czarist imperial government for its nonrecognition of nationality, and flamboyantly granted autonomy to national groups. Immediately thereafter, however, the latter were forged into a "higher union," completely dominated by the Russian Republic, which in turn fell under the strict control of the Communist party.

Composed of a mere 1 percent of the Soviet population, the party was a small, well-disciplined oligarchy of professional revolutionaries—the revolutionary *élite*, advocated by Lenin at the very onset of his political career. The function of the Communist party, the only party allowed in the USSR, was to actuate the dictatorship of the proletariat, provide for the realization of state socialism, and promote governmental efficiency. Those honored with party membership took orders without question or reservation, devoted themselves completely to the state, became experts on Communist policy, and mastered the most intricate details of farming and manufacturing so that they could credibly give authoritative leadership and assistance to the mass of nonparty members, who composed the bulk of the USSR's population. Like a thin stream of lifeblood, circulating through the body politic, the Communist party kept the Union of Soviet Socialist

Republics unified, vital, and alive. As the Bolshevik tyranny grew thus more consolidated, Red leaders became increasingly willing to maintain cordial relations with the outside world. Summarizing the continuation of Communist pragmatism that had begun with NEP, Stalin once declared: "Those who want peace and seek business relations with us will always have our support."

Nor was this message ignored. In 1924, England, France, and Italy formally recognized the Soviet Union, to which a number of new republics were added shortly thereafter. In 1925, Japan followed suit, while Turkey joined Lithuania and Iran in signing nonaggression pacts with the USSR. Hence during the middle years of the 1920s Russian military weakness, combined with the failures of the Comintern, had generated conditions that led to an atmosphere of guarded mutual confidence between the Soviets and their neighbors. Two full decades would have to pass before the understandings, reached by Russia and the European democracies, degenerated into a Communist-non-Communist cold war.

In 1918, a young working class woman named Fanny Kaplan, convinced that Lenin had betrayed the revolution, attempted to assassinate him. Although she failed, the wound sustained by the Bolshevik dictator in this abortive effort permanently weakened him. Several years later, overwork caused Lenin to suffer strokes, possibly complicated by a social disease he may have inherited from his mistress (and later wife), Nadezhda Krupskaya. With the spring of 1922 came the coup de grâce, a cerebral hemorrhage, from which he never recovered; and in January 1924, the architect of the Bolshevik Revolution died in his bed.

The heirs apparent to Lenin were Trotsky, the paradigmatic creator of the Red Army and Stalin, a hitherto modest political organizer who had quietly become General Secretary of the Communist party. Vain, domineering, and overconfident, Trotsky urged a renewal of the international revolutionary movement despite its colossal failures. Likewise unwilling to acknowledge the major contributions to the Soviet State made by NEP, he castigated Stalin's tolerance of the Russian middle classes and wealthy farmers. Hinting, moreover, that Lenin, lethargic in his declining years, had wrongly fostered a bureaucratic ossification of the Communist party, Trotsky demanded that he be allowed to rejuvenate the proletarian movement in the USSR, accelerate Russian industrial development, collectivize agriculture, and preside over the entirety of Soviet economic life.

Sensing that rank and file party members were offended, if not horrified, at Trotsky and his cohorts, Stalin let them pursue their strident criticisms of Russian communism until he felt ready to strike. His opportunity came at the Congress of Soviets in 1927, on which occasion the General Secretary stigmatized the "Trotskyites" as leftist deviationists, called for and received a no confidence vote against them, and thereupon ordered that they be exiled to Siberia. Trotsky himself had to flee from the USSR, eventually relocating in Mexico, where he was assassinated in 1940.

Once firmly established in power, Stalin did not hesitate to adopt fragments of Trotsky's program. Crediting himself with having devised these trail-blazing policies, the new Red dictator decreed an end to the NEP. In its place he inaugurated a "New Socialist Offensive," which would provide for speedy industrialization of the USSR through the introduction of several successive Five-Year Plans, the first beginning in October 1928. Under Stalin's heavy hand, the national economy was accordingly strengthened by the rapid development of heavy industries, most of which produced war materiel. Less change took place in the area of consumer goods production because this was and would remain a low priority matter until the 1970s.

Stalin knew what he wanted and tolerated no external frustration of his designs. Infuriated at the inefficiency and recalcitrance of those manufacturers who openly resented government control over their business enterprises, Stalin tried and executed numerous "technicians" for mismanagement and sabotage.

The agricultural counterpart to the creation of a modern industrial system was the socialization of farming through consolidation of individual peasant land holdings into large concerns. Justified by government propaganda, this agrarian collectivization was carried out through naked force. Well-to-do peasants who refused to cooperate were summarily wiped out. Hence within a few years Stalin saw his objectives substantially attained, and the Communist regime now controlled agricultural output.

Stalin's stranglehold on the USSR was assured in 1936, by which time he had completed a systematic purge of the Communist party. Well over a million members were expelled from its ranks, and undetermined numbers, executed after brief but spectacular trials. Consequently, Stalin could mark the tenth year of his dictatorship with the knowledge that he had suppressed Trotskyism, destroyed all rivals, and made great strides in rebuilding the Russian state according to a Communist blueprint. Furthermore, since he felt no benefits would result from a resumption of militant communism on the international scene, Stalin pursued peaceful coexistence with non-Communist Europe. Indeed, during most of the 1930s the Comintern became virtually inactive, as the USSR concluded nonaggression pacts with Poland and several Baltic states. Appreciating Russian attempts to stabilize relations with European neighbors and pursue active participation in the sixty-nation Disarmament Conference of 1932, the United States formally recognized the Soviet State in November 1933. During the following year, the USSR joined the League of Nations and worked for the furtherance of collective security in Europe.

When Hitler and Mussolini began to engage in saber rattling, Stalin offered to join with the European democratic states in an attempt to curtail expansionist fascism. At the outbreak of the Spanish Civil War in 1936, the Russian government sent airplanes, troops, and supplies to the Loyalists in order to thwart General Franco's scheme to convert Spain into a Fascist state. Unfortunately, Franco could not be stopped, and the resultant demise of Spanish democracy was attributed by Stalin to half-hearted Anglo-French-American support, which he disdainfully contrasted to the major efforts put forth by Fascist Italy, Nazi Germany, and of course the Soviet State. Embittered and disillusioned at what appeared to be Western indifference, the Russian dictator then began to fear that England and France cared less about his friendship than promoting a Nazi-Soviet war.

Determined to guarantee the security of the USSR by whatever means necessary, he did not take kindly to an Anglo-French refusal to form an effective alliance with Russia in 1939. His anger was compounded by disgust when he learned of a large English loan, apparently earmarked for Germany at the end of July.

Stalin accordingly decided that the best interests of Russia would be served by signing a Nazi-Soviet nonaggression pact the following month. By its terms, the signatories promised to refrain from attacking each other and pledged neutrality in the event that a third state attacked one or the other. Secretly appended to the Nazi-Soviet nonaggression pact was an agreement to divide up much of Eastern Europe in case of a territorial and political rearrangement. Finland, Estonia, Latvia, Bessarabia, and eastern Poland would become a Soviet sphere of influence, while Lithuania and the lion's share of Polish territory would fall to the Nazis. Viewing the treaty with cold pragmatism, Stalin never dreamed it would last the ten years for which it was concluded. No less than Hitler, he saw inevitable conflict between Germany and Russia. Hence the Russian tyrant interpreted the Nazi-Soviet nonagression pact as merely a convenient time-buying device.

Stalin's breathing spell lasted approximately two years. On September 1, 1939, Hitler began World War II by invading Poland, which he crushed in short order along with Holland, Belgium, and France. After crippling, but not defeating England, the German war machine turned against Russia; and on June 22, 1941, the expected invasion took place.

The Russians were ready. During the period of Nazi-Soviet neutrality, they had equipped and trained their large armies for proficiency in tank, artillery, and paratroop combat. With two million men under arms, an indefinite reserve, and a tremendous expanse of territory, the Russians could counteract German superiority in war materiel and battle tactics.

Significant assistance was rendered the Red Army by the United States and Great Britain. By the terms of the First Russian Protocol, both nations agreed to supply materials necessary to the Russian war effort from October 1941 through the following July. Furthermore, purchase of nonmilitary supplies from the United States was expedited by an American loan to the Soviet government in the amount of one billion dollars. Supplementing this arrangement in June 1942, the United States and USSR negotiated a Master Lend-Lease Agreement, whereby the American president authorized massive distribution of supplies to support the Russian resistance to the German invasion. Through this system, 1,500,000 tons of foodstuffs alone traveled from American to Russian ports.

The cooperative venture worked. By winter 1941, German armies had reached the suburbs of Leningrad and Moscow, but could press no further in the face of a vigorous counteroffensive by the central Russian army. During the following autumn, another German offensive sputtered at Stalingrad, a vital communications center, because of overstretched lines. Again a Russian counterattack repelled the invaders, and this time at a cost of half a million German lives. By the summer of 1943, the military advantage passed irrevocably to the Soviets, who utilized increasing Anglo-American assistance to close a vise around the German war machine. Less than two years later, the Russians, British, and Americans, with token French help, swept through Germany and stormed the capital city of Berlin.

On May 8, 1945, the killing finally stopped. At this point, Russian military deaths numbered approximately seven million, more than twice that sustained by Germany, while twenty million Russians had been rendered homeless. But the USSR had won the war! From 1941 to 1945 Russia used her inherent strength to withstand the terrific shock of the Nazi invasion and contribute to Hitler's ultimate debacle. In the postwar era, despite the widespread devastation of Russian soil, she would utilize this formidable resource to exploit international poverty, hatreds, and confusion for the expansion of Soviet strength in Europe.

At the end of World War II, the Soviets controlled what, prior to 1938, had been eight independent European countries: Estonia, Latvia, Lithuania, Poland, Czechoslovakia, Hungary, Rumania, and Bulgaria. In addition, East Germany, euphemistically renamed the German Democratic Republic, along with Albania also fell into the Soviet orbit. In all these states, with only the possible exception of Albania, Communist-dominated "satellite" governments were established, resulting in the descension of an "iron curtain" around much of Eastern Europe, now effectively cut off from Western democracy.

The consolidation of the Red hold on Eastern Europe proceeded according to a simple but effective pattern. Liberated from the Germans by Russia or her allies, each state received an anti-Nazi coalition government, the predominant characteristic of which was a Communist minister of the interior, who of course controlled the police. Before long this powerful government official outlawed noncoalition parties under the pretext that they had been pro-German during the war. Having established a foothold in the ruling bureaucracy, the Communists intimidated and/or arrested non-Communist members of the coalition. Once all government officials who had demonstrated signs of independence were cowed into submission, the structure of the state was reorganized to establish a Communist political monopoly. Civil liberties were suppressed. All means of communication fell under direct Communist control. Forced labor camps, which were opened or expanded, bulged with recalcitrant citizens, some of whom were shot outright. Finally, after the consolidation of the Red dictatorship, any opposition to the dominant faction in the Communist party was systematically wiped out.

The architect of the "iron curtain" system was none other than Joseph Stalin, who in less than three decades had converted communism into the strongest single movement in Europe. Feared and detested by the free world because of his power, ruthlessness, and blood thirst, Stalin also eventually terrorized even his closest associates, who watched him gradually lose mental stability and succumb to self-feeding paranoia.

On March 5, 1953, shortly before he planned to initiate yet another wholesale purge, Stalin died suddenly; and a great sigh of relief went up inside as well as outside the USSR. Immediately thereafter, Soviet leaders repudiated most of the old dictator's brutal policies. Expressing horror at the latter's "crimes," they popularized government in the Soviet Union, released hundreds of political prisoners, restricted the secret police, and closed slave labor camps.

Yet, despite this softening of official policy, Russian strength is still on the increase, and communism, as an international movement, has probably not yet attained its historical apex. Beginning almost imperceptibly at the dawn of the twentieth century with Lenin and two dozen or so followers, European communism now impinges upon millions of individuals, can boast of its courageous leadership, and enjoys an increasingly popular base. Built on an efficient institutional structure, it exhibits unity of purpose, dynamism, and an uncanny knack for expanding its political power. Since its inception, the aims and methods of Bolshevik communism have remained virtually unchanged; and were it not for the present-day threat of nuclear holocaust, the USSR would be working actively to revolutionize the entire world. As it is, the Soviet interpretation of peaceful coexistence can be reduced to a demand that non-Communist states refrain from interfering in their affairs while the Communists do what pleases them!

Although after Stalin's death it has become more difficult for communism to spread, expansion has nonetheless taken place as a result of aggressive Soviet diplomacy, saber rattling, and brinkmanship. Furthermore, in every area that has fallen under Russian control, a Soviet society has been forcibly established. In sum, today, more than ever before, Bolshevik communism presents a grave threat to Western civilization. In retreat since the end of World War II, its future can only be assured if the free world succeeds in containing the Red Star over Europe.

Suggested Readings

The following book list is intended to provide the introductory student with some additional works to consult to broaden his or her knowledge of the various topics dealt with in this chapter.

Basic bibliographic materials appear in Paul L. Horecky, ed., *Basic Russian Publications* (1962) and, by the same editor, *Russia and the Soviet Union* (1965).

Easily available books presenting various interpretations of the nature and importance of the Russian Revolution are the following. E. H. Carr, *The Bolshevik Revo-lution, 1917-1923* (3 vols., 1951-53), based on official documents, is highly detailed and very scholarly. The first volume deals with Communist theory and practice, the second with Soviet economics, and the third with interna-tional communism. The standard history of the revolu-tion is W. H. Chamberlin, *The Russian Revolution, 1917-1921* (2 vols., 1952). This study is exhaustive and clearly anti-Soviet. *The Great Russian Revolution* (1936) is an analysis of the political, social, and economic con-vulsions of the revolutionary period by a moderate re-former, V. Chernov, who feared and detested bolshevism. M. Florinsky, a World War I Russian Army veteran, pre-sents a vivid account with valuable information on the czars in *The End of the Russian Empire* (1931), but he includes only rather ephemeral coverage on the Soviets. *The Catastrophe: Kerensky's Own Story of the Russian Revolution* (1927) is a self-justifying account of the revolu-tion by the man who led the Provisional Government to disaster in 1917. V. Lenin and J. Stalin, *The Russian Revo-lution* (1938) presents a mine of information on the revolu-tionary strategies employed by two of the most remarkable figures of the twentieth century. The masterwork of the brilliant creator of the Red Army, L. Trotsky, *The History of the Russian Revolution* (3 vols., 1937), is not as tenden-tious as one might expect, although it is decidedly pro-Soviet. For a serious, highly critical analysis of Allied bungling during the revolution and civil war period, see R. Warth, *The Allies and the Russian Revolution* (1954). B. Wolfe has written a semipopular description of the lives, hopes, and *raisons d'être* of Lenin, Trotsky, and Stalin in *Three Who Made a Revolution* (1948).

Good biographical introductions for the general reader on the Russian Revolution and USSR are A. Ulam, *The Bolsheviks* (1965); L. Fisher, *The Life of Lenin* (1964); and I. Deutscher, *Stalin: A Political Biography* (2nd ed. 1967), *The Prophet Armed: Trotsky, 1879-1921* (1954), *The Prophet Unarmed: Trotsky, 1921-1929* (1959), and *The Prophet Outcast, 1929-1940* (1963).

For the post-Stalinist period, useful studies include W. Leonhard, *The Kremlin Since Stalin* (trans. 1962); M. Tatu, *Power in the Kremlin: From Khrushchev to Kosygin,* (trans. 1969); Z. Brzezinski, *The Soviet Bloc: Unity and Conflict* (rev. ed. 1967); F. Barghoorn, *Politics in the USSR* (1966); and A. Meyer, *The Soviet Political System: An Interpretation* (1965).

British Prime Minister Chamberlain leaving for Munich to appease Hitler, September 29, 1938. *(Courtesy of the National Archives)*

Europe Between
the Wars

The period between the world wars was probably the
most exciting, teeming, varied decades in the entire history of Western civilization. Between 1919 and 1939, Europe evolved from peace to war, from stability to instability, from order to chaos. In 1919, the future of European
society looked bright and promising, for the war to end all
future wars had ended, democracies had been established
throughout most of Europe, and a new organization, the
League of Nations, gave promise for international stability. But the emotions and hatreds unleashed by World War
I had not abated, and together with new grievances and
new animosities, the entire European continent was again
engulfed and swallowed in world war.

In the first essay in this section, Thomas F. Hale
examines the democracies of Western Europe between the
wars. He provides a much-needed revision of the traditional historical view that the 1920s and 1930s witnessed
a betrayal of democratic institutions and values by
England and France. He argues, instead, that the democratic states of Western Europe survived the great crises of
the 1930s and reaffirmed Woodrow Wilson's hope that
World War I would make the "world safe for democracy."

J. W. Baird, on the other hand, examines the strange phenomenon of fascism in Europe between 1919 and 1945, particularly the two most important Fascist movements, those of Adolf Hitler and Benito Mussolini. In the third essay in this section, Professor C. Robert Cole critically analyzes European diplomacy between the wars and its responsibility for the origins of World War II. Cole is especially effective in describing the revisionist foreign policies of the Nazis, and the various factors that contributed to the emergence of the British and French policies of appeasement toward Hitler. In the final essay in this section, Francis H. Thompson describes the course and consequences of World War II in Europe and the world. He describes in kaleidoscopic sequence the major military campaigns, the new weapons spawned by the war, the economic effects of the conflict in Europe and, finally, the emergence of the two new super powers of the world, the United States and the Soviet Union.

CHAPTER 4

The Triumph of Democracy Between the Wars

Thomas F. Hale

> Democracy is a form of government based upon self-rule of the people and, in modern times, upon freely elected representative institutions and an executive responsible to the people . . . Though democracy has a long and ancient history as the modern fruit of Western civilization and of its two component elements, the Athenian and Roman legacy and the Judaeo-Christian tradition, it is the most delicate form of political organization and the most difficult to achieve. It has therefore come to fruition only with very few peoples and in relatively short periods of history.

These remarks of the late Hans Kohn are indicative of the faith a free society must have in the *ultimate* efficacy and triumph of democracy. Professor Kohn witnessed the undeniable weaknesses of democracy in his native Czechoslovakia, which was not able to defend itself against the combined pressures of the Nazis, Fascists, and ineffectual democratic foreign leaders who in 1938 worked out the Munich Pact, which sealed the fate of Czechoslovakia's first experiment in democracy. Similarly, Kohn witnessed Soviet suppression of the briefly resurrected Czechoslovakian democracy after World War II, yet he retained his confidence in the democratic form of government. Professor Kohn's attitude is explained by the comments quoted above from his *Political Ideologies of the Twentieth Century* (1949).

Like Professor Kohn, we must, in order to discuss democracy properly, understand what it is, and what it is not, and especially understand its occurrence in the general history of mankind. First of all, what is democracy? It is a delicate type of government which relies on the self-rule of the governed. It is based on the undeniably correct assumption that the governors must be checked by some mechanism which will prevent an otherwise inevitable drift toward tyranny. The mechanism it uses is, in its essential form, a regular recourse to the participation of the people in their own governance. Its inestimable excellence is the ability to preserve maximum freedom and prevent tyranny. It need not make many other claims concerning its superiority over other systems of government. It is part of its inherent nature that democracy be paradoxical and contradictory in its goals, methods, and achievements. It is undeniable that its record is mixed at best. Its excellence is therefore relative in comparison to the ideal, but at the same time absolute in relation to the merits of authoritarian forms of government. As Winston Churchill observed, ". . . democracy is the worst form of government, except for all those other forms that have been tried from time to time."

Secondly, what is it that democracy is not? It is not efficient and expeditious in its day-to-day conduct of affairs. It does not usually provide mechanisms conducive to rapid changes and reforms. It is not generally bold in its leadership. It is not immune to floundering miserably in emergency situations. It is not the best vehicle for the impatient "Man of Destiny" who seeks revolution and war. It is not able to measure itself consistently in terms of many obvious achievements. Its goodness is best measured in one fundamental way: survival alone. Other gauges of its merits are often extraneous. For democracy to exist and survive, even briefly, is a triumph. This is so, from the Western European perspective at any rate, simply because freedom is the greatest good, the *summum bonum* from which all other blessings ultimately flow. The history of democracy is part of the history of liberty, and this in turn is truly the history of Western civilization. This can be properly appreciated when the overall record of democracy is examined.

Democracy must be understood in its historical context. It appears infrequently in history and until recently almost never outside the West. Even more rare have been the periods during which it flourished and achieved successes for all classes. For vast periods of the human past, there were no working models for imitation, and for equally significant amounts of time, democracy has only been a memory. Its tradition has been tenuous in the extreme, and in general, democracy has existed as a radical dream. As recently as the eighteenth century, Edmund Burke, a British advocate of liberty in the American colonies, could say without fear of censure that a pure democracy is "the most shameless thing in the world." At roughly the same time, Alexander Hamilton, one of the American architects of constitutional liberty, could also say unashamedly that the people are a "great beast." During most periods of history in fact, democrats were eccentrics and persons held suspect for their treasonable ideas; men who were comparable to the much-hated anarchists of the nineteenth century and the Communists of the twentieth. Accordingly, the context for a discussion of democracy's triumphs and failures between the wars and after must include the knowledge that democracy has always had severe and sincere critics as far back as Plato; that many glib people have been content to view its shortcomings without in the least bothering to contrast them fully to the manifest and manifold failures of despotisms and dictatorships. Realizing this, it should be no surprise that many people in Europe lived under various forms of monarchical government before World War I, and therefore were not anymore receptive to the establishment of democracies by the Paris Peace Conference than were the men of the eighteenth century. (Similarly and more recently, the newly liberated peoples of Asia and Africa have often repeated this pattern.)

It is fashionable to belittle faith in the promise and principles of democracy. It is *de rigueur* in some circles to point to the undeniable disasters of the twentieth century as if our time had a monopoly on cataclysmic events. It is commonplace to hear that the democratic creed and its concomitant, the hope for human progress, must be abandoned. It is popular to preach that only despair and cynicism can be affirmed in view of the unparalleled destructiveness of two world wars and the Holocaust. It is stylish to see only darkness in our midst and on the horizon, and therefore to foreswear the traditional Whiggish view of history which relates the story of liberty and its triumph over evil in its natural and human forms. It is chic to assert the wrong-headedness of great historians from Herodotus to Macaulay who saw liberty as the great theme of history. This is unfortunate, and especially so because it is based on the premise that the twentieth century is unique and that man has never before witnessed, endured, and survived gross calamities such as ours. Yet in truth, we must realize that Western standards of living in this century have created the greatest material and idealistic expectations that man has ever known. As a result, our sorrows are more intense by way of contrast with our daily pleasures, but no greater than the constant grinding hardship man has had as his ever-present companion in the past. Even the sickening, shattering horror of the Nazi holocaust is, ugly as it is to think it, part of the recurring story of man's inhumanity to man. It is gross in all its aspects, especially in its numbers and technological methods, but we cannot say that the Holocaust of the twentieth century has a separate significance apart from the enormity of man's crimes against his fellowman which is a constant factor throughout history. The important variable factor in our time is the increased development of a reliable mechanism for the diminution of man's inhumanity, i.e., democracy. This accomplishment is the great theme of our period and the interwar years are a crucial episode in the course of history's grand theme of liberty. We must restore a commonsense view of democracy without the pessimism of Oswald Spengler and Arnold Toynbee. Our studied and stylish skepticism has perhaps already created some of the most severe carping of all time. It should be noted parenthetically, however, that carping is a significant ingredient in the creation of a healthy democracy because it provokes the discourse and eternal vigilance required for success. It should also be realized that this carping occurs ironically in the environment of an earthly utopia which we are too blind to see as in large measure the result of the growth of democratic institutions in the West.

Interestingly, much of the criticism of democracy revolves around the mammoth economic and social problems which confronted all governments in the twenties and thirties and the supposed ease and success with which the Fascist and totalitarian governments cured the economic and social evils before which the democracies cowered and stumbled. This critical attitude is perhaps best epitomized by the flip statement that at least Mussolini made the Italian trains run on time. This remark was regularly repeated between the wars, but despite its currency it was nonetheless untrue. The Italian railways did not become models of punctuality under *Il Duce*. More important than the literal statement itself is the assumption that underlies it; namely, that efficiency and functionality are the most important criteria of success. The totalitarian regimes of the Right and the Left had their undeniable achievements, yet they cannot be viewed as more than ephemeral successes. A mystique of insidious proportions has grown up about them, and a corrective is greatly needed before totalitarian success myths further undermine democratic sentiments. Mussolini's Italian state was not a model for other Fascists in terms of efficiency and accomplishments. Italy's economic growth charts and other measures of prosperity were not impervious to the financial storms which afflicted the democracies. During the 1929 crash, for example, while "the major European economies bobbed up and down during the crisis, the Italian economy was engulfed," and by 1933 one million workers were unemployed. Even militarily, Italy scored only easy "triumphs" such as the conquests of feudal and penurious Ethiopia and Albania. Very early in World War II, it faced virtual collapse and had to be shored up by the Nazi regime. The story of Mussolini cannot be characterized as one of success, only one of audacity and cruelty.

Similarly, Hitler's Third Reich is given credit for the restoration of German prosperity. In popular conversation one hears that the little Volkswagen was part of this incredibly successful economic story. This is a distortion of reality originally fostered by the Nazis and still in our midst. The democratic Weimar Republic had already initiated the experiment with successful public work projects before the accession of the Nazis in 1933. At best, the Brown-shirted regime of Adolph Hitler only furthered this economic recovery. Their efforts to promote prosperity consistently took the form of shameless preparation for aggressive war and surely it is wrong to commend them for this. To do so would be to assert "better fed than dead"; that the end justifies the means. Ironically, those who justifiably condemned the democracies for their "peace at any price" mentality in some cases slipped into implicit praise for the Fascist policy of "stability and prosperity at any price." As late as 1940 for example, Churchill said of Mussolini, "that he is a great man I do deny. . . ." The critics of the democracies also point to the military flabbiness of the democracies and by implication praise the dictators for their military preparedness and rapid successes on the battlefield. This praise is again uncalled for simply because the democracies emerged victorious on the battlefield. Even the totalitarian Soviet Union, which made it a point to prepare for "defensive" war through Stalin's many programs and purges, very nearly succumbed to the Nazis.

Much of the blame for the disorders and crises between the wars is placed at the feet of the democracies. It is said that the Fourteen Points of Woodrow Wilson held forth the promise of peace and prosperity in 1918, but that these hopes were dashed almost immediately by the Paris Peace Conference and its implementation. Clearly the peace was defective and President Wilson's Fourteen Points were regularly sabotaged by the leaders of the other victorious democracies who had reveled in an orgy of demagogic rhetoric after the Armistice in 1918. But just as surely as the Treaty of Versailles had a dark side, so also did it have a bright one. It is perhaps true that the peace was stillborn and that it made war inevitable, yet the Paris Peace Conference was at the same time the midwife for the world's greatest and most extensive experiment in democracy. History records nothing like it in all its annals. Democracies sprang up everywhere as a result of the efforts to achieve Wilson's self-determination of nations. For the first time in history, democratic constitutions were adopted by a majority of European peoples. The monarchical institutions of more than a thousand years were abandoned almost overnight. A veritable democratic revolution occurred. This phenomenon, remarkable in itself, is all the more noteworthy when we consider the brief success of the fledgling democracies which by all predictable standards should have completely collapsed overnight without leaving a trace since there were no democratic traditions in many countries on which to build.

The example of Czechoslovakia is of particular interest in this regard. For centuries the Czechs and Slovaks of this region had been subject to the alien Germans and Magyars of the Austro-Hungarian Empire. Its post-1919 democratic government was grafted onto a monarchical stock, and thus its growth should have been impaired by an anti-democratic plutocracy, and retarded further by the friction which was endemic between the rival nationalities that made up its population. Leadership and sound economic and educational systems, however, made up for these deficiencies and under the guidance of men like Tomas Masaryk and Eduard Beneš, Czechoslovakia flourished and its democracy was remarkably well established within twenty years. What other countries took centuries to achieve, Czechoslovakia accomplished in two decades. Other less fortunate East European democracies eventually crumbled on all sides, yet Czechoslovakia by 1938 was ready to meet the test of Hitler's bullying and bluffing. Unfortunately, the major democracies, Britain and France, did not have the will to resist Hitler's demands at Munich. Instead, the West lost the well-trained divisions of the Czechoslovakian army which it might have used to intimidate or at least weaken the still uncoordinated legions of the Nazi Wehrmacht. The Munich betrayal was all the more disheartening in view of the active participation of democratic leaders. Yet despite this sorry chapter in the history of appeasement, democracy did triumph nevertheless. In the context of the general history of democracy, it was enough for the democratic tradition to have seen light in Czechoslovakia. It is more remarkable that it flourished and grew strong as well.

After the Soviet army defeated the Nazis in Czechoslovakia, the pre-Munich democratic government was briefly restored and though it soon succumbed to the irresistible embrace of the Soviet system, this short-lived revival of democracy was a consequence of the success of the 1919-38 experiment. Similarly, the democratic spirit was apparent in the "Prague Spring" of 1968 under Premier Alexander Dubček who attempted unsuccessfully to liberalize the Czechoslovakian political and economic system imposed by Russia. This ill-fated "Prague Spring" revealed nevertheless that the democratic spirit had been carefully nurtured between the wars even though it had been forced underground. If Czechoslovakia were the only example of democratic success, it would be of sufficient importance to tilt the scales toward democratic triumph rather than democratic failure, but there are other illustrations which are not so singular, yet of great importance in the growth of the democratic tradition in Europe.

Even in Germany, which collapsed into hideous tyranny in 1933, one can see that democracy was beginning to have some successes. It is the context once again that makes this understandable. In 1919, German governing classes had a tradition of general contempt for democracy. Centuries of Prussian authoritarianism and militarism had gained control of the German state since its unification in 1870. Its legislature had the trappings of representative democracy, but was at best an organ of a pseudo-democracy; the kaiser bragged that he had never read the German constitution or newspapers. Even though the forces of democracy helped engineer the abdication of the kaiser in 1918, they were often blamed, rather than praised, for helping end the war by those who insisted that the old imperial army was "stabbed in the back" by "unpatriotic" elements at home. Consequently, the democratic forces in Germany had a constant uphill struggle to win the meagre tolerance that the Weimar Republic eked out from the antidemocratic *Junkers*, the middle classes, the old imperial officer corps, the judiciary, and the bureaucracy which Weimar had to contend with throughout its existence. Likewise, most of the political parties lacked true sympathy for even the most rudimentary democratic principles. This German hostility to the democratic process is further indicated by what became the military character of the political parties which adopted strong-arm tactics by choice or out of self-defense. Eventually each of the parties possessed its own street-fighting organization based on the model of the *Freikorps* of demobilized, unemployed veterans. It redounds to the credit of the few democratic elements in Germany, such as the Social Democrats, that the government achieved anything in such an adverse environment.

The achievement is there, but even today it is hidden by many misconceptions and half-truths. The Weimar Republic attained at least a degree of reasonable stability despite a multitude of disorders, and it should be realized that it had to rely on a disaffected and antidemocratic army which was at times insufficient in size to suppress easily the many rebellions and putschs which threatened it from the beginning. The Weimar government consequently trusted to maneuvering rather than to manpower, but it achieved general order nevertheless. It acted strongly during the French occupation of the Ruhr in 1923 and secured an evacuation. But the Weimar leaders are not adequately recognized for their decisiveness in promoting the work stoppages which discouraged the French intruders. Instead, the hyper-inflation of 1922-23 overshadows its record of performance. The German governments from 1918 to 1933 cleverly encouraged the financing of the crippling reparations payments with short-term credits from America which paved the way later for a moratorium on the payments altogether. The Weimar Republic's democratic Cabinets also initiated the recovery from the depths of the Depression for which Hitler is usually given the credit. But the most important achievement was the nurturing of a weak democratic tradition; a task that was difficult in the extreme. The antidemocratic forces could appeal to a past based on military and nationalistic glory whereas the champions of democracy had to engage in a massive reeducation process which appealed to an unknown and alien future. As British Prime Minister Attlee later observed, the devil had all the best tunes in Weimar Germany.

Obviously democratic sentiment grew among tares, on stony ground, and much of it was choked out by the Nazi Revolution; yet few of us doubt today that Germany has turned its back on nondemocratic traditions. The undeniable success of German democracy in the recent third quarter of the twentieth century is partly due to the efforts of the democrats, like Konrad Adenaur and Willy Brandt, who made democracy work despite the odds. Trial and error is an important part of the building of a fully democratic society and it is therefore not at all surprising that the democratic Weimar Republic was destroyed by Nazi tyrants who, like the ancient Greek and Roman demagogues before them offered bread, circuses (i.e., pageantry), and imperialism as the means to fulfill the state's destiny. Instead, it is remarkable that the German democratic experience, with its worthy attempts to help the individual satisfy his own destiny (not the state's), existed and survived as long as it did. Furthermore, it is ironic that this democracy in Germany achieved so much despite the opposition of domestic despotic elements, the particular vengefulness in the twenties of the French who sought a crippled Germany, the relative indifference of the British, and the determined isolationism of the Americans. Weimar democracy was undercut by both domestic and foreign forces which were beyond its control. Conversely, after 1945 the support of the foreign democracies in the form of the Marshall Plan, for example, made the task of the democrats in Germany much easier.

One of the great problems for the Western democracies between the wars was their own loss of faith in democracy. The Victorian confidence in the spread of the parliamentary process and its concomitant, the blessings of progress, was lost. The old Palmerstonian-Gladstonian insistence on the furtherance of constitutionalism in foreign affairs was also forgotten. The last expression of this full confidence, perhaps the swan song, was Wilson's Fourteen Points, which were only halfheartedly endorsed by the Allies. President Wilson even had to threaten to make a separate peace with Germany to win this limited acceptance of the Fourteen Points. In any case, the old direction of foreign policy toward the accomplishment of democratic goals was replaced after World War I by a continuation of the late nineteenth century emphasis on nationalistic objectives. Accordingly, the Western democracies failed to see that their own particular interests were inextricably tied up in the fate of democratic governments in general. Partly as a result of this, the democracies were unable to develop a sound basis for the coordination of foreign policies—something which the French sought earnestly but in vain throughout the twenties and thirties. The British, in part disdainful of the ability of non-English-speaking peoples to govern themselves properly, concentrated their best efforts on the democratic governments of its empire and commonwealth. The Americans, embittered by their experience in the Great War, sought a return to the ideal of a self-sufficient republic set apart from the storms created by European warmongers. The Western democracies turned their backs on the ideal of democratic solidarity to such an extent that they were more interested in anti-Communist governments and capitalistic economic systems than in democratic governments per se. This made them "soft" on fascism whether it took the form of Italian fascism, German nazism, Spanish falangism, or one of its many forms in eastern Europe. Almost the only area of consistent democratic agreement was the necessity to encourage capitalism and undermine bolshevism. Most other matters paled into insignificance. These remarks by Churchill concerning British Cabinet Ministers could be applied equally as well to the inability of the democracies to coordinate their efforts: "So they go on in strange paradox, decided only to be undecided, resolved to be irresolute, adamant for drift, solid for fluidity, all powerful to be impotent." This failure of the democracies to develop a coherent policy in the face of the totalitarian menace revealed itself in many ways.

The folly of the going-it-alone attitude on the part of the older democracies put severe strain on the new ones created at Paris. An omen of folly was apparent at the peace conference itself when the Big Four excluded the German delegation from the proceedings. This and other regular rebuffs weakened the position of the German democrats at home. The imposition of the Versailles Treaty with its repugnant war-guilt clause tainted the democrats with the responsibility for accepting the

Diktat—the hated dictated peace. To these insults the Allies later added the injury of the final computation of a horrendous reparations debt and the humiliating occupation of the Ruhr when the payments were not made punctually. Regularly during the twenties, the Weimar Republic was punished by the democratic guarantors of the peace for the sins of the autocratic Hohenzollern monarchy, the *Junkers*, and plutocratic industrialists. This punitive policy only served the interests of the antidemocratic parties within Germany and continued until the collapse of the republic with the accession of Hitler in 1933. Then appeasement took the place of punishment. In a very real way, the self-serving nationalism of the democratic countries significantly contributed to the death of the Weimar Republic. When the Nazis destroyed German democracy, they were abetted by democratic Britain and France.

Perhaps the most dramatic betrayal of a fellow democracy occurred in Spain, where the cause of democracy was championed to no avail by such literary figures as Ernest Hemingway *(For Whom the Bell Tolls)* and George Orwell *(Homage to Catalonia)*. In keeping with standard diplomatic practice, the democracies adopted a policy of nonintervention when civil war broke out in 1936 between the army under Francisco Franco, and the government of Spain, which armed the citizenry of Madrid to preserve the republic. To their discredit, Britain and France held fast to their policy (in a rare instance of solidarity) while acquiescing in the overt military support made available to Franco by Mussolini and Hitler. Ironically, the Spanish republic was forced into the embrace of another dictator, Stalin, who both weakened the democratic elements in the Spanish government and fought fascism on the battlefield as well. Unfortunately, Spain's democratic republic was not the only republic abandoned by the older democracies and thus forced to embrace a dictatorial bedfellow. The Czechoslovaks, who were so shamelessly betrayed by the democracies, were actually deterred from implementing the defensive pacts they had arranged against the menace of German imperialism.

It is, however, too easy to dwell on the failures of the major democratic powers between the wars. The merits of the major and minor democracies can be easily overlooked. Some signal events are often discussed as part of the history of the interwar period, but are not considered properly in the context of humanity's quest for liberty. This is the case with regard to the restructuring of the European system in 1919. A mere listing of the nations which adopted more democratic parliamentary constitutions after the war cannot help but make an impression, and will no doubt be seen eventually as an important episode in the history of parliamentary democracy: Finland, Estonia, Latvia, Lithuania, Germany, Poland, Czechoslovakia, Austria, Hungary, Rumania, Yugoslavia, Bulgaria, Albania, and interestingly, Turkey. It should also be noted that when one adds to the list the prewar parliamentary democracies, Britain, France, Italy, Switzerland, Spain, Portugal, Norway, Sweden, and Denmark, the impression is reinforced that this period represents a flood tide for liberty. It is also important to remember that Iceland and Ireland received their independence and restored their native parliamentary governments. In fact, there was only one obviously autocratic government on the horizon in 1919, and its fate was uncertain: Soviet Russia. Ironically, the Allies through their halfhearted military intervention and occupation helped preserve Lenin's regime by supporting czarist holdouts and thus provoking a xenophobic reaction.

The peacemakers at Paris can be praised for their efforts to promote what is called the "Wilsonian heresy, the idea that liberal democracy was the only desirable form of government." Fault can be found with them, however, not because they committed themselves to democracy, but because they encouraged the adoption of constitutions based on the model of the French Third Republic, which established relatively weak executive branches of government. This was an error inasmuch as strong leadership was necessary if the governments were to survive the normal political, social, and economic problems which confront new nations. The Paris peacemakers also encouraged excessive centralization rather than federalism in these new political entities with the result that minority ethnic groups within the various states were ripe for discontent. The outstanding example of this was the twelve million Germans who had over the years settled outside of the boundaries of Germany. This error would especially haunt the democracies in the shape of the German Sudetenland in Czechoslovakia. We must not be harsh on the peacemakers, however, or attribute their failure to naiveté. Given the ebullience of the democratic victors, and their perhaps inevitable self-satisfaction in having defeated the autocracies which had bedeviled European politics for centuries, they could not predict the trials and tribulations which the new democracies had before them. There were few precedents which might have directed them to promote different constitutional models. Only a few people foresaw what John Maynard Keynes called *The Economic Consequences of the Peace* and the problems which waited on the horizon ready to throw European economics and politics into a tailspin. The Allies in 1919 did very well, considering the uncharted territory into which they embarked.

The interwar democracies made important breakthroughs in the realm of diplomatic affairs. This period witnessed the world's first limited experiment in world democracy, namely, the League of Nations. Never before had different nations organized themselves by means of democratic goals and machinery. Closely associated with the work of the League of Nations was the effort to achieve lasting peace. The world had never before witnessed such a flurry of plans and principles for the keeping of the peace. Admittedly some of the treaties were somewhat simplistic, like the Kellogg-Briand Pact which required a renunciation of war and an endorsement of conciliation, yet the scale of such efforts was unprecedented and in itself indicative of a commitment to peace that was entirely novel in its proportions. Never before had nations in such large numbers agreed to reject what for centuries had been "the sport of kings" according to George Bernard Shaw. It now became a major concern to beat swords into plowshares, and this was not just a matter of lip service. As it turned out, the best efforts of the League and individual nations failed, but not because of insufficient commitment to the ideal. This is an accomplishment worthy of recognition.

Democratic achievements can also be seen in matters other than constitutional structures and international treaties. Positive contributions took many forms, not the least of which was the extension of the franchise. For the first time in history, universal manhood suffrage became the order of the day. Uniform electoral districts were also introduced as a means of achieving the ideal of one-man-one-vote. The efforts of the prewar suffragettes bore fruit in the granting of the female franchise in some countries and a good many new rights to women. Greater tolerance of disparity and less insistence on homogeneity also became firmly rooted at least in theory. The new democracies, for example, generally eschewed the establishment of the official religions which had been a hallmark of Europe since the late fourth century. Social reforms facilitated the work of democracy in some areas by making education and social welfare systems a matter of right and an obligation of the state. Land reform schemes pushed the populace toward the egalitarian ideal. This, however, was a mixed blessing as aristocratic and bourgeois elements became disaffected, and thus receptive to demagogues who promised something for all classes. Nevertheless, the striving for these democratic goals was a commendable enterprise which should not be ignored.

By 1939, on the eve of the Second World War, the record of democratic attainments had virtually come to an end. The great hopes of many Europeans had long since been dashed. Almost all of the new democracies had succumbed one way or another to the onslaughts of despotism. In most cases, democrats were forced underground or into exile by the new states with their new fascistic or semifascistic systems. The prewar democracies in Italy, Spain, and Portugal had also fallen. Franco in Spain and Salazar in Portugal would survive along with their dictatorships until the 1970s as living reminders of this interwar period of experiment and turmoil for democracies. From one perspective, however, this should not be viewed as a true defeat for the spirit of democracy. Perhaps, it could be said that the democratic tradition was dormant for a time. This had happened before when in some times and places there existed no living memory of democracy among men, when democratic sentiment was nourished only in books. Fortunately, man's taste for democracy was not destroyed by the Second World War, and the tradition of democracy can still be traced back without interruption to the interwar period. In fact, in post-1945 Europe, there has been a veritable "Democratic Renaissance" in Europe.

This renaissance manifested itself in the restoration of democratic constitutions immediately after the war. Since then, not one of these liberated countries outside the Eastern Bloc, with the exception of Greece, has had a serious flirtation with antidemocratic forces. Furthermore Spain, Portugal, and Greece are now reinstalling democratic governments. There can now be little doubt that the experiments of the twenties and thirties, combined with harrowing experiences during World War II, have created a commitment to democracy which may prove difficult to subvert. Europe underwent a catharsis which has steeled its resolve, as is the case clearly in Italy, which continues to meet successfully the threat of widespread terrorism which it had been unable to cope with in the twenties. In fact, Western Europe has been transformed. Whereas in 1918 it represented a vast preserve of autocracies and had been the cockpit of war for more than a thousand years, it has been moving since 1945 toward a remarkable stabilization and entrenchment of democratic and peace-keeping systems. The degree of harmony and liberty now present in Western Europe would not have been possible without the democratic traditions of the interwar period.

Similarly, most East European countries briefly experimented with parlimentary systems after they were liberated by the Russian army. Stalin soon subverted and perverted the democratic systems, yet the taste for democracy was and still is there. The riots and rebellions which have since occurred in the Eastern Bloc, although some were mercilessly repressed by the Soviet army, are nevertheless testimonials in part to a renewed faith in democracy as well as nationalism. Even in the Soviet Union, the foul despotism of Stalin has been repudiated, and the drift toward liberalization is quite evident and may be symbolized by Leonid Brezhnev's insistence on the drafting of a "new," though equally useless, Soviet constitution. It is appropriate to speculate that the grim experience of both Nazi and Communist oppression may eventually help East

Europeans develop an appetite for democracy which is even more pronounced than that of West Europeans.

It is possible that the interwar democratic experiment can be given too much credit. Even if this were the case, democracy has recently been too little championed and as a result our perspectives have gone so far out of focus that Fascist myths have altogether too much currency even today. It is lamentable that there are those who deny the lessons of the chronicles that reveal that despotism confers no benefit on mankind. Conversely, the chronicles of democracy consistently reveal a pattern, often interrupted for long periods, of creating a foundation on which humanity can build its hopes. One of the finest minds of the nineteenth century, John Stuart Mill, once remarked that "Marathon was a more important battle in English history than Hastings." Mill's idea is also applicable here. One could say that the First World War and the Paris Peace Conference of 1919 were just as important in the annals of liberty as the battle of Marathon, which helped preserve Athenian democracy from Persian despotism in 491 B.C. This is true in the sense that the war ended the tyranny of the old order and the peace conference created the greatest democratic experiment of all time and planted the democratic tradition in places where it might never have grown otherwise.

Parenthetically, it should also be noted that the interwar democratic experiment has indirectly influenced Africa and Asia as well as Europe by providing object lessons and models. The European ideal of government has been transplanted, and even imposed, in the Third World in ways which are not always obvious. The goal or at least the facade of a democratic government has been adopted throughout many parts of the world, as can be seen in the repetitious regularity with which the label "Democratic Republic" or "People's Republic" is applied to all types of government. In a few instances, such as India and Iran, there is an insistence on the full substance of democracy that is genuine. This is underscored by the rebuff of the voters to Indira Ghandi after her distortion of executive powers as the Indian premier, and in the inadequacy of the Shah's paternalistic reforms to forestall meaningful progress toward Iranian democracy. The interwar years are therefore still strongly influencing the contemporary world.

There are some important lessons to be discovered from the history of liberty between the wars. The point which deserves the greatest emphasis and repetition is that the weakest democracy is ultimately preferable to even an "enlightened despotism" which generally cannot, by its very nature, prevent its inevitable drift into tyranny. There is a significant qualitative difference between the weakest democracy and the best dictator in terms of consequences. The distinction is that democracies out of their weaknesses generally fail to do good whereas almost all dictatorships eventually inflict great injuries. There are, of course, instances when democracies and republics have done their share of injury to mankind. Two of the most obvious examples would be the imposition of the death sentence on Socrates and the excesses of the guillotine during the French Revolution. The despot's capacity for mischief is infinitely greater, however, and is seen clearly in the horrors and exterminations perpetrated by Stalin and Hitler. Very few outrages can in any case be blamed on the democracies between the wars. Are there any serious historians who would dare tote up the atrocity scores for democracies and despots in the hopes of vindicating the humanity of dictators? It should also be stressed that the failings of the democracies in the twenties or thirties eventually bore fruit in terms of a new resolve after 1945 to establish and preserve democratic systems, whereas the failings of dictatorships have not produced tangible benefits. As has been noted, the weaknesses of the democracies helped produce a climate which made the aggressive wars of the dictators possible, yet the positive side of this is that the democracies did overcome their weaknesses and triumph over the dictators, who for all their strength and preparedness could not win the wars they had started. It must be remembered that the totalitarian system under Stalin contributed an overlarge share of its men and might to the victory over the Fascist dictators, but the success of the victorious democracies in 1945 was no less great than the Athenian victory over the mighty Persian Empire with the help of the despotic Spartans in the fifth century B.C.

As the remarks by Hans Kohn pointed out earlier, democracies are not easily achieved and have only been highly successful with relatively few people and in relatively short periods of time. The twenty-year period between the wars was very short indeed, yet fantastic strides toward the goals of democracy were made. This should be the center of our focus in examining these two decades and the twentieth century in general. It should not be otherwise. Man cannot allow his highest aspiration to be subverted by a squalid acceptance of the evils generated by autocracies and despotisms. We must realize that although World War I was not the "war to end all wars," as President Woodrow Wilson had hoped, yet it was nevertheless, in conjunction with its peace conference, the war which made "the world safe for democracy."

Suggested Readings

For general introductory information, Raymond J. Sontag, *A Broken World, 1919-1939* (1971) is recommended, as is E. H. Carr, *The Twenty Years' Crisis, 1919-1939* which is still standard for diplomatic history. The background for a discussion of democracy per se can be found in David Thomson, *The Democratic Ideal in England and France* (1940) and in Hans Kohn, *Political Ideologies of the Twentieth Century* (1949) which also deals with the loss of confidence in the West. The relevant perspectives of the social scientist can be explored in Joseph A. Schumpeter, *Capitalism, Socialism, and Democracy* (1950) and Zevedi Barbu, *Democracy and Dictatorship: Their Psychology and Patterns of Life* (1956). Studies of democratic institutions in particular countries can usually be found as parts of more general considerations. Great Britain is covered judiciously by Charles Loch Mowat in *Britain Between the Wars, 1918-1940* (1955) and somewhat controversially by A. J. P. Taylor in *English History, 1914-1945* (1965). Arnold Wolfers' *Britain and France Between the Wars* (1940) is still valuable for foreign policy. A personalized account by a participant is given in *The Gathering Storm* (1948) by Winston Churchill whose latest biographer, Henry Pelling, gives a more detailed and demythologized account of this staunch critic of appeasement. George Orwell, *Road to Wigan Pier* and *Down and Out in Paris and London,* recounts his eyewitness experiences of the desperation which provoked flirtations with fascism rather than socialism. *The Long Weekend: A Social History of Great Britain, 1918-1939* (1940) by Robert Graves and Alan Hodges describes the distractions and apathy of the comfortable classes. France is treated at length by David Thomson in *Democracy in France Since 1870* (1969) and D. W. Brogan, *France Under the Republic, 1870-1939* (1940). William Shirer's works on the Third Republic and the Third Reich should be avoided by the novice. Rudolph Binion's biographical approach on France's *Defeated Leaders* (1960) is quite valuable. *Weimar and the Rise of Hitler* (1968) by H. J. Nichols is a good place to begin on interwar Germany as is S. William Halperin, *Germany Tried Democracy* (1965). The "politics of acceptance" is treated in Klaus Epstein, *Matthias Erzberger and the Dilemma of German Democracy* (1959). *Bread and Democracy in Germany* (1943) sketches the social and economic difficulties of the Weimar period. The "man on the street" viewpoint is explored by Milton Mayer, *They Thought They Were Free* (1955) whereas the local history perspective is presented by Rudolf Heberle's study of Schleswig-Holstein, *From Democracy to Nazism* (1970). Peter Gay, *Weimar Culture* (1968) integrates many topics thoroughly. Italy is handled quite well in Adrian Lyttleton, *The Seizure of Power: Fascism in Italy, 1919-1929* (1973). Gabriel Jackson, *The Spanish Republic and the Civil War, 1931-1939* (1964) is a most thorough treatment. For Eastern Europe, Karl J. Newman, *European Democracy Between the Wars* (1971) should be consulted along with Anthony Polonsky, *The Little Dictators* (1975). Both explore the weaknesses and difficulties of parliamentary governments. R. L. Wolff, *The Balkans in Our Time* (1967) is still standard. Czechoslovakia is treated admirably in V. Olivova, *The Doomed Democracy* (1972). Hugh Seton-Watson's work is still valuable, especially *The East European Revolution* (1950) which treats the democratic interlude after the defeat of the Nazis.

CHAPTER 5

The Spirit of Fascism

Jay W. Baird

Fascism, which was a dominant force in politics from 1918 to 1945, was an international movement. It was not a peculiarly German or Italian phenomenon, although it took its most virulent form in those two countries. Fascist movements were found throughout Eastern and Western Europe, in the United States and Latin America, in Japan and the Far East. Each Fascist group joined local and national characteristics to a fairly stable core of ideology. Fascism was stronger in some areas, weaker in others, but there was hardly a single major or minor country which was not infected with the virus.

To be sure, international fascism harbored some strange bedfellows. Adolf Hitler in Germany, Benito Mussolini in Italy, Oswald Mosley in Great Britain, Jacques Doriot in France, Leon Degrelle in Belgium, José Antonio Primo de Rivera in Spain, Konrad Henlein in Czechoslovakia, Ferenc Szálasi in Hungary, Corneliu Zelea-Codreanu in Rumania, and Fritz Kuhn in the United States were the most outstanding leaders of Fascist movements. Their character, personalities, and style were as divergent as the widespread geographical areas from which they came. Yet they all adhered to a nearly uniform set of ideological principles.

This essay will focus on these principles of the Fascist movement in three stages. Commencing with a description of its reactionary program of alienation, followed by an analysis of its ideological tenets, a discussion of Fascist organization will demonstrate how its ideology was translated into practice. Attention will be directed throughout to the two strongest leaders and movements, those dominated by Hitler and Mussolini.

First of all, what characterized the Fascist movement? What groups, what ideologies did they choose to attack? Against whom did they vent their seemingly boundless wrath and hatred? The Fascists themselves identified four enemies, but their primary foe was world Jewry. The Fascists hated the Jews with an irrational, immeasurable hatred, with a contempt and derision which knew no bounds. The Jews were the beginning and the end of all that was evil. The Jewish parasite drained one's pure blood, and he siphoned off the national wealth with his time honored, stealthy, cheating business practices. Most Fascists were united in their attacks on the Jews. By appealing to this prejudice, they could direct all the hatreds, fears, and disappointments of rootless, industrialized mass society against the enemy within, symbolized by the eternal Jew.

Futhermore, the Fascists were able to link political anti-Semitism with a deep-seated religious anti-Semitism traceable to the earliest days of the church. After all, "the Jews killed Jesus Christ," the Son of God, and the heavens decreed that the Jew would be damned by all mankind. It was charged that the Jews did not have souls and were motivated entirely by materialistic impulses. A race without a soul was a parasite on the folkish body politic and as such was fit only for extermination.

Julius Streicher, perhaps the most notorious of the Nazi anti-Semitic propagandists, wrote in 1933 in his newspaper *Der Stürmer*:

> The Jew has miscalculated. The hero has not come too late. He took up the struggle against Jewry and achieved victory. . . Facing the Führer and his blows, the Jew fell to the dust. He now sees the enormous danger threatening him. He is exposed; his criminal plans are revealed. And now a struggle begins the like of which the world

has never seen. World Jewry is up against Adolf Hitler.
The Jews are going to wage this conflict without mercy.
We must also wage it against Pan-Jewry without mercy.
The Jews are a people of the devil. They are a people of
criminals and murderers. Therefore, the Jewish people
must be exterminated from the face of the earth. . . .

With this sort of background, one can better comprehend
the antecedents of the Holocaust, the Nazis' liquidation of
nearly six million Jews.

The Fascists trained their guns on another enemy, international communism. According to them, the Marxist-
Leninist tenets led to nothing but the degradation of the
individual, and the degeneration of the nation. Fascists
tended to equate communism with Jewry and their propaganda guaranteed that mention of the one conjured up
images of the other. According to Hitler, knowledge of the
Jews was the only key where one could understand the
inner nature and real aims of Marxism, and he charged
that the Marxist pest could be laid at the door of that
"ferment of decomposition of race and society—
international Jewry." It followed, then, that Russian bolshevism was the twentieth century attempt of Jewry to
gain control of the world.

The motif of "Jewish bolshevism" opened the way to the
wildest fantasies of the Nazis. According to their theories,
the "Jewish-Bolshevik" was a subhuman. A subhuman
was defined as that which biologically appeared to be a
man but in reality differed fundamentally, representing a
lower order than the animal kingdom. The swamp was the
natural element of the subhuman, and he too was fit only
for extermination.

Bolshevism, then, was Jewish, and represented a danger
for the Aryan. Bolshevism, it was held, destroyed the
spirit of the individual, of the race, of the nation, and all
that was worthwhile in man. It was the Fascists' goal to an-
nihilate Jewish bolshevism before the pestilence could
spread. Marx, Trotsky, Zinoviev, Radek, Kamenev, among
others, were the Jews behind international bolshevism,
and Stalin was guilty because he had a Jewish mistress.
"Clear the streets of the Reds" was the cry, and it was a
slogan with a wide appeal, because millions of people,
who under normal circumstances would never identify

with the Fascists, looked to them to save their lives and their property from communism. This motif was one of the best horses in the Fascist stable.

Of less importance as a drawing card for the Fascists was their hostility to big business and to middle class people of more than ordinary wealth. Theirs was the voice of the little man, mass man, who suffered because of high prices blamed on the cartels and monopolies of the great capitalists. The Fascists could look toward winning support of countless people who tended to blame the wealthy factory owner or property holder for all their ills. These were individuals whose ancestors might have been craftsmen or landed people but who, with the coming of industrialization, had lost their identity and self-respect. In the age of the machine, they seemed to have no place, and the capitalist was the symbol of their hatred of modern life. Thus the cry of the Fascists to break up the great industries also found widespread support.

It was no coincidence that both Hitler and Mussolini came from the lower stratum of society, and early in their careers they were firmly committed to this plank. Indeed, the opportunist Mussolini had spent many years as a leader of the radical wing of the Socialist party of Italy, and it was only later that he came to understand that to attain power and to maintain his hold over the nation, he must drop his socialist notions. As it worked out, no class enjoyed the fruits of Fascist power more than the men of great wealth. At the time when the Fascists were climbing to power, however, this was an effective slogan, because there was widespread sympathy for the Bolshevik revolution and a rather naive belief in the Communist mystique which spread throughout Europe after Lenin fought his way to power in November 1917. Furthermore, the Fascists could win many adherents among those searching for extreme solutions to problems which otherwise seemed insoluble. If the extreme left—communism—could not offer the answer, perhaps the radical right—fascism—could.

The fourth major enemy of the Fascists after the Jews, the Bolsheviks, and the great capitalists, was democracy and liberalism. Fascists were quite explicit in their rejection of liberalism, which they found to be one of the most disturbing aspects of modern life. They found liberalism and democracy detestable because this world view was diametrically opposed to their concept of a hierarchically ordered, elitist, one-party state ruled by a Führer. The leading Nazi ideologist, Alfred Rosenberg, decried the results of modernity in his work *The Myth of the Twentieth Century* (1930), a brutal attack on the development of liberal ideas since the French Revolution. As the Fascist philosopher, Giovanni Gentile, pointed out in *The Origins and Doctrines of Fascism* (1929):

> Liberalism sets the individual against the state and liberty against authority. It wants a liberty which limits the state, thereby resigning itself to the inevitable evil of a state which limits freedom... But it is one of Fascism's merits that it has set its face vigorously and courageously against current liberal prejudice and has stated loud and clear that that sort of freedom benefits neither a nation nor its individual members. Moreover, inasmuch as the corporative state tends to realize a closer and more substantial unity or circle of authority and liberty by means of a more honest and realistic system of representation, the new state is more liberal than the old one.

Thus, Fascists argued that liberalism degraded the individual, and democracy was nothing more than rule by the mob. They pointed to the "effeminate"democracies—to England, France, and the United States—nations wallowing in the trough of liberalism, ruled by tired sons of rich fathers, who were leading their nations to destruction. Democracy was equated with cowardice, and in the troubled atmosphere of the 1930s, fascism did seem to offer a viable alternative for a great many people. Strength lay in the virtue and heroic life of fascism, weakness in the cowardice of liberalism. The nineteenth century German philosopher, Friedrich Nietzsche, served to inspire them when he wrote in *Thus Spake Zarathustra* (1883):

> My brothers in war, I love you... You should have eyes that always seek an enemy—*your* enemy... You should love peace as a means to new wars... War and courage have accomplished more great things than love of one's neighbor.

If Jewry, communism, monopoly capitalism, liberalism, and democracy were the enemies of fascism, what were the virtues which they praised so highly? Above all, truth and virtue lay in one's race and nation. Blood and nation—these were the two pillars upon which fascism rested. God or Providence spoke to man through his blood and his nation, and it was the sacred duty of the Fascist man to stand guard for these racial and national principles against both foreign and domestic enemies.

The Italians looked back in awe to the great days of Rome, once the center of Western civilization, and it was Mussolini's ardent wish to reincarnate those days of bygone glory. Hitler, on the other hand, looked not so much to the heroic years of German power in medieval Europe as he did to the virtues of the early German tribes, when he thought that men lived and died as men—not "effeminate" democrats—under a Führer such as himself, warriors of strength and virility—not as fearful, craven twentieth century people interested only in material gain, breathing the air of fetid cities and inspired only by values of decadence. Both Hitler and Mussolini were determined to write a new chapter in the glorious history of their peoples, the one by overturning the dictated peace of Versailles and establishing the German Reich as the arbiter of Europe, the other by returning Italy to the glory of the Roman Empire.

Whereas the spokesmen of the radical right castigated liberals for allowing their nations to disintegrate into a collection of mutually hostile groups, where self-interest ruled the day, they offered the authoritarian state in the guise of racial and national unity as an alternative. Allegedly there were no class differences in their states. Greed, the acquisitive instincts, and a national soul devoid of higher ideals had characterized life in pre-Fascist Italy and Germany. Now, according to their propaganda, individualism which had ruled the day since the French Revolution was to give way to the Olympian principles of justice, folkish equality, and service to the nation. Thus the racially pure, national, organic state offered the unity for which the masses longed to offer them salvation from the chaos and divisiveness of modern life.

While the nineteenth century had offered the Hegelian-Marxist dialectic or Darwinian evolution to explain change and movement in history, the Fascist posited the fulfillment of the racially pure state—struggling against its enemies until the final victory was won. Victory would come because it *had* to come. National socialism and Italian fascism were thus movements, sweeping through history to carry out their cosmic functions. They were not to be compared to the corrupt liberal parties vying for popular favor. Instead, their Fascist movements were spearheading the march of truth and morality through world history. The party names taken by these "movements" were significant, and reveal a great deal about them. The party of Hitler, the National Socialist German Workers' party, was at once nationalist, socialist in terms of the peoples' interests, German in its struggle for the *Volk,* and the party of workers in its broadest sense. The party was all-encompassing. It represented the Germanic whole, free of Jewish and Freemason impurities and sinister international conspiracies.

The Fascist party of Mussolini purported to represent an organic political union as well. Mussolini once remarked that "Mankind cannot be divided. Instead of being separate, the proletariat and the bourgeoisie, indeed all sectors of the Italian nation, are integral parts of a single whole." The pattern of the development of political institutions in Fascist Italy lent new life to this fiction. Mussolini governed the "corporate state," in which each sector of the population was united within a column of the nation, a corporation. In any particular industry, for example, both labor and capital were included in a corporation which represented that industry. Although propaganda about the corporate state tended to reinforce the myth of unity within the Italian whole, the fact was that Mussolini's Italy brought little amelioration of the condition of either rural or industrial labor. In fact real wages declined in many sectors. The corporate state was a corporate state in name only.

Besides race and nation, there was a third vital factor in the development of the Fascist mystique—the place of the leader. The leader, who took the name of Führer in Germany and Duce in Italy, was the quintessence of race and nation. Indeed the Fascists claimed that he was the best of the race and the best of the nation. He was destiny incarnate, the first among many, who lead the great struggle between light and darkness, and whose very presence was a guarantee of victory. The leader was all good; he was Christ, Siegfried, and the greatest of the Caesars. He was conceived of as a nearly divine personage and as such was to become a figure of worship. There was nothing that the leader could not do. As the slogan went in Italy, "The Duce is always right." The Duce was the doctor to the sick, the source of ideology for the intellectual, the lover of Italian womanhood, the heroic figure to inspire youth, the soldiers' soldier. Indeed, he was Italy. As a Fascist poster demonstrated, he was every Italian boy's and girl's pal. According to one caption: "Benito Mussolini loves little children; the little children of Italy love the Duce. Hail the Duce!" In every classroom there was a photograph of Mussolini, flanked by a crucifix, and a photograph of the king of Italy. He was thus the three in one, the one in three, the central component of a new Trinity. Hitler had no such competition in the Third Reich; all devotion was directed to him personally.

The Nazi film *Triumph of the Will*—a documentary on the Nuremberg Party Rally of 1934, directed by Leni Riefenstahl—was a propaganda masterpiece which serves as a case study in Fascist ideology and practice. Throughout the film, the attention of the viewer is focused on the charismatic and mystical qualities of Hitler. It begins as the Führer rides through the clouds in his personal aircraft, coming directly from on high, the physical manifestation of the will of Providence. In the background the strains of *The Meistersinger of Nuremberg* by the great German composer Richard Wagner sets the proper heroic tone for the magnificent accompanying footage of medieval Nuremberg. This pure Aryan specimen—a true Siegfried figure—has come from above to cleanse the nation of the "Jewish-Bolshevik racial enemy," and to eradicate the hated Peace of Versailles. His loyal SA and SS comrades wait for him below in seemingly endless columns. The army awaits him as well, standing guard with the entire German nation—women, children, Hitler Youth, farmers, and workers. As Rudolf Hess, the Führer's deputy declared before the assembled masses: "My Führer, you are Germany. You are the guarantee of victory."

Triumph of the Will creates a new reality, much in the manner of fascism itself. Life is approached from a romantic perspective, and race is viewed as the prime force determining the character of individuals and of nations. Racial consciousness is heightened in scene after scene of well-scrubbed Hitler Youth, of blond Germanic maidens, of SS men who look like Greek sculpture, and of peasants whose eyes reflect the eternal truths of blood, soil, and work. This organic union of Führer, Volk, and Fatherland was total fulfillment, and smiling face after smiling face conveys the message that life in the Third Reich was a deliriously happy experience.

But *Triumph of the Will* also conveys a deadly seriousness. Footage celebrating the beauty of Romanesque towers, Gothic spires, and historic squares transmits the idea that nazism represented a historical continuum traceable to the Greco-Roman-Christian heritage. More importantly, it celebrated the greatness of the Germanic tribal past—the warrior ethos, racial comradeship, courage, bravery, and loyalty to the death. This loyalty was extended to the hero worship of the German dead in the Great War. One of the very moving scenes in the film memorializes Hitler's comrades of 1914-18 who died at Verdun and Langemark, on the Somme and the Marne. In an act of devotion to the memory of those who perished fighting in the streets for the Nazi ideal, Hitler blesses the standards of new Nazi units with the "Blood Flag," drenched in the blood of Nazi "martyrs" who died that the nation might live. The viewer actually sees one of these heroes—the famed Horst Wessel who died fighting bolshevism as a storm trooper in Berlin—resurrected and marching through the clouds, banner flying in the breeze, united in spirit with his comrades marching below. One sees column after column of various Nazi and military units marching through Nuremberg, past the reviewing stand of Adolf Hitler. The message of the film—as of nazism itself—was: "Führer command, we will follow!"

The Führer was viewed as the realization of the prophecies of Houston Stewart Chamberlain, Paul de Lagarde, and Julius Langbehn, all cultural pessimists, racial ideologists, and forebears of nazism. He was the embodiment of Nietzsche's will to power and to victory. In his person, he seemed to be the antithesis of all that was hated in modern civilization, and in him the masses could lose themselves and give full reign to the delights of mysticism. One could worship at his feet as people of earlier centuries turned to Christ and the Virgin Mary.

It was claimed that he shared many of the attributes of Christ. The Reich propaganda minister, Joseph Goebbels, was not alone in thinking that Hitler's career was even more important than that of Christ, although admitting that he could not say that to the public without being horribly misunderstood. According to Goebbels:

> I am absolutely certain that Hitler has performed more than one miracle. Without any doubt whatsoever he has performed many miracles, actual miracles. But if I should announce that in my propaganda, it would be unbelievable. . . The Führer does not want that to be divulged. I think I know the reason. . . I couldn't swear who he really is, whether or not he really is a man.

Hitler encouraged this blind faith and trust throughout his career.

Like Mussolini, Hitler's greatest appeal was to the youth of the nation. Nazi propaganda appealed to the naive trust of children who were taught to believe that Hitler was a God-sent leader, a messianic figure not unlike Jesus. He had been sent to love and protect them from dangers perpetrated by the Jews, the Communists, and even the French and English, who in Germany's hour of desperation after World War I had conspired to starve little children with a "hunger blockade." Hitler was seldom happier than when cavorting with children, or speaking to groups of Hitler Youth. He made it clear to them that as Germany's young people they were to become soldiers of destiny. Accordingly, the ideals of courage and bravery should inspire them to emulate the greatness of those who had been martyred in the fields of Flanders and the streets of Munich. They represented the future of the nation. They were to mature in a Germany which knew no class antagonisms, where their common Aryan blood guaranteed them a position of stature in the *Volk*.

It was the dream of great numbers of German children to

meet the Führer. An elementary school textbook of the period played on the natural fantasies of children in order to win them for Hitler. One passage read like a fairy tale:

> Far from our homeland, our Führer Adolf Hitler has a beautiful villa. It is located high up in the mountains and is surrounded by an iron fence. Often many people who would like to see and greet the Führer stand in front of it.
>
> One day the Führer came out once again and greeted the people in a very friendly way. They were all full of joy and jubilation and reached out with their hands to him. In the very first rank stood a little girl with flowers in her hand, and she said in her clear child's voice: "Today is my birthday." Thereupon the Führer took the little blond girl by the hand and walked slowly with her through the fence and into the villa. Here the little girl was treated to cake and strawberries with thick, sweet cream. And the little one ate and ate until she could eat no more. Then she said very politely: "I thank you very much!" and "Good-by." Then she stood as tall as she could, put her little arms around the Führer's neck, and now the little girl gave the great Führer a long, long kiss."

With such indoctrination as this, the seduction of youth was complete.

Along with race, nation, and a charismatic leader, action and violence formed the fourth component of fascism. Indeed, Fascism is almost synonymous with action. Contemplation, reason, logic, scientific objectivity, and pure thought—all these were hated by the Fascists. With a world view such as this, one can understand why Nazi anti-intellectualism evoked this notorious outburst: "When I hear the word culture, I grab for my revolver." Force, action, violence, and blind intuition replaced reason as the ultimate arbiter of life.

Mussolini's Black Shirts made a fetish of action—action for its own sake. It was of little consequence what one was doing, just as long as action, movement, and spontaneity characterized one's activity. In this way, the passions of the beast in man could be fulfilled, untrammeled by middle class conventions and morality. The tedious life of the workaday world with its time clocks and punch cards, the assembly lines and monotonous hum of the factories—all this was to be rejected. Instead, the spirit of the front generation of World War I stalked the land, leaving violence, lawlessness, and death in its path.

The front generation set the tone for the Fascist era of alienation, and it was the war which acted as a catalyst in bringing into play the emotions and desires of the frustrated. For the millions who had served in the trenches, life would never be the same again. Service at the front with its mass slaughter did something to men which affected them at the core of their being, and they could not adjust to what they felt to be the philistine values of bourgeois materialism. Millions of people who could never be integrated into the world of peacetime Europe found their spiritual home with the Fascists. Nineteen-eighteen had been the point of no return for them. Ernst Jünger, a German writer of the front generation, spoke for these veterans when he wrote in *The Storm of Steel:*

> War, father of all things, is also our father. It has hammered us, chiseled us, and hardened us into what we are. And always, as long as the swirling wheel of life revolves within us, this war will be the axis around which it will swirl . . . We shall remain fighters as long as we live. . . . Below the surface of cultural and technical progress we remain naked and raw like the men of the forest and of the steppe . . . This is the new man, the pioneer of the storm, the choice product of central Europe. . . . This war is not the end but the new ascendancy of force . . .

This spirit of lawlessness and violence was very infectious after the war, a period characterized by political and economic instability, and social unrest.

Thus far our attention has been focused on Fascist ideology, myth, and political programs. It remains for us to analyze the means by which this ideology was translated into political power. This entails a discussion of the three major areas which the Fascists utilized to gain and maintain power—the elitist hierarchy, the propaganda network, and organized terror.

Central to any discussion of the Fascist elitist hierarchy is its organization. The will of the leader, at the top of the pyramid, was as good as law. His words were commands, and he expected that his every wish would be carried out according to the strictest principles of military discipline. Those who were not blindly obedient were dealt with mercilessly. The party—in Italy the Fascist party, in Germany the National Socialist party—was the organization endowed with the authority to carry out the leader's will. The party in both states was the elite guard of nation, race, and leader.

The party man was a very special kind of man, not to be confused, as one Nazi said, with members of bourgeois parties whose meetings had the tone of rabbit-breeding societies. The party man was the Fascist "whole man" and he was part of the elite chosen to fulfill the ideology of the movement. Fascist party men were imbued with the spirit that they were the nation's best, people who knew the meaning of battle, struggle, and reality, in contrast to the shirkers who had sat out the war before a fireplace with a degenerate novel in their hands, or who had used the war as an opportunity to amass illicit fortunes. Their songs were stirring martial airs. The "Giovanezza" of Mussolini's Black Shirts and the "Horst Wessel Song"—written by the martyred fighting troubadour of Hitler's Brown Shirts—offered encouragement in their battles with political enemies, comfort for their suffering, and a visionary goal for the future.

Hitler's most important organization on the road to power was the SA, the Brown Shirts (storm troopers). This paramilitary organization was in reality the fighting arm of the Nazi party. Composed of war veterans and young men with fighting spirit, the SA waged a bloody struggle in the streets, squares, and beer halls against Communists and other political enemies throughout the years of the Weimar Republic. For them, battle was life itself, to die for the cause, noble. Without the SA, there is reason to believe that Hitler never would have become Reich chancellor of Germany. "Clear the streets for the Brown Battalions" was their byword for action.

The party men were trained as children in the Hitler Youth and the Italian youth organizations, the Balilla and the Avanguardisti, where they were given extensive education and indoctrination in their future roles. For, after all, they were some day to be party men, and the party controlled the state. There were several grades to climb before one finally was accepted as a party member, and could enjoy all the rights associated with this privileged position. One of the most festive occasions each year—the Fascist Levy—was held in Rome, when new members of the various party groups stepped forward to be knighted by Mussolini, the twentieth century Caesar, who carried out his ceremonial functions atop a giant white stallion. Each member saluted his superior in an ascending pyramid, until the highest ranking gave his salute to the Duce. From the beginning, when the child entered the Balilla, a type of Fascist Boy Scout organization, until his promotion at a later age to the Avanguardisti and the Young Fascists, until ultimately he climbed the ladder to full membership in the Fascist party, he was schooled in the virtues of loyalty, honor, and obedience.

Hitler also had at his service a highly disciplined organization for young people, the Hitler Youth. Hitler realized that if he could win over the children of Germany, he would have his party men and soldiers for future battles. The best of the Hitler Youth could one day look forward to becoming members of the elite corps of Nazi Germany, the SS.

The SS—who have been stereotyped as blond beasts—developed and trained by Heinrich Himmler, a former poultry farmer from Bavaria, were to be the vanguard of the war against "international Jewry." Therefore, they had to pass rigorous biological tests to demonstrate that they had no Jewish background, and to undergo extensive physical training before they could proudly wear the tailored black SS uniform.

The SS was based on the principle, "Loyalty is my Honor"—loyalty to one's Aryan race, to the *Volk*, to one's superior, to Reichsführer SS Himmler and to Adolf Hitler. SS men were indoctrinated with the idea that they were soldiers of good in a titanic struggle to the death against the "racial underworld." They were to be the bravest of the brave, models of courage and heroism, and they enjoyed great prestige in the Third Reich. The Führer's favorite military unit was the "Leibstandarte SS Adolf Hitler," and the SS governed and policed a vast network of concentration camps. No assignment was to be too difficult for the SS, not even the extermination of the Jews in the "Final Solution of the Jewish Question" undertaken during World War II. Loyalty and honor, blood and soil—these were the ideals of a generation of young men who were trained to kill like wolves of prey.

Fascist uniforms conveyed a sinister aura of fear, and none more so than those of the SS. Uniforms had a two-fold purpose: they gave those who wore them a sense of unity and esprit de corps, and secondly, they ranked each individual in an ascending order of hierarchy and authority which ended with Hitler. Insubordination was brutally suppressed when Hitler felt that his authority was being questioned. To cite the most outstanding example, on the "Night of the Long Knives" in June 1934, Hitler gunned down the commander of the Brown Shirts, Ernst Röhm, along with several hundred SA men and others of questionable loyalty. Hitler's party organizations generally carried out his commands expeditiously. Mussolini was able to accomplish the same ends, although he did it without the frightening efficiency of the Germans.

A second component of the Fascist drive to power, and subsequent concentration of power, was their propaganda. According to Hitler, the most important principle of propaganda was to direct one's words to the masses, not to the intelligentsia. Themes should be simple so that the least intelligent person in any audience could understand them. The larger the audience, he said, the lower the intellectual level of the speech. One is not addressing professors of international law, or aesthetic adolescents, he declared, one is addressing the German nation. Furthermore, propaganda had to appeal to the emotions, never to reason or objective analysis. The more violent the emotional impact of the propaganda, the more successful it would be.

Hitler's technique was based on other principles from which he never wavered. Realize, he said, that your audience consists of a collection of doubting, fearful individuals. Give them something to lean on; say to each what he wants to hear. Secondly, never theorize. Thirdly, capitalize on the weaknesses of one's audience. Realize that the "feminine nature of humanity" is essentially weak, leaving the way open for strong leadership. He operated from the principle that the masses want to be impressed, to surrender their individuality, to seek the sweet balm of consolation for their wounds of insecurity, and to be dependent on a leader.

There is no question that both Hitler and Mussolini put their ideas to work in a refined manner. Their favorite medium was the mass meeting. In mass meetings, individuals seem to forget their fears and can easily be swayed by the emotions of the moment. At such mass meetings they are particularly vulnerable to the suggestive techniques of a skilled orator. A common experience was for individuals to merge with the group, joining in with shouts of "Sieg Heil!" or "Duce, Duce, Duce!" signaling their surrender to the stronger man, the stronger leader. One expert on fascism, Karl D. Bracher, has referred to the meetings as "religious-psychological phenomena" characterized by a biological mystique. When one sees film footage of the ranting crowds gathered before Mussolini, weaving and shouting in a tidal wave of ecstasy and exaltation, or the hypnotic effect of a Hitler rally, one knows that these leaders fulfilled Jakob Burckhardt's fearful prophecy of the consequences of mass man's falling victim to the seductive powers of a cunning demagogue.

The use of symbols played an important part in Fascist propaganda, and both Mussolini and Hitler employed them to lend unity to their movements. The *Fasces*, a bundle of rods surrounding an ax with a projecting blade, had been carried before Roman magistrates as a sign of authority, and Mussolini adopted this symbol as well. One saw this *Fasces* symbol everywhere in Italy, but nowhere more striking than when flanking the Duce on the veranda of the Palazzo Venezia, his favorite podium on an impressive piazza in downtown Rome. The Fascist salute, dagger outheld, was a rather fearful symbolic gesture. The Roman eagles, the black shirts, and Fascist monuments cast against the background of the ruins of ancient Rome all served as visual symbols to reinforce Fascist ideology.

Hitler also utilized many symbols. The most striking was the swastika itself, a symbol of the racial struggle of the Aryans against the Jews. The alphabet and customs of the barbaric Germanic tribal ancestors—such as the winter and summer solstice festivals—were resurrected as well.

Uniforms, flags, insignia, monuments, and even the names of military units—e.g., the 9th S.S. Panzer Division 'Hohenstaufen'—were replete with historical or folkish connotations. Wherever one looked in the Germany of the Third Reich, he came into contact with Nazi symbols.

The third component of fascism was organized terror. Terror went hand in hand with propaganda in the authoritarian system, and the one complemented the other. Both worked from the same premise—that modern man is weak and a show of force, a demonstration, or a threat will coerce any person into submission or apathy. Whether or not the individual becomes a true believer is irrelevant, because the terror apparatus acts to guarantee that he does not oppose those who are. The frightening genius of the Fascists was that they were able to make it appear as if the authoritarian terror apparatus was acting in the best interest of the *Volk* and the nation.

Both Hitler and Mussolini used terror and the threat of reprisals to their advantage. The Duce's Black Shirts went into action against the Communists and their other enemies almost from the beginning of the movement. Their terror acted at once to intimidate and console a weary nation. Great numbers of people were sympathetic with the excesses of the Fascists because they acted to liquidate the Communist threat to their cherished rights of private property. Others found violence for its own sake an answer to the troubles of the times. Still others were frightened; their response was apathy, which played into the hands of the radicals.

Nazi terror developed a mystique of its own, and the golden age of the party was the 1920s, the "period of struggle," when much of the energy of party members was devoted to beer hall and street brawls fighting Communists and Socialists. At that time the spirit of the desperado ruled the day, and the Brown Shirts were enthusiastic about their life of combat. They were convinced that their struggle and blood sacrifice would guarantee Germany a more happy future, when the shackles of the Versailles Treaty would be cast off, and honor returned once more to the German flag.

Once in power, Hitler had the entire communications and power apparatus under his control. He proceeded to employ it to neutralize the Communists and his other internal enemies. Throughout the history of the Third Reich, the SS and police were a specter to be reckoned with, and the SS became the vehicle for the persecution and liquidation of the Jews.

In the question of race, the Nazis cast their practical power interests into an ideological framework. According to their tenets, terror was the realization of the law of movement in history, because it set free the forces of nature and history which must be fulfilled. In practical terms, this meant that Nazi terror must be utilized to strike down the impure racial enemies who blocked the path of truth and light. The Aryan race was purported to be the weapon of Providence in this struggle of cosmic proportions. In the National Socialist context, terror was redefined and became equated with lawfulness; terror was seen to be in the service of the law of nature. To become free was to get into step with the forces of history, and to merge oneself in the racial whole. In this way, terror and ultimately the annihilation of world Jewry took on a new meaning. The death of the racial enemy was a service to one's folk brothers and sisters, to God, and to history. It was the party's supreme task to see that Aryan blood emerged victorious in the racial struggle.

The Fascist era was a period when neo-romantic political ideology and mystical ideals regained currency in the political arena. Europe between the wars saw leaders turning from material reality to a new reality defined intuitively, when emotion was prized over reason, the irrational over the rational. Fascist leaders were the inheritors of the cultural pessimism so rampant in the late nineteenth century. They gave political form to a widespread revolt against the modern world, against the decadence of the city, against widespread immorality, against liberalism and free thought. Both Hitler and Mussolini stepped onto the stage of history after World War I when violence, social unrest, and instability were the order of the day. They saw themselves as men of destiny and were determined to exploit the opportunity which political chaos had opened up to them. It was their goal not only to dominate their eras, but to set the stage for grand Fascist empires which would control Europe for centuries to come.

Mussolini was above all a man of action. Ideology was of secondary importance to him. It is significant that the ideological foundations of Italian fascism were not developed until long after Mussolini was in power. Ideology always took second place to violence and action in the Duce's Italy. On the other hand, just the opposite was the case with Hitler. Ideology determined the Führer's every thought and action, and his central focus was on world Jewry. For Hitler, propaganda, terror, and violence were always means to an end—to further the goals of his racial world view. Even as the Third Reich lay in ruins, he held to the idea that the "Jewish Bolsheviks" and "Wall Street Jews" were united in a worldwide conspiracy which had to be destroyed.

The Fascist leaders who exalted violence were themselves to meet a violent death. Mussolini, whose career had been devoted to a blind glorification of force, faced a despicable end. He was hanged upside down in a square in Milan, his mistress beside him. Hitler's heroic view of life was based upon the principle of "either victory or death," which drove him to the destruction and nihilism of 1945. When final victory eluded him, Hitler committed suicide, thus signifying the end of the Fascist era. Germany lay in ruins, and the survivors were to endure great material losses and psychological suffering.

Suggested Readings

There is a vast literature on fascism, and the student's problem is one of choice. Fritz Stern, *The Politics of Cultural Despair* (1961) and George Mosse, *The Crisis of German Ideology* (1964) offer an excellent background on the historical roots of fascism. Broadly ranging studies on the subject are: Alan Cassels, *Fascism* (1975), F. L. Carsten, *The Rise of Fascism* (1967), Eugen Weber, *Varieties of Fascism* (1964), John Weiss, *The Fascist Tradition* (1967), and S. J. Woolf, ed., *European Fascism* (1968). Advanced students seeking a real challenge are encouraged to read a work which merges history and philosophy, Ernst Nolte, *Three Faces of Fascism: Action Francaise, Italian Fascism, National Socialism* (1966). Students writing term papers are urged to consult Walter

Laqueur, *Fascism: A Reader's Guide* (1976) for assistance in locating the best works available.

Alan Bullock, *Hitler: A Study in Tyranny* (1961) remains the best single biography on the life of Hitler, although Joachim Fest, *Hitler* (1975) is also recommended. Robert G. L. Waite, *The Psychopathic God: Adolf Hitler* (1977) is an exciting and provocative addition to the growing literature of psychohistory. On the Jewish question, see Lucy Dawidowicz, *The War Against the Jews 1933-1945* (1975). For a study of the Nazi elite, the SS, see Heinz Höhne, *Order of the Death's Head: The SS* (1969). The propaganda machine of Joseph Goebbels is the subject of Jay W. Baird, *The Mythical World of Nazi War Propaganda, 1939-1945* (1974).

The following works are recommended on Mussolini's Italy: Adrian Lyttleton, *Seizure of Power: Fascism in Italy 1919-1929* (1973); Ivone Kirkpatrick, *Mussolini: Study of a Demagogue* (1964); Edward R. Tannenbaum, *The Fascist Experience* (1972).

CHAPTER 6

European Diplomacy and the Origins of the Second World War

C. Robert Cole

The Second World War began for Europe in September 1939. In five and a half years it killed 37,000,000 people, cost nearly a trillion dollars, introduced atomic terrorism into international relations, and destroyed Europe as the arbiter of global politics for all time. Yet apocalyptic though these consequences were, the war was conventional in origins. It resulted from the Germans' desire for redress following the First World War, from traditional political and diplomatic juggling among the European states in response to this desire, and from the most enduring feature of modern European history, the place of Germany in Europe.

The Versailles Treaty of 1919 ended the First World War. Those who made the treaty spoke of great new principles in international relations: open diplomacy, self-determination of peoples, pacification through international agreement, that is, through collective security, and above all, the new League of Nations through which all future disputes would be arbitrated and future wars avoided. But from the beginning there was tension between victors and vanquished, which over the years would be compounded by economic and diplomatic crises. German representatives had participated in the conference only when they were required to sign the treaty, and Germany saw in it not hope for the future but an act of vengeance and Allied aggrandisement at its own expense. This view was more or less constant down to 1939. Under the Treaty of Versailles, Germany was allowed an army of only 100,000, a small navy without submarines, no air force, and was required to demilitarize the Rhineland, a key portion of her frontier with France and Belgium. Significant areas of German territory were taken away for reasons both of defense and self-determination. From the outset the losses, especially of the Polish Corridor with its Baltic port of Danzig, were seen as a national humiliation. Also, Germany was held responsible for causing the war and was assessed reparations of $5 billion in gold to be paid by 1921, and a much larger sum to be determined and paid later. It was hoped that the military sanctions would pacify Germany, and thus Europe, and the territorial losses, coming in part through the creation of new central and eastern European states on Germany's frontiers, would reduce German preponderance in Europe. These new or revitalized states were to act as buffers against a resurgent Germany and against the Bolshevik menace coming out of Russia.

The huge reparations bill was mainly a matter of vengeance. It was regarded as harsh and unjust by the Germans and served into the 1930s as an object for blame whenever anything went wrong. This view was shared by many outside of Germany who both doubted the justice of reparations and feared that the issue might contribute to bringing about a future war. Among these critics was John Maynard Keynes, an economist who had resigned from the British delegation at the peace conference in protest. In his book *The Economic Consequences of the Peace* (1919), Keynes attempted to show that a large reparations debt would be disastrous for the economies of all European states, a danger equally to peace and the revival of trade. Later, German claims that territorial sections of the treaty likewise were vengeful and unjust, violating for example the spirit of the principle of self-determination, also fell on sympathetic non-German ears.

The two decades following the First World War divide

evenly at 1929, the year in which the Great Depression began. Before 1929 hope for a new and better Europe dominated politics and international relations. After 1929 the European mood changed to uncertainty and fear for the future. Disagreement over the role Germany was to play in Europe was the principal cause of the Second World War, and the diplomacy of the 1930s set up the situation in which that debate came to a head. Behind it all lay the Great Depression which shattered hope, stifled expectations, and altered dramatically European perceptions of what was possible and acceptable in politics and in foreign policy.

During the 1920s, statesmen and others operated on the assumption that from Versailles would emerge a new Europe dedicated to peace, prosperity, and democracy. These expectations were reinforced from time to time by apparent victories for the new order in international affairs: the Washington Naval Conference in 1921-22 produced three treaties; ongoing military disarmament conferences kept alive hopes for a general European pacification; the Locarno treaties of 1925 saw both Germany and the victors of 1918 making concessions; conferences in 1924 and 1929 reduced reparation payments; and the idealistic Kellogg-Briand Pact in 1928 proposed to outlaw war. Appallingly naive in the view of foreign policy experts, this pact nevertheless was enormously popular and by 1933 had been endorsed by sixty-five nations.

But these victories were illusory. Offsetting them were some very real failures. The British-inspired Genoa Conference in 1921 collapsed for want of support. In 1922 Germany and Russia signed a treaty at Rapallo which included secret military agreements. The German economy collapsed in 1923-24, the result of attempts to resist French occupation of the resource-rich Ruhr Valley. Fascist and other antidemocratic movements took root in every European nation, actually producing governments in some of them. Italy was the most notable of these when Benito Mussolini became premier following the march on Rome in 1922. Above all Germany, despite the efforts of Chancellor Gustav Stresemann who participated at the Locarno Conference, remained dissatisfied with her economic, political, and diplomatic position in Europe. Suddenly the economic crash of 1929 intruded a mood of fear and hopelessness into this mixture of reality and illusion.

The economic crisis of 1929 was worldwide. It wrecked most of what had happened for the good since 1919, not only bringing about economic dislocation but also creating uncertainties and reinforcing antagonisms. In *Origins of the Second World War* (1961), historian A. J. P. Taylor characterized the impact of this crisis when he wrote that: "Men who are well off forget their grievances; in adversity they have nothing else to think about." Before 1929, Europeans clung to a hopeful internationalism through which they believed adversities could be rectified and grievances reconciled. After 1929, they were gripped by a mood of apprehension, rising despair, and ultimately weakness. The campaign slogans of the British Conservative party under Stanley Baldwin were typical: "Safety First!" and "Don't Rock the Boat." Only the revisionist states, Germany and Italy, showed initiative and were assertive. The Western powers, Britain and France, seemed suddenly to lack the will to make the new international order work. Their response to Japanese aggression in Manchuria in 1931-32 makes the point clearly. The League of Nations raised the question of imposing sanctions on Japan. But Britain, the League member most involved in Pacific affairs, hinted that perhaps sanctions in this case were inexpedient. Despite pressure from the United States, Britain decided to remain neutral in the controversy, and other League members gladly followed her lead. Similarly, Anglo-French reticence provided the lead when the League responded weakly to Italian aggression in Ethiopia in 1935. The Western powers had lost confidence in themselves with the onslaught of economic depression. Consequently they also lost confidence in the new internationalism and reverted to policies of national self-interest. In the context of 1929-33 a sort of negative *realpolitik* emerged. After 1930, Britain and France paid only lip service to the concepts of Versailles for which they mainly had been responsible.

Germany too felt the impact of the Great Depression in terms of rising self-interest. The Germans, however,

spurned passive leadership and found a charismatic dictator prepared to use the circumstances of uncertainty and
unrest to repudiate in the name of Germany all vestiges of
the "humiliation" of 1919. In 1933, the National Socialists, or Nazis, secured the German chancellorship for their
leader, Adolph Hitler. They had risen to prominence in
German politics by suggesting simple solutions to Germany's many complex problems. These solutions included blaming the nation's ills on a variety of scapegoats.
They attacked recklessly such democratic statesmen as
Gustav Stresemann, and made the Communist party and
the Jews objects of national hatred. Nazi success generally
was due to the frustrations felt by the German people. In
particular in 1933 it resulted from political chaos. The
German system of government under the Weimar Republic, like that in Britain, depended upon either a party
majority or a coalition of parties which could produce a
voting majority in the German parliament, the Reichstag.
Without one or the other, the chancellor who was appointed by the president could not form a viable government. In the elections of 1932 Adolph Hitler lost the pres-
idency to Field Marshall von Hindenberg in a run-off, but
the Nazi party gained a plurality of Reichstag seats. Its
members subsequently were able to convince right-wing
nationalist parties to support them. This combination
wrecked all efforts to form a government without Nazi
members, and it was only a matter of time before Hitler
had to be appointed chancellor.

Many historians and others writings since 1945 have
argued that the Second World War resulted from Hitler's
wickedness as a politician and statesman. This simplistic
argument does not take into account all of the relevant
facts of European politics and diplomacy after 1929. Hitler
came to power with the consent of the German people and
on the strength of his ability to give voice to their determination to again dominate European politics. War came
only when the Western powers refused to concede the
final diplomatic move that would make this dominance a
reality. Hitler's platform rested upon the constantly reiterated complaint that the rebuilding of Germany was
necessary because the Germans had been the victims of an
international conspiracy carried forward by France, Rus-

sia, and Britain, and their postwar clients, Czechoslovakia and Poland. With this the Germans agreed, and he had their broad support whenever he denounced Germany's former leaders and other European states. Hitler's success rested upon his ability to articulate and satisfy German grievances. It was not his intention from the start to have war, but to achieve what he understood to be German national goals: (1) reasserting Germany's "natural weight" in Europe, and (2) gaining for Germany political and economic hegemony over central, if not over all of Europe. Hitler meant to reverse everything the Versailles Treaty had established, both in principle and in fact. He was successful beyond even his expectations. Between 1934 and 1939, he took Germany out of the League of Nations, repudiated reparations, rebuilt Germany militarily, and recovered much of Germany's lost territory, as well as reducing Britain and France to feelings of fearful impotence. His success simply demonstrated to the Germans that they had been right all along. Hitler was the catalyst, not the inspiration, for German policy, and thus for the events and decisions which produced the Second World War. To be sure he was a dictator with few scruples. But the same could be said for certain of his contemporaries. Hitler appeared to the German people as a savior who could accomplish what other German statesmen had failed to do, and what the rest of Europe presumably had conspired to prevent. Only in this manner does he bear primary responsibility for the Second World War.

The story of the war's origins centers on the assertive policies of this revisionary German leader and the passive response to them from the Versailles Treaty powers, with Italy, Russia, and Poland playing secondary yet vital roles. There are two distinct periods to consider: 1934 to 1937 and 1938 to 1939. Both were characterized by Anglo-French efforts at forming diplomatic combinations to contain Germany. In the first period Britain and France sustained hope of success, especially with regard to their courtship of Italy. In the second period their efforts had failed and the Western democracies faced what appeared to be a choice between submission to German revisionism or war. Throughout both periods the Great Depression worked its malevolent influence. British and French policymaking was plagued by pessimism and malaise born out of economic dislocation and political unrest. This mood contributed to the lack of a unified Anglo-French viewpoint on the German problem. Of equal importance was a similar lack of agreement between Germany and Italy as the two leading Fascist powers, at least until 1937, on what constituted their mutual interests. Both factors worked a vital effect. Down to the outbreak of war, Anglo-French disunity encouraged Hitler to believe that he always could count on British and French policy to collapse if only he were sufficiently willful. Until 1937, and perhaps wistfully for some time after, the Western powers viewed it as still practicable to work toward a Western orientation for Italy.

At the outset of the years of Hitlerian diplomacy, the British and French gave little evidence that they understood what game was being played. Hitler knew, at least in outline, but as full-scale German rearmament had not yet begun he was dealing from a position of relative weakness. His early successes resulted therefore not from the actuality but from the illusion of resurgent German power, created by his bold, skillful, and daring tactics. In the Saar Plebiscite in 1935, held to determine the future of this rich coal area which had been taken from Germany in 1919, the Nazis' skillful use of anti-French propaganda produced a stunning pro-German vote of more than 90 percent. The remilitarization of the Rhineland in March 1936, succeeded as a result of a consummate bluff. An Austro-German understanding, also in 1936, in which Austrian Chancellor Kurt von Schussnigg recognized the German national character of Austria was carefully orchestrated by Hitler in preparation for the eventual union of Austria with the Reich. Though many Austrians had long believed that their proper place was with Germany, the aim here was not sentimental so much as strategic. Hitler regarded unification with Austria as he did remilitarization of the Rhineland: both were essential to German security, and to the assertion of German dominance in European politics. There was little resistance to any of these moves beyond Anglo-French attempts to convince Mussolini to commit Italy to a Western combination against Germany.

Anglo-French courting of Fascist Italy points to a vital

problem in prewar diplomacy which ultimately had a great deal to do with the coming of war in 1939. In the first place, both Britain and France perceived themselves as being weaker than Germany. In the second, they could not agree on the extent or manner of their commitments in Eastern Europe. For example, France had made defensive agreements with the Little Entente (Czechoslovakia, Yugoslavia, and Rumania) and Poland during the 1920s, and had looked with increasing favor on cooperation with Soviet Russia. Britain had no such involvement and even the Anglo-Russian trade agreement sponsored by the first British Labour government had long since been dropped. Finally Britain and France had no common viewpoint on what constituted the greater danger to European security, and they could not agree on a general security system. In place of such a system, they concentrated between 1934 and 1937 on Italy, overlooking the fact that Italy also was a revisionary state. It is inescapable that in lieu of options, Mussolini finally would seek friendship with whatever power could offer both security and a free hand to pursue Italian goals. Britain and France might have managed the former, but the latter was beyond what their interests and commitments could permit.

Disagreement over fundamental perceptions of the European security problem and what constituted their individual European interests was the key to Anglo-French policy from 1934 to 1938, and especially to their courting of Italy. Britain was a maritime and France a continental power. Traditionally the British worked for a European power balance which did not commit them to continental involvement. The French always had attempted to maintain a position of dominance within any continental balance of power system. Britain's European perspective was more objective than that of France owing to the perculiarities of her insular position. Also Britain tended to favor Germany over Russia because of the geographical and historical relationship of Russia to British imperial interests in India. In the 1920s and 1930s, except for the brief periods of Labour governments, Britain regarded Soviet Russia as an extension of imperial Russia, now with the disagreeable addition of a revolutionary bent. Thus the British consistently regarded German resurgence as a lesser evil than Russian communism, and worked for a Western orientation for Germany and the exclusion of Russia from European politics. Still, Britain's policy in the 1930s was to pacify Europe. By 1934 she distrusted the internal systems both of Germany and Russia, and saw no reason to make hard commitments to either unless in the context of a general security system. France meanwhile regarded Germany as her constant enemy and was prepared to encourage Russian entry into European affairs as a counter to German power. She would accept nothing short of the diplomatic isolation of Germany. The French shared a common frontier and a long history of conflict with the Germans, and consequently regarded European security as dependent upon whether Germany or France was in ascendance. From the French viewpoint bolshevism appeared less frightening than German industrialism and the German army.

To effect French hopes for German isolation, French Foreign Minister Louis Barthou in 1934 proposed an "eastern Locarno" which would ally the Western powers with the Little Entente, Russia and Poland. The British saw this as upsetting the idea of collective security. They argued that by isolating Germany the circumstances of 1914 would be recreated. They countered by proposing a general security system that would include Germany and possibly Russia. The British believed that there was no possibility of security for Europe without German participation, but that security could be achieved without Russia. To France this alternative plan and concept was out of the question. In French eyes Russia was the only land power in Europe capable of countering German weight, and without Russian participation no security system was practicable. Due to this impasse, the proposed "eastern Locarno" which in retrospect might have prevented war in 1939 never reached fruition. Instead France and Russia signed a mutual assistance pact in May 1935, without reference either to Germany or to Britain—in some respects an admission of diplomatic defeat for France.

The failure of "eastern Locarno" produced an undercurrent of mutual distrust in Anglo-French relations after 1934. The result was evasiveness in their diplomatic and and especially military discussions thereafter, a weakening of their resolve when facing German pressures, and finally, in combination with growing internal economic and political difficulties in France, Britain taking the initiative in Anglo-French relations with Germany and others. These developments occurred in this fashion. In 1935, Britain and France met with Italy at Stresa to enlist Italian support against Germany. While this conference was in session, Britain was negotiating a private naval arms treaty with Germany and France its mutual assistance pact with Russia. When the Anglo-German Naval Treaty was announced in June 1935, the French protested that it sanctioned German rearmament and thus constituted a threat to French security. To this charge Britain replied only that "it was a realist contribution to peace similar to the Franco-Soviet Pact." The irony was not missed in Paris. Now the French felt insecure in their relationships with Britain, and despite their Soviet alliance felt incapable of acting independently in foreign policy. Their mood only encouraged British reluctance to trust their judgment. By 1937, it was clear to Britain that France could provide little initiative, and indeed hardly could survive in the increasingly jungle-like atmosphere of European diplomacy without British support. At the same time, Britain believed that she could survive with the assistance of the empire and commonwealth (providing she maintained freedom of the seas) even if the entire continent fell to a hostile power. The French had little choice but to fall in line with Britain, whatever their private reservations.

Now Anglo-French policy was conceived largely in London. This was made clear when British Prime Minister Neville Chamberlain sent Lord Halifax to meet with Hitler at Berchtesgaden in November 1937. Halifax complimented Hitler on his contribution to German recovery, proclaimed him the European bulwark against communism, and suggested that "possible alterations might be destined to come about with the passage of time" with regard to Austria, Czechoslovakia, and Danzig, so long as "methods should be avoided which might cause far-reaching disturbances." This statement amounted to acknowledgement of redress for all German territorial grievances since Versailles. It was a statement France should have protested had she been capable of divorcing herself from Britain's foreign policy leads. The Halifax statement represented an unrealistic if not actually foolhardy policy line, for it contravened French commitments in Eastern Europe and came close to contradicting Britain's own continental outlook. Despite its flexibility, British policy assumptions always included denying to Germany a free hand in Eastern Europe. Certainly the Berchtesgaden meeting revealed that in his own way Chamberlain could be tough-minded—at least where the French were concerned. But it showed also that he was naive regarding Hitler. A dangerous paradox resulted. By acknowledging that Germany might seek territorial redress even at the expense of existing treaties, Britain provided Germany exactly the leverage she needed to gain European hegemony. It would be a mistake to assume that Hitler did not see this, or that he might not use it to Germany's advantage. In the end, Hitler's leverage after November 1937 forced Britain into the guarantees of 1939 which led directly to the September war. France was compelled out of her own weakness to support them even though she had grave doubts concerning their wisdom.

The failed "eastern Locarno" also produced Anglo-French courting of Fascist Italy as part of a Western European alternative to the security system the Western powers had failed to achieve in 1934. It seemed natural that Europe's leading Fascist states ought to come together. But in 1935, Mussolini did not consider Hitler a suitable partner for Italian fascism and Hitler, who in any case held the Italians in contempt, did not completely trust the Italian dictator. Hitler recognized that Mussolini was ambitious for Italy. This was fine so long as these ambitions were pursued outside of Germany's sphere of interest. But there was a potential area of both Italian and German expansion in southeastern Europe. The key to this was Austria which bordered on Germany, Italy, and the Balkans. Concern over Austrian national integrity led Mussolini in 1935 to participate in the Stresa Conference which discussed and rejected Hitler's demands regarding European boundaries. Concern over Italian influence in Austria led Hitler to make the Austro-German agreement in 1936. A shared commitment to Fascist political principles was not enough to hold these revisionary states together. In 1935, Britain and France stepped hopefully into the breach created by Italo-German tensions over the question of the future of southeastern Europe.

The first move came in January 1935, when France acknowledged Italy's right to seek concessions in Ethiopia. In return, Italy indicated her willingness to favor the Western democracies against Germany, and to respect Anglo-French Mediterranean interests. The next move was a meeting of these three powers at Stresa in April, where they jointly denounced German efforts to repudiate the Versailles Treaty and promised to guarantee Western and Eastern European boundaries. No mention was made of the January acknowledgement. Several months later Italy attacked Ethiopia. When Emperor Haile Selassie appealed for help to the League of Nations the Western powers were in a quandary. On the one hand, Italy had been encouraged to seek concessions in East Africa, not to commit acts of aggression. On the other hand, Britain and France feared to alienate Mussolini. The Western powers simply had been outmaneuvered. When the League voted for economic sanctions, they held out until oil, among other commodities of vital military importance, were stricken from the list of prohibited trade items. Further, in November 1935, Britain and France signed the Hoare-Laval Pact, an agreement whereby Italian gains in Ethiopia were to be recognized in exchange for Italian guarantees against further aggression. However a wave of popular protest in Britain and France forced cancellation of the pact. This was a defeat which the concept of a Western combination, or to give it a name the "Stresa Front," did not survive. The breakdown was a victory for Germany. Italy emerged from Stresa permanently estranged from Britain and France and moving toward a relationship with Germany in which Italy would be the weaker partner. By losing Italy, Britain and France were weakened also in relation to Germany. The following year the Austro-German understanding placed Italy at a disadvantage with regard to southeastern Europe, while the remilitarization of the Rhineland put Britain and France on the defensive in Western Europe. The extent of the Italian drift into the German orbit was indicated by Mussolini's announcement of the Rome-Berlin Axis Agreement in November 1936. The Anglo-Italian "Gentleman's Agreement" the following January could not bring Italy back.

By January 1937, a definite shift in European diplomacy was in progress. While the Rome-Berlin Axis was a superficial agreement, it did signal that Britain and France were in the process of being isolated in Europe, just as once Germany had been. Both the direction of the diplomatic shift and the degree of flux in European politics while it was taking place can be seen in Anglo-French policy regarding the Spanish Civil War. This conflict represented a European ideological struggle, a test of wills between fascism and democracy, but its principal impact was in diplomacy. The war began in the summer of 1936 when an anti-Republican mutiny led by General Francisco Franco broke out in the Spanish army in Morocco. Initially France's leftist Premier Leon Blum wished to support the Republican cause openly as a gesture of anti-Fascist defiance, and hoped to persuade Britain to back him. Britain informed Blum he could do what he wished, but also expressed a strong desire that the war be localized and that others keep hands off. Blum agreed but proceeded to send aid unofficially to Madrid. This action embroiled him in such domestic conflict with various rightest supporters of Franco that he too soon came down in support of nonintervention. By September, Britain and France agreed upon the principle of closing the Spanish border to arms traffic. They managed even to gain acceptance for this principle from Italy and Germany who had responded to the outbreak of war with moral and material aid to the rebels, and from Russia who was no less anxious to help the Republican cause.

Britain's primary concern was that Italy not use the war as an excuse for revising the status quo in the Mediterranean, a concern compounded by an exaggerated assessment of Italian air and sea-power capabilities. The British were determined to submit to no pressure which would involve them in a Mediterranean conflict with Italy. To this end they took over leadership in Anglo-French advocacy of nonintervention in the Spanish war. But to advocate neutrality and to enforce it were not the same thing.

A supervisory committee on nonintervention was established in London on September 9. Soon it had to recognize that Germany and Italy regularly were violating the neutrality principle. This continued throughout 1936 and into 1937. In March 1937, after further negotiations, a multilateral agreement was made for the withdrawal of all non-Spanish "volunteers," and for setting up an international blockade to prevent further arms shipments. Again evidence appeared of violations, even to the extent of attacks on British warships and other vessels manning the blockade in the Mediterranean. The situation had become critical, and another conference was organized at Nyon in September to deal with it. In what historian W. N. Medlicott describes as "an error in tactics," the Germans and Italians boycotted Nyon because Soviet Russia had been invited. In their absence, arrangements were agreed to by which the signatory powers could counterattack. The shoe suddenly was on the other foot. Italy found it expedient to participate in these arrangements, though she had not signed the agreement. Likewise Germany now demonstrated a more restrained attitude, withdrawing her warships from the Mediterranean and instructing her "advisers" in Spain to become inconspicuous. However, despite adherence to the Nyon convention, Italy was determined that Franco should win the war. Britain, still worried over the security of its Mediterranean interests, negotiated a separate agreement with Italy in April 1938 by which she would work for recognition of Italy's position in Ethiopia and Italy would adhere to Britain's plan for the withdrawal of "volunteers" from Spain. The British stipulated that the agreement should not come into force until the Spanish Civil War was settled, and Italy disclaimed any territorial interests in the Mediterranean. Later, feeling secure following the Munich agreement in September 1938, Hitler sent reinforcements to Spain which enabled Franco to begin the final defeat of Republican forces. Italy withdrew her forces in February 1939 and her position in Ethiopia conveniently was forgotten as an issue in European politics. Through all of this the French went quietly along. Once she had accepted the nonintervention principle France's policy simply was to follow Britain's lead.

Britain's generous treaty with Italy in April 1938, followed by one month the German-Austrian *Anschluss*, the union of Austria with the German Reich. These two developments indicated that the fateful 1938-39 period of Anglo-French relations with Germany had begun. Germany had taken the step which removed Italy once and for all from the Western European combination. The Anglo-Italian treaty had been a vain attempt to weaken the impact of this fact. It did not. With Austria firmly in Germany's grasp, Italy faced on its northeastern flank an assertive power far greater than herself. After March 1938, the door was open for revision of Czechoslovakia and for German domination in Eastern Europe without interference from the West. Revision of Czechoslovakia, the key to this domination, became Hitler's next goal virtually from the moment German troops entered Vienna. Czechoslovakia, created in 1919, was an amalgam of minorities held together by the political and economic predominance of Bohemia. Its existence constituted a limitation to German ambitions in Eastern and Central Europe. Mapped out at Versailles, Czechoslovakia consisted of former Habsburg territories including the Sudetenland, the home of some three and a half million Germans. Though they had never belonged to Germany, these Germans were clamoring in 1938 to be united with the Reich. They were the specific issue in the Czechoslovakian crisis in the summer and early autumn of 1938.

The Sudetenland was a strip of territory in northeastern Czechoslovakia having a common frontier with Germany. Its German inhabitants charged that Czech rule over them was oppressive and intolerable. They were supported in these allegations by the German government which demanded some actions from the Czechs. Britain and France became fearful that the Czechs might act irresponsibly, that is in a manner that would precipitate war, in the face of German pressure. In April and May 1938, British and French military talks had taken place regarding Czechoslovakia, and it was the opinion of the experts that despite having a strong army of its own, Czechoslovakia was indefensible in the case of an all-out German attack. The ball was in the diplomatic court. Given a picture of disaster should a general war come, Anglo-French leadership

agreed that the Sudeten problem would have to be resolved through compromise and used the Franco-Czech
Treaty of 1925 as an opening to force mediation of the
crisis on the Prague government. Veteran British diplomat
Lord Runciman was sent to Prague to arbitrate an agreement between the Czechs and the Sudeten Germans. If he
succeeded, war might be avoided and Czechoslovakia still
protected.

Lord Runciman, astute in a scholarly way, was not the
diplomatic realist this situation required. He labored
throughout August to no avail. Instead of cooperating, the
Sudeten Germans increased their propaganda and resistance to Prague until negotiations broke down completely.
Meanwhile, Prague was compelled to use force to quell
anti-Czech riots in the Sudetenland. Sudeten refugees
poured into Germany where they were welcomed as victims of oppression. Berlin now demanded unilateral concessions from Prague and threatened drastic measures if
the Czechs refused. Faced with an intolerable situation,
Czech President Eduard Benes decided to mobilize the
army. His aim was to force the Western powers to inter-
vene directly, and thus to secure his country against what
appeared to be Germany's intention to dismember it.
Terrified that this act would precipitate war, Britain and
France demanded that the Czech army stand down and
that the government prepare to make concessions to the
Sudeten Germans. Benes had no choice but to give in.
Neville Chamberlain took charge of negotiations which
began at Berchtesgaden on September 15. He agreed with
Hitler that the Sudetenland ought to be turned over to
Germany. The French played their part by threatening to
terminate the 1925 treaty if the Prague government balked.
Benes, realizing the hopelessness of his position and
claiming that his only thought was to guarantee peace,
capitulated on the 21st. On the same day Runciman sub-
mitted a memorandum to Chamberlain in which he expressed sympathy for the Sudeten Germans and at the
same time blamed them for the final breakdown of his
attempts at arbitration. It is doubtful if his views directed
Chamberlain's thinking, for the prime minister's mind already was made up. But they most surely encouraged
Chamberlain's personal conviction that Hitler could be

dealt with rationally and that the German case against the Czechs contained merit.

On September 22, Chamberlain met with Hitler at Godesberg to work out the details of the Sudeten transfer. Now the German chancellor set forth unexpected demands: the Sudetenland must be occupied at once by German troops, and all Czech military and economic installations must be left intact. In short, Czechoslovakia was to be left completely unprotected on its German frontier, and a significant portion of its economic structure was to be incorporated wholesale into the Reich. Here again Chamberlain felt there was little choice and so informed Benes. Hitler then invited Britain, France, and Italy (but not Russia, a treaty power with Czechoslovakia), to Munich at the end of September. There the transfer of the Sudetenland was formalized as an international agreement, and the remains of the Czech state were guaranteed on the strength of Hitler's claim that as "all German blood now flows into the Reich" Germany had no more demands to make. Everyone went home relieved that war had been averted. At Heston Airdrome outside of London, Chamberlain announced to an emotional crowd: "I have it! I believe it will be peace for our time." But this proved to be the case only for the Czechs who when war began in 1939 already had been eradicated as a political entity. As journalist Lawrence Thompson described the scene in Prague when the signing of the Munich Pact was announced: "The news of surrender was kept from the people . . . until five o'clock that evening . . . When they heard it, some wept, some got drunk, a few shot or gassed themselves. The rest, thanks to Benes and Chamberlain, went on living."

There were more wolves than merely Germany in the European sheepfold. One of these was Poland which finally would drag Britain and France into war. Soon after Munich other states acted to seize coveted "national" portions of the now defenseless Czechoslovakia. Poland occupied Bohumin on October 9 and Hungary took parts of Slovakia and the lowlands of Ruthenia on November 2—both acting with German approval. Then on March 15, 1939, Germany scrapped Munich and occupied Bohemia. The next day Hungary seized the remainder of Ruthenia and the Slovaks, claiming German protection, declared their independence. Czechoslovakia had disappeared; German power now extended down the Danube to the Rumanian border. Yet Britain never intended to capitulate totally to German demands and after March 15, Anglo-French policy reversed. Chamberlain genuinely believed in redressing legitimate German grievances. But he believed also in opposing those which were not justified. After October 1938, Britain set in motion for Eastern Europe what Elizabeth Barker has called "a limited policy of insurance against Germany monopoly in the area, which the Foreign Office sought to implement by economic means until such time as British resistance could be strengthened."

Following the Munich agreement, only Danzig and the Polish Corridor remained to be regained by Germany, and before the end of 1938 Germany was pressuring Poland to negotiate. As Hitler noted, Danzig was a German city in composition and the Corridor, though Polish, did separate Germany from East Prussia. German claims appeared to be legitimate, and indeed were more so than those had been regarding the Sudetenland. Initially Hitler asked only for a plebiscite on the Corridor, and apparently would have settled for rights of passage across it. But Józef Beck, the Polish foreign minister and a pirate in his own right, refused even to consider German arguments. In fact, he held the trumps in the diplomatic situation, for the key factor was not the Corridor and Danzig so much as it was Poland's position between Germany and Russia. For this reason alone neither Britain nor France could abandon the Poles, and Beck knew it. His refusal to negotiate with Hitler was designed to force a crisis and win commitments from the Western powers. The moment would come when the West would have to protect the Poles or else see them disappear into a German sphere of dominance. The proof of Beck's logic came in March 1939, when Britain issued a unilateral and unconditional guarantee of Poland against German aggression. Beck had to commit Poland for very little in return.

The Polish guarantee was announced on March 31, following the German occupation of Prague on the 15th. The considerations behind it were basic to Britain's longterm view of the German threat to European security. There was the fact that compromise with Germany was no longer likely. Morale in the Balkans was also slipping: Greece, Turkey, and Rumania, fearful that Britain might abandon them, were indicating they would not hesitate to abandon Britain. In addition, Germany and Japan seemed to be drawing together in the Far East, and Italy by now had gone wholly into the German camp. British defense capabilities had not yet reached acceptable standards, even though since 1936 military appropriations had increased from 21 to 48 percent of the annual budget. The Polish guarantee was seen as buying needed time for building up armaments and for strengthening the resolve of the Eastern Europeans to aid the West in resisting German domination. Finally, there was the fear that unless Beck was supported he might negotiate an agreement favorable to Germany and harmful to British policy in Eastern Europe.

The Polish guarantee was an unwelcome surprise to Germany. Propaganda at once was geared up and Western policy was denounced. Germany's 1934 nonaggression pact with Poland was scrapped, the "pact of steel" with Italy was announced, Italian occupation of Albania was approved by Germany, and Hitler declared that the future of Greece, Yugoslavia, and Rumania still was to be decided. Also the frequency of German talks with Russia increased. These talks were vital because they were aimed at isolating Poland from the West. They were predicated on the assumption that without Russian help it was unlikely that Britain and France could defend Poland, and would not even make the attempt unless Russia was firmly on the Anglo-French side. In light of past experience, notably the Czechoslovakian crisis, Germany was certain that the Western democracies would not risk a general war merely for the sake of a diplomatic declaration. Russo-German talks were at a critical stage in the late spring and early summer of 1939 because then the Russians were also talking with the Western powers and with Poland. Anglo-French diplomats talked hopefully of a "peace front." If a Western agreement with Russia had been reached, it would have denied to Germany the advantage of Western disunity in the event a German war with Poland became necessary.

Britain naturally hoped that the March guarantee would accomplish its purpose. But the problems were enormous because there was the unfulfilled need to give the guarantee some teeth. France was incapable of doing more than defending its own frontiers, if that, and the Russians made impossible demands. Russia wanted to keep a substantial force in eastern Poland in order "to facilitate retaliation in the event of a German attack." Beck argued that this would destroy Poland as effectively as would a German war, and the Western powers were inclined to agree. In any case, Britain still distrusted Russia and refused to meet the Soviet demands.

By mid-summer Russia and Germany were on the verge of agreement. Joseph Stalin, the Russian leader, hoped to buy time, and Hitler a free hand to move in Eastern Europe. Hitler was now confident that Russia would stand aside, and that Britain and France would collapse diplomatically before they could agree upon a declaration for war. Germany believed that the possibility of war was now remote. W. N. Medlicott has noted that Hitler was "absolutely convinced that the Western democracies would, in the last resort, recoil from unleashing a general war," and that General Franz Halder, a Wehrmacht chief, thought the "utmost possibility" of Western resistance would be the recall of ambassadors, embargos on German commerce, promotion of Polish trade, and appeals to the League of Nations. War seemed even less likely when on August 23, Hitler announced the signing of the Russo-German Non-Aggression Pact in which Russia declared that it would not participate in a war over Poland, and Germany promised Russia a free hand in eastern Poland. The hope for a "peace front" was broken, and it was now up to the Western democracies to capitulate or to risk war.

The immediate Anglo-French response was to hurry preparations to defend Poland which were completed on August 25. Though a somewhat surprising response to the Non-Aggression Treaty this did not alter Hitler's conviction that Britain and France would not fight for Poland. On that day he again assured the Western powers that Germany would still be content with resolution of the Danzig and Corridor questions, and they again accepted his assurance. With hopes for a peaceful solution to immediate problems still flickering, they turned to Beck, upon whom the future seemed now to hinge. Would he negotiate with Germany now that Hitler had guaranteed Poland once the Danzig and Corridor questions were resolved? During the following week the problem of war or peace came down to these possibilities: (1) on the side of peace, Beck would negotiate or else the West could collapse diplomatically and Hitler would get what he wanted without negotiating; (2) on the side of war Beck could stand firm and the West with him, and Hitler would have to fight for his objectives.

Beck did not move, and though military talks between Poland, Britain, and France were progressing slowly, the West did not collapse. Hitler remained courteous to Western diplomats, but German newspapers stepped up their campaign of vilifying Poland. A stalemate had been reached. It was broken on August 29 when it was claimed that Poles had murdered six Germans in the Corridor: Hitler demanded that a Polish plenipotentiary appear in Berlin within twenty-four hours, prepared to negotiate all German grievances. The message was relayed through the British who unaccountably were hours late in delivering it. Thus Beck replied only after the midnight deadline on the 30th, refusing compliance with the claim that he had not had time to prepare. Privately he assured the British that he would not have complied in any case. Over the next twenty-four hours diplomatic messages flew back and forth between the various embassies in Berlin. Hitler declined to act, perhaps because he still hoped for a break in British, French, or Polish resolve or else because the Wehrmacht could not be ready to attack before September 1. Actually, whether or not war would begin on September 1, still rested on the success or failure of last-ditch diplomatic efforts. In the early hours of September 1, Josef Lipski, Polish ambassador in Berlin, requested a meeting with Hitler. But the chancellor was informed that Lipski was not authorized to speak officially for the Polish government and refused to meet with him. With the failure of this last maneuver, German air and land forces began the attack. Three days later, after further debate among themselves, Britain and France honored the March guarantee and the Second World War began.

Had Hitler planned war all along, as many historians

claimed after 1945? Probably not, though surely he was not averse to war if that was the only way Germany's ambitions could be realized. Was it purely the result of failure to satisfy all German grievances left over from Versailles, of Hitler's policy of brinksmanship in the final months, of the irresolution of Western statecraft beginning with the remilitarization of the Rhineland in 1936 or, as A. J. P. Taylor wrote in 1961, of a diplomatic maneuver launched on August 29 which ought to have been launched on August 28? All of these factors were contributory. But the primary factor was that as had been the case in 1914 a particular diplomatic problem remained unresolved: That Germany from its own weight was bound to seek mastery over Europe, and that just as surely Britain and France must seek to prevent it.

Suggested Readings

Only a tiny fraction of the voluminous writing on European diplomacy and the origins of the Second World War may be noted here. For the Italian role, there is Elizabeth Monroe, *The Mediterranean in Politics* (1938), and M. Toscano, *The Origins of the Pact of Steel* (1967). The French position is treated insightfully by John Dreifort, *Yvon Delbos at the Quai D'Orsay* (1973) and Geoffrey Warner, *Pierre Laval and the Eclipse of France* (1968). Britain is treated kindly in W. N. Medlicott, *Britain and Germany: The Search for Agreement, 1930-1937* (1969), but critically in Keith Middlemas, *Diplomacy of Illusion: The British Government and Germany, 1937-1939* and Roger Parkinson, *Peace in Our Time* (1971). The German position, usually presented as an indictment, may be found in Herman Mau and Helmut Krausnick, *German History, 1933-1945* (1936), Alan Bullock, *Hitler: A Study in Tyranny* (1953), and Joachim Fest, *Hitler* (1975). The great argument over appeasement is laid out in Martin Gilbert, *The Roots of Appeasement* (1966), John Wheeler-Bennett, *Munich: The Prologue to Tragedy* (1964), and Arthur H. Furnia, *The Diplomacy of Appeasement: Anglo-French Relations and the Prelude to World War II, 1931-1939* (1960). International relations analysts have worked on prewar diplomacy almost as much as historians: E. H. Carr, *The Twenty-Years Crisis, 1919-1939* (1964), William J. Newman, *The Balance of Power in the Interwar Years, 1919-1939* (1958), and Arnold J. Wolfers, *Britain and France Between Two Wars: Conflicting Strategies of Peace from Versailles to World War II* (1966); from historians there is Keith Eubank, *The Road to World War II* (1973) and A. J. P. Taylor's highly argumentative *The Origins of the Second World War* (1961). Recent archival openings in Britain have produced numerous new studies of interest and value. These include M. Cowling, *The Impact of Hitler: British Politics and British Policy 1933-1940* (1975), Sidney Aster, *1939: The Making of the Second World War* (1973), Simon Newman, *March 1939: The British Guarantee to Poland* (1977), and Lawrence R. Pratt, *East of Malta, West of Suez: Britain's Mediterranean Crisis, 1936-1939* (1975).

American soldiers landing at Normandy, D Day, June 6, 1944.
(Courtesy of the National Archives)

CHAPTER 7

The Course and Consequences of World War II

Francis H. Thompson

On September 1, 1939, forces of the German Wehrmacht crossed the Polish border and thereby initiated the most widespread and destructive war in modern history—a war that touched not only the armies involved but the civilian populations as well. Mankind had devised the most sophisticated weapons of destruction the world had ever seen, and they were used with precision and effectiveness. As a result, thirty million people lost their lives, and those who survived would forever endure the scars of six years of total war. Despite considerable skepticism to the contrary, Europe would survive the Holocaust, but she would never be the same again.

Hitler, as he indicated in *Mein Kampf* (1925) and elsewhere, quite evidently planned to start a major war. He had already demonstrated a fanatic desire to fight as early as 1938, even though Germany was, at that time, ill prepared to wage such a war. Hitler had certainly not been discouraged by either Britain or France, both of whom had acquiesced to his earlier bombastic demands. But it is naive to assume, as some historians have done, notably A. J. P. Taylor, that the British and French policy of appeasement forced a reluctant Germany into war. In any case, the era of appeasement came to an end with the German seizure of Czechoslovakia in 1939.

As the German government began to make its first demands against Poland, there was a euphoric notion evident among a few Western observers that Hitler had at last overstepped himself. A German attack against Poland would bring the Third Reich into direct conflict with the Soviet Union. The resulting war between the two great evil powers would, it was surmised, end with the destruction of both. More astute Western diplomats, however, felt that the USSR in 1939 could not stop the Germans. Joseph Stalin, harboring no illusions, evidently felt likewise. The ensuing Nazi-Soviet Non-Aggression Pact of August 24, 1939, abruptly ended any hopeful expectations, and opened the door to the German invasion of Poland.

If the Nazi-Soviet agreement was a shock, which it surely was, the rapidity with which the Germans disposed of Poland caused even more dismay. The Wehrmacht introduced the *blitzkrieg*—an attack that began with the use of air power to break up enemy defensive positions and to destroy communications, followed by the swift deployment of armored divisions. It worked to perfection on the broad plains of Poland. Though Warsaw held for ten days, the Poles, with Russia attacking from the East, were crushed in a matter of weeks. On October 6, Hitler, with Stalin's blessing, requested a conference to conclude peace.

The attack against Poland brought a declaration of war against Germany from both Britain and France, but neither power made any significant offensive move. French military strategists, committed to the idea of defensive war, were content to remain behind their expensive and well fortified Maginot line; the British, also thinking defense, were simply not prepared. In addition, the rapid collapse of Poland would have rendered futile any attempt to aid that country.

Although the powers were technically at war, there continued to be little evidence of that fact during the winter and early spring of 1939-40. It was, as one United States observer noted, a "phony war." With the exception of the Soviet Union's aggression against Finland, which started November 30, 1939, and continued for three months, there was little or no significant military action between October 1939 and April 1940. Hitler perhaps hoped that the Western democracies would once again revert to a policy of appeasement. In all probability, however, the inclement weather had more to do with the inactivity of the German army than any other factor. During those winter months, Hitler developed plans for his Western blitz.

In April, British efforts to mine Norwegian waters were abruptly frustrated by the swift Germany occupation of Oslo and five Norwegian ports. Though Hitler more often than not ignored the advice of his generals, in this instance they convinced him that control of Denmark and Norway was necessary to protect the German flank, and to ensure the uninterrupted flow of Swedish steel to Germany. Denmark fell quickly but the Norwegians resisted, and issued a call for British help. The latter did land small forces in central Norway but they were soon forced to evacuate. Norwegian resistance crumbled and the way was paved for the invasion of France.

By May 1, 1940, the Western Allies, with a combined force of some 124 divisions, faced 134 well drilled and heavily armed German divisions. Though not outnumbered to any conclusive degree, the lack of unity among the Allies proved fatal against the disciplined German troops. On May 10, 1940, the Wehrmacht struck swiftly and convincingly through the Ardennes forest in southern Belgium. Both Holland and Belgium capitulated within a matter of days, and the British expeditionary force of 200,000 was trapped at the port of Dunkirk. Hitler, believing that the German Luftwaffe could destroy the British army, did not move decisively against it. He was mistaken as the majority of British troops, plus over 100,000 French, were successfully evacuated back to England in one of the most remarkable operations of the war. It was a serious blunder on the part of the German Führer as the survival of the British expeditionary force in France was indeed vital to the survival of Great Britain.

Despite all evidence to the contrary, many Western observers continued to believe that France would rise to the occasion and put a stop to the Nazi onslaught. The French were, however, quite evidently finished. On June 10, 1940, Italy declared war on France. The following day, the

French government departed Paris for the city of Tours where, on June 18, 1940, France capitulated. The armistice was concluded on June 22, 1940, at Compiègne. The world was stunned and it is perhaps not an overstatement to conclude that the surrender of France was, to that point in time, the greatest psychological shock of the twentieth century.

Those same Western observers who had so much hope for the survival of France, became after June 18, extremely pessimistic about Great Britain's ability to stand alone against the seemingly invincible German forces. The new British prime minister, Winston Churchill, with his particular adeptness at phraseology, addressed himself to the British task in a speech before the House of Commons on the day of the French surrender.

> If we can stand up to him [Hitler], all Europe may be free and the life of the world may move forward into broad, sunlit uplands. But if we fail, then the whole world, including the United States, including all that we have known and cared for, will sink into the abyss of a new Dark Age made more sinister and perhaps more protracted, by the lights of perverted science. Let us therefore brace ourselves to our duties, and so bear ourselves that, if the British Empire and its Commonwealth last for a thousand years, men will say: 'This was their finest hour.'

The events of the next several months would prove Churchill's eloquent words most prophetic.

Plans for the invasion of Britain, Operation Sea Lion, were not formally inaugurated until July 1940. In the interim, Reich minister Hermann Göring convinced Hitler that Great Britain's will to resist could be broken by the German Luftwaffe. On August 13, 1940, the Battle of Britain commenced. The British air force, with only 900 planes available, seemed hardly adequate against the superior German force of over 2,000 fighters and bombers.

The first daylight raids, directed specifically at military targets, proved almost fatal. The British were indeed making the Germans pay a heavy price, but their own losses were staggering and could not be easily replaced. Suddenly, for reasons known only to the Führer, the thrust of the German assault shifted from airfields and other military installations to British cities. Perhaps Hitler felt he could break the morale of the British people. It was, in any case, a crucial miscalculation. Britain suffered heavy casualties and had some of her cities reduced to rubble, but the morale of the English people remained resolute throughout. And all the time the production of British fighter aircraft increased. The German losses in turn grew to such proportions that the Luftwaffe was forced to change from daylight to night raids, with the latter still producing less than tolerable loss of German aircraft.

Although air attacks on British cities continued into the spring of 1941, the Battle of Britain was, for all intents and purposes, finished after the British destroyed over 250 German planes during a massive raid on September 15 against London. Göring's grandiose dreams of a shattered England were far from realized. On September 17, Hitler "postponed" Operation Sea Lion indefinitely, with his thoughts already directed toward an invasion of Soviet Russia. In tribute to the Royal Air Force, Churchill would say:

> At the summit the stamina and valour of our fighter pilots remained unconquerable and supreme. Thus Britian was saved. Well might I say in the House of Commons, 'Never in the field of human conflict was so much owed by so many to so few.'

Hitler had never really lost his ambition to invade the Soviet Union. Once he became firmly committed to the task, it became an obsession which took precedence over all else. In a global conflict, such centrality of thought was a definite liability. At the time the Russian operation was in the planning stage, German troops in Africa, under the command of Field Marshall Erwin Rommel, were moving convincingly against the British. Hitler, with his mind fixed on the Soviet Union, never fully appreciated the significance of the African campaign.

Operation Barbarosa, the code name for the invasion of Russia, was set for May 1941. It was delayed, however, for over a month as German troops were diverted to Greece and Libya to aid their faltering Italian allies. The timing was critical because of the Russian winter. On June 22, 1941, with 4,000,000 men, 3,300 tanks, and 5,000 aircraft,

Barbarosa was finally implemented. The German general staff had recommended an invasion by stages, with an all-out attack against Moscow. Hitler insisted on the same *blitzkrieg* tactics employed in Poland, with one major thrust toward Leningrad and another south into the Ukraine. The Führer had his way.

The Red Army, suffering from the Stalinist army purges of 1937-38, performed poorly in the first stages of the campaign. Within three months, the German Wehrmacht had surrounded Leningrad and isolated over 600,000 Russian troops in the south. However, as the Germans approached Moscow, Russian resistance stiffened. With the aid of Soviet troops from the Far East, the Red Army launched, in subzero cold, a counteroffensive on December 5, which stopped the German advance. There was to be no quick victory in Russia.

December 1941, marked the high tide of Nazi success. The Germans were far from defeated, but from that moment on the Allied powers began to take the offensive. Before proceeding with a discussion of Allied military resurgence, some of the more pertinent consequences of World War II should be examined—the role of science, the German occupation, the underground resistance movements and, not least, the economic factors.

The German failure to achieve a swift, decisive victory in Russia meant, quite simply, that it was to be a long war. From the initial German mobilization in the 1930s, Hitler had chosen to utilize the existing economic structure rather than expand it—to mobilize in breadth rather than depth. His thinking was based entirely on the notion that when war came, it could be won quickly. Certainly the Wehrmacht's initial successes in Poland and France seemed to indicate that the Führer was correct in his assumptions. The failure in Russia, however, pointed out the deficiencies in Hitler's strategy and necessitated a broader economic undertaking.

Fritz Todt, minister of armaments and munitions, was the first to attempt to broaden the German economic base. His successor, Albert Speer, proved a near genius in expanding German production under the most trying circumstances. Despite the fact that Speer succeeded in continuing the flow of armaments to the bitter end, the

Germans would eventually be overwhelmed by the lack of manpower and sufficient fuel to run the machines being produced. The longer the war lasted, the more the advantage shifted to the Allies.

The British, on the other hand, recognized from the first that it was going to be a long war. The German blitz in the West shocked them into action. On the last day of the Dunkirk evacuation, British economists attached to the War Cabinet presented a plan for an all-out mobilization of the British economy. In the early part of the war, the English placed far too much reliance on their ability to strangle Germany with an economic blockade, a strategy that Britain had so successfully employed in the past war. Eventually the blockade became an integrated and more successful part of a greater economic undertaking. The British ability to mobilize an antiquated economic system for total war, and to do it within a period of three years, was one of the outstanding achievements of World War II.

The Soviet Union had from the beginning of the war a special economic adaptability. Of particular importance, Stalin's third Five-Year Plan had emphasized the industrial development of the eastern regions of Russia. From 1934 to 1939, the Russians miraculously transferred, or constructed, thousands of manufacturing establishments in the Ural Mountains. Without such an Eastern base, which was geographically secure from attack, the German invasion in 1941 might well have been fatal. In any case, the Russian ability to survive economically, with over half of her industrial and agricultural resources in enemy hands, was a notable economic accomplishment.

In the area of science, as with the mobilization of the economy, the Germans lagged behind the Allies. This was somewhat surprising because of the prestige and influence of German scientists. The fault was certainly not with the scientists, but with Hitler who steadfastly refused to give any precedence to scientific development until it was too late. The Führer, always guided more by personal moods rather than cold analytical facts, was certain the war could be won quickly and with conventional weapons. As one observer noted: "One reason Hitler failed is that he was out-of-date." Among other factors, the British were the first to make effective use of radar.

German scientists had actually perfected a superior radar system before the war began, but it was the British who made the first use of radar. Fearful of the kind of attack that eventually came in the summer of 1940, the British endeavored to perfect a workable radar system that would render their island less vulnerable to attack. Unlike Germany, there was unity of effort between soldiers and scientists as exemplified by the informal gatherings of experts in both fields held at the home of radar expert A. P. Rowe throughout the 1930s. By the spring of 1939, the British had successfully installed twenty radar stations along the channel coast—installations that would prove invaluable during the Battle of Britain.

Radar was also developed as an offensive weapon. During the course of the air war over Britain, the Germans perfected a complex beam that could be used on several frequencies to avoid jamming by British ground radar. This system was used most effectively in the devastating raid on Coventry, England, in November 1940. The British quickly rendered the new German system less efficient with the installation of radar sets in fighter aircraft.

The British also made excellent use of radar as an offensive arm with various systems employed to guide British planes to the designated target. In order to avoid detection by German radar, British scientists developed the so-called window which consisted of pieces of tin foil, dropped from bombers, which appeared as an aircraft blip on German radar screens. The British were at first reluctant to use the new system, fearing the Germans might copy it and use such a device in attacks against Britain. When the decision was finally made to use the "window," it cut British bomber losses significantly. The Germans did, in fact, copy the system but too late to be of any use as an offensive weapon.

Still another remarkable scientific achievement in World War II was in the area of missiles. A number of unorthodox scientists had been experimenting with the idea of rockets long before the war, with the research directed more in the area of transportation. At the beginning of the conflict, the Germans had a clear edge in missile development. But once again, Hitler refused to give any serious priority to such weapons until 1943. One week after the Normandy invasion on June 6, 1944, the Germans launched the first of over 9,000 V-1 rockets, dubbed buzz bombs by the English. Though terrifying, the V-1 was slow and soon became easy prey to British radar-installed fighters and to anti-aircraft batteries, utilizing shells with proximity fuses. The latter were detonated by noise from the approaching aircraft.

On September 8, 1944, the Germans fired the first and more effective long-range V-2. They continued to fire the new supersonic rocket, over 4,300 in seven months, until the German crews were driven from their launching areas by the advancing Allied troops. During that seven-month period, the British were unable to develop a successful counter to the V-2. It is shuddering to contemplate what might have happened had Hitler given serious attention to such weapons much earlier.

The Führer also refused to give high priority to the development of jet aircraft. The Germans, five days before the invasion of Poland, actually put a jet-propelled Heinkel in the air. In 1942, the Messerschmitt firm successfully tested the ME 262 turbojet fighter, and proposed immediate plans to mass-produce the new aircraft. Hitler preferred, instead, to emphasize production of a new bomber. As a result, the ME 262 did not become fully operational until the summer of 1944. Again, it was a matter of too little, too late.

Perhaps the most important weapon developed during World War II, certainly from a long-range view, was the atomic bomb. Building on the work of many late nineteenth and twentieth century scientists, there had been enough research conducted by 1939 to lead a number of physicists to conclude that such a weapon was possible. Many individuals both in and out of the field of science remained unconvinced, but the work continued. An important breakthrough occurred in early 1940 when it was demonstrated that one pound of U-235, not tons as previously surmised, would suffice to create the "critical mass" necessary to cause a chain reaction. The British, aware that the Germans were making progress, mounted a major effort in the area of atomic research in late 1941. Two factors contributed to delay the German endeavor—British sabotage of the German heavy water facility in Norway, the only such installation on the continent, and fortunately for the Allies, Hitler's neglect of the project.

By late 1942, the United States assumed the lead in the development of atomic energy. Spurred by the exigencies of war, progress was made in a period of five years that would, in all probability, have taken decades to achieve in normal times. In July 1945, the United States successfully tested the first atomic bomb. One month later the bomb was used against the Japanese cities of Hiroshima and Nagasaki. The world has not been quite the same since. Writing on the significance of atomic weapons, historian Gordon Wright succinctly noted that "henceforth the world would know only lesser wars—or greater ones."

One of the more important technological achievements in World War II was the British development of "Ultra." By fortuitous circumstances, British scientists acquired information that allowed them to reconstruct "Enigma"— the German code machine. From that point, the British were able to interpret virtually every move the Germans planned to make. The whole operation was such a well-kept secret that it has only recently come to light. The existence of Ultra was so significant that it may require a serious reevaluation of World War II historiography.

As in all wars, scientific technology is most often applied to the completion of more sophisticated weapons of destruction. Yet, there were, in World War II, some more humane achievements in the area of medical research. On the Allied side, two of the outstanding medical breakthroughs occurred in the use of sulfa drugs and penicillin. Both were known to medical scientists before the war but the healing properties of each had not been explored.

German medical scientists also made significant progress in the development and use of sulfa. Important advances in the prevention and cure of typhus, a scourge on the Eastern front, represented another German accomplishment in the area of medicine. One of the more abhorrent aspects of German medical research was the use, by some German doctors, of human guinea pigs to test various scientific theories, none of which did much to push back the barriers of medical knowledge. Such barbarism was part of the unhappy price a great many

Europeans were forced to pay for German occupation—for the establishment of the so-called new order.

German propagandists stated from the outset of the conflict that "we did not cross our frontiers in order to subdue other people in blind madness for conquest. . . . We came as the heralds of a new order and a new future." It cannot be stated with any degree of accuracy exactly what plans the Nazis had for conquered territory. In a vague sense, it might be assumed that Hitler, as his proposed thousand-year Reich progressed, had in mind the colonization of most of Eastern Europe, to provide *Lebensraum* for the German people, and the creation of satellite states in the West. For millions of Europeans, the German new order meant only subjugation, starvation, and death, especially to those considered racially inferior.

Nazi racial policies became clearly evident with the invasion of Russia. For the first time, propagandists began to use the word *Untermenchen*, referring to what the Nazis regarded as the subhuman character of Eastern Europeans. Such a policy of racial superiority reached its apogee with the Nazi treatment of European Jews. By 1939, several million had been herded into various camps throughout Europe. There was talk of deportation to some faraway place such as Madagascar, but the war precluded any plan for such a mass exodus. The German "final solution" to the Jewish problem was extermination. Several death camps were established for just that purpose, with Auschwitz, located in Silesia, as a prime example of the most horribly efficient. Using the new zyklon gas, at its peak, some 15,000 persons a day were marched to their death at Auschwitz. Although figures vary, perhaps as many as six million Jews perished in concentration camps. Certainly there were barbaric acts committed by all participants in the war, but Nazi atrocities, especially those committed against Jews and other Eastern Europeans, established a new level of hideousness.

There was, from the first, a minority of native collaborators in each of the occupied countries. But there was always an equal, if not greater, number of people who resisted Nazi subjection. Depending on the terrain, the resistance ranged from sabotage to all-out guerrilla warfare. The British wisely encouraged and aided the

European underground forces through, what Winston Churchill described as, the "ministry of ungentlemanly warfare." As the Nazi war machine began to falter in Russia, resistance activity increased and was a major contributing factor in the final Allied victory.

In the spring of 1942, the German Wehrmacht, after enduring the bitter winter of 1941-42, launched what was hoped would be its final decisive campaign on the Eastern front. At that moment, the German Africa Corps was prepared to move against Cairo and to seize control of the Suez Canal. Rommel was doubtless chagrined when he received word that the Russian campaign was to be given precedence.

The German attack in Russia moved well initially but ran into stiff resistance near the Russian city of Stalingrad on the lower Volga River. After weeks of intensive fighting, with heavy casualties on both sides, the Germans failed to seize the city. On November 19, 1942, the Red Army launched a counterattack that successfully isolated the German Sixth Army at Stalingrad. After several unsuccessful attempts to break out of the trap, and in defiance of Hitler's specific orders to fight to the death, the Sixth Army commander, Field Marshal Friedrich von Paulus, on February 2, 1943, surrendered the remnants of his army. The German failure at Stalingrad, combined with the even more significant loss of a major tank battle at Kursk in the summer of 1943, foreshadowed the total collapse of Nazi Germany.

Eighteen days before the Russian counterblow at Stalingrad, British General Bernard Montgomery's tank forces shattered Rommel's Africa Corps of El Alamein. Rommel, with his supply line constantly harassed by British raiders operating from Malta, Gibraltar, and Alexandria, was unable to hold, and began a sustained retreat. If Rommel did not have enough difficulty with Montgomery, on November 8, 1942, an Anglo-American armada, under the command of United States General Dwight D. Eisenhower, landed in Morocco. The result was the eventual destruction of German and Italian forces on the continent of Africa.

Stalin had for some time been pushing his American and British allies to open a second military front, and the generalissimo left little doubt that he meant Western France. United States General and Chief of Staff George C. Marshall had actually proposed a small-scale attack along the channel coast as early as September 1942. President Franklin Roosevelt, fearing a possible Russian collapse, pushed for a major invasion of the continent of Europe in 1943. The British reluctance to support such a proposal led a number of ranking United States military advisers to propose a shift of American emphasis to the Pacific theatre. Roosevelt refused to consider the latter advice. In the meantime, Churchill had successfully convinced Stalin that the proper military move was to strike at the enemies' "soft-belly," Italy, while preparing to hit him in the "snout," France. The United States agreed to Churchill's strategy only because an invasion of France in 1943 was no longer a possibility. It was assumed, however, that military action would not extend beyond Sicily or at the very most southern Italy. Later events would lead General Marshall to conclude that the British had led the United States "down the garden path."

On July 9-10, 1943, Allied forces landed in Sicily. On July 25, King Victor Emmanuel of Italy replaced Benito Mussolini with Pietro Badoglio who immediately began to seek a separate peace with the Allies. This proved difficult because of the "unconditional surrender" demand issued by Churchill and Roosevelt from their meeting at Casablanca in January 1943. In this instance, the rigidity of the term unconditional surrender proved flexible and Italy, for all purposes already out of the conflict, officially withdrew from the war in September 1943. It would make the task in Italy no less difficult because German forces under Marshal Albert Kesselring had occupied all but the southern part of the Italian Peninsula.

A few days before the conclusion of the Italian armistice, Anglo-American troops landed in southern Italy. The initial Allied advance, with the British up the east coast and Americans the west, moved well until they ran into heavily fortified German positions along the Rapido River south of Rome. In January 1944, the Allies, in an attempt to outflank the German defense, forced a landing at Anzio. The failure to break quickly inland from the initial beachhead almost nullified the entire operation.

Nevertheless, Allied troops managed to fight their way out of Anzio and, on June 4, 1944, entered Rome. The city surrendered on June 8, 1944, two days after the Normandy landing in France.

After the defeats of 1942-43, the Germans best hope to prevent or at least delay an assault on France was to shut off the flow of supplies to Britain with the use of the submarine. When the war started, the German navy had only fifty-six such craft in operation, which seemed to indicate that Hitler had indeed hoped to avert war with Great Britain. In the spring of 1940, the Germans accelerated production of their undersea arsenal. As a result, the British counterforce seemed less than adequate against the increasing number of German submarines plus the 115 Italian U-boats operating in the Mediterranean. In June 1940, the British navy had less than 200 destroyers available, compared with the 339 she had at the height of submarine warfare in 1917. As a consequence, the English suffered heavy losses in ship tonnage from mid-1940 through December 1941, with a comparable loss of desperately needed Lend-Lease material from the United States.

After Pearl Harbor, much of the American Atlantic fleet was transferred to the Pacific which further heightened the strain on the British. By January 1943, the Germans had a force of nearly 400 U-boats operating in the North Atlantic. The sinkings continued to increase throughout 1943, especially after the elevation of Admiral Karl Doenitz, a strong proponent of submarine warfare, to head the German navy. By the summer of 1943, however, American shipyards were producing more ships than the Germans could sink (one Liberty ship was launched every fifty-five days). In addition, the installation of microwave radar in search aircraft increased the Allied ability to locate and destroy German submarines. Although U-boats continued to harass Allied shipping, any chance of delivering a decisive blow against the British had long since vanished, if indeed it ever existed. American and British air assaults against submarine pens and fuel storage areas was also beginning to take a toll.

The overall effectiveness of the air war against Nazi-held Europe is still a matter of debate. There is one point, however, on which there is general agreement. The British idea that the German people would break under intense air bombardment was totally false. They responded, in fact, with much the same fanatical determination to survive that characterized the British response during the air war over Britain in 1940-41. There is also agreement that the air war, whatever its effectiveness, would have been even more productive if American and British air squadrons had, to a greater extent, coordinated their efforts. At times, both acted more like rivals than allies.

The British, after suffering heavy losses in daylight raids, switched to night assaults, much as the Germans had been forced to do in 1940. Always skeptical of precision bombing, the British chose to attack larger targets, i.e., cities such as Hamburg and Berlin. The British policy was guided in part by a revenge motive, and finally by the stubborn belief that such raids would destroy the morale of the German people.

American squadrons entered the air war over Germany in January 1943. The Americans, flying daylight raids, concentrated on precision bombing of specific military targets. Despite the fact that the American B-17 was heavily armed and the American squadrons flew in tight formation for maximum protection, the losses from German fighters and anti-aircraft batteries were prohibitive. In one massive six-day raid against German ball-bearing plants at Schweinfurt, the Americans lost 148 bombers. The development of the P-51, a long-range fighter that could accompany the American bombers to the target, made the losses at least tolerable. Through 1944, the raids increased in intensity.

In the final analysis, the air attacks against Germany did not shake German morale, but did hamper the German war effort, to what extent remains a matter of conjecture. German production did, in fact, continue at a surprisingly high level throughout 1944. But according to Albert Speer, the American raids against sources of fuel were the most effective. The Germans might well have continued to produce tanks and aircraft, but without an adequate supply of fuel, they were worthless. This fact became clearly evident when only a handful of German planes appeared over the beaches of Normandy on June 6.

Plans for the invasion of France had been underway for

months, with the finalization of specific details at the Tehran conference in November 1943. Normandy, which required a much longer water route, was chosen as the site of the proposed landing because of the element of surprise. The months of planning, coordination, and staging reached fruition on D Day, June 6, 1944, with the largest amphibious operation in history.

The Germans, aware that the invasion was imminent, had made exhaustive preparations to meet the assault, with the full knowledge that whatever faint hope remained for a German victory rested with their ability to deny the Allied forces the beaches of France. When the invasion came, the strongest German Panzer divisions were far to the north at Calais. Hitler, convinced that there was to be a second invasion, refused to commit the German tank divisions until an Allied beachhead was firmly established.

In July 1944, as the Allies broke inland from Normandy, a group of German conspirators, including some distinguished members of the Wehrmacht, attempted to implement a plot to assassinate Adolf Hitler, a plot that had been in existence in one form or another since 1938. At a staff conference on the Eastern front, Colonel Claus von Stauffenberg entered the staff room, deposited a brief case containing a bomb, and quietly departed. Hitler, by a stroke of luck, emerged from the block house shaken but very much alive. In spite of his own paranoia, and the chaotic conditions in Germany at the time, the Führer remained firmly in control. In the aftermath, some 7,000 persons were arrested, with 5,000 of those eventually executed. The legendary "Desert Fox," General Erwin Rommel, who was implicated only, was forced to take poison. In retrospect, the elimination of Hitler at that point might well have brought peace in the summer of 1944. But it was not to be. The people of Europe would be required to endure ten more months of costly war.

On August 25, 1944, American troops liberated Paris. Although the fighting was fierce, the Allies were moving inexorably toward the German border. In the East, what had started as a slow German retreat after the surrender of the Sixth Army at Stalingrad had, by the summer of 1944, turned into a rout. The Red Army was racing across

Eastern Europe, much to the consternation of some Western observers who feared the future consequences of Communist penetration into Central Europe.

In December 1944, the Germans, taking advantage of deplorable weather conditions that grounded Allied air power, launched their last offensive in the West. Driving a wedge in the Allied lines in the Ardennes area in Belgium, the German forces succeeded in completely surrounding the United States 101st Airborne Division at Bastogne. After ten days, the weather cleared, the beleaguered defenders of Bastogne were relieved, and the German advance halted. It was the once proud Wehrmacht's last hurrah. The Ardennes offensive cost the Germans over 100,000 men and 600 tanks which might have been better utilized to defend the fatherland. A short time after the Allies resumed the offensive, the Supreme Allied Commander, General Dwight Eisenhower, decided to halt the eastward advance at the Elbe River. It was a purely military decision but one that contained serious, long-range political implications because it opened Berlin to Russian occupation.

On April 30, 1945, as Soviet troops pushed through the eastern sector of Berlin, Hitler, from his bunker in the German capital, named Admiral Karl Doenitz as "President of the Reich." He then married his longtime paramour Eva Braun and within a matter of hours, shot himself to death, with orders that his body be burned. On May 7, at Reims, a representative of Admiral Doenitz accepted the Allied terms of unconditional surrender. On the following day, May 8, 1945, the war in Europe came to an end.

The problem facing Europe in May 1945, were many and complex. The physical destruction alone defied comprehension, with Germany reduced to virtual rubble. Millions of displaced persons wandered the continent with the prospect of mass starvation an ever-present menace. The economies of Europe were shattered and any hope of immediate recovery did not appear bright. Politically, the military presence of the Soviet Union in East and Central Europe alarmed many individuals, and necessitated a long and hard look at future policy options. The problems were of such magnitude that many wondered not when Europe would recover, but if recovery was in fact possible.

But, as noted by one historian:

> Perhaps men are always inclined to underestimate the resilience of the human race, its stubborn capacity to scramble back from the pit into which it has been cast by its own follies. Perhaps those observers who in 1945 had talked gloomily of the 'end of Europe' have overlooked the possibility of a new beginning.

Suggested Readings

Three good general accounts of the war are Gordon Wright, *The Ordeal of Total War* (1968); B. H. Lindell Hart, *History of the Second World War* (1970); and Winston Churchill, *The Second World War*, (6 vols., 1948-1950). On wartime diplomacy, see John L. Snell, *Illusion and Necessity; The Diplomacy of Global War, 1939-1945* (1963). There are numerous scholarly works on specific military aspects of the war: Robert M. Kennedy, *The German Campaign in Poland* (1956); Major L. B. Ellis, *The War in France and Flanders, 1939-1940* (1953); Telford Taylor, *The Breaking Wave* (1967), which gives a good account of the Battle of Britain; Albert Seaton, *The Russo-German War* (1970); W. G. F. Jackson, *The Battle for Italy* (1967); and Cornelius Ryan, *The Longest Day* (1957), which is an interesting chronicle of the Normandy invasion. On the air war, see D. Richards and H. S. Saundby, *Royal Air Force, 1939-1945*, (3 vols, 1953-54), for the British view. On the role of the United States, consult Wesley F. Cravens and James L. Cate, *The Army Air Forces in World War II*, (7 vols., 1948-58). For an account of the naval war, consult Captain S. W. Roskill, *The War at Sea*, (3 vols, 1954-61). On the subject of economics, see W. K. Hancock and M. M. Gowing, *British War Economy* (1951). For an informative and interesting discussion of German mobilization, see Albert Speer, *Inside the Third Reich* (1970). On the role of science, consult C. P. Snow, *Science and Government* (1961), Robert M. Page, *The Origins of Radar* (1962), Ronald W. Clark, *The Birth of the Bomb* (1961), and Rudolf Lusar, *German Secret Weapons of the Second World War* (1960). For a discussion of Nazi racial policies, see Paul Hilberg, *The Destruction of European Jews* (1961), and Gerald Reitlinger, *The Final Solution* (1953).

European Society After World War II

In 1945, at the end of World War II, much of Europe lay in ruin. Fascism was dead and Hitler and the Nazis had been defeated, but at a staggering cost. There were millions of refugees clogging the roads, there were thousands of cities reduced to rubble; European industry and commerce had been reduced to pathetic levels and much of the great wealth of western Europe had disappeared; Europe had been liberated from the Nazi tyranny, but this had been achieved essentially by American and Russian power, not European armies. It was all of these factors that prompted many European and American scholars to predict in books about the *Passing of the European Age* and the *Farewell to European History*. It was these factors that prompted General Douglas MacArthur to state bluntly in 1944 that "Europe is a dying system. It is worn out and run down . . . The lands touching the Pacific with their billions of inhabitants will determine the course of history for the next ten thousand years." The obituary of Europe's death has, however, been a bit premature. Europe has, indeed, undergone a remarkable economic, political, and social resurgence since World War II, a resurgence that has forced scholars today to think in terms of a new Europe, united together by common cultures, common goals, and, most important of all, common sense.

James M. Laux examines Europe's dramatic economic, political, intellectual, and cultural recovery from the disasters of the Second World War, or, as he puts it, from "ashes to affluence." In the second essay in this section, M. B. Lucas analyzes Europe's new political role between the two great super powers of the world, the United States and the Soviet Union, and describes Europe's reactions to the threat of Russian power, Russian Communist ideology, and its reliance on the Americans for Europe's security. William J. Miller surveys the impact of the collapse of the European colonial system on Europe and the world, an event that is still shaping and directing world history. The section closes with a conclusion, Thomas E. Hachey's critical discussion of Europe in the 1970s.

CHAPTER 8

Europe After the Second World War: From Ashes to Affluence

James M. Laux

As the Second World War ended in Europe in May 1945, powerful forces pushed for major political and social changes in the war-torn continent. In Britain, the voters expressed this in August 1945 when they repudiated their great wartime leader Winston Churchill and elected a heavy majority of Labour party members to the House of Commons. This forced Churchill out of office and brought the Labour leader, Clement Attlee, to the prime minister's office at 10 Downing Street. In France, in October 1945, the public by a proportion of 25 to 1 chose not to return to the political system of the Third Republic that had fallen in 1940 and selected an assembly to write a new constitution. In Italy, in June 1946, the voters repudiated the Italian monarchy, tainted by its association with Mussolini, and opted for a republic.

These events proclaimed a widespread desire not to return to the good old days but to try something new. In Germany too, few wished to continue an authoritarian regime of the Nazi type that had brought so many disasters on themselves and their country. This desire for change came in part from unappealing memories of the 1930s, because for many people those old days were not so good.

Also, the events of the war had often discredited old leaders, on the continent especially, and allowed new people—especially those from the Resistance—to rise to prominence. In this new leadership in France, Italy, and Eastern Europe, Communists and Socialists were strongly represented and of course they wished to bring major changes to their countries' politics and societies. What happened to this wave of renovation? How far did it carry up the shores of Western Europe?

In Britain, Labour's victory in August 1945 gave it almost a two to one majority in the House of Commons. When, after resigning as prime minister, Churchill first reappeared in the House, his Conservative colleagues greeted him with "For He's a Jolly Good Fellow." But the Labour members showed where their sympathies lay by singing "The Red Flag," a party anthem written by an Irish Socialist in the 1890s. As events would show, such choral rhetoric did not mean that Labour would embark on a major social revolution, but it did have a program, a series of measures to move the country toward a moderately Socialist society. This meant national government ownership and control of some major sectors of the economy and the spread of a government-operated welfare system to all citizens. In the six years that Labour held power, it nationalized the Bank of England, electricity and gas industries, over-the-road trucking, railways, coal mining, and the steel industry. Social reform included a reorganization and expansion of social insurance programs including family allowances, retirement pensions, and unemployment insurance, but its centerpiece was the National Health Service, a system of publicly operated medical care that had begun in 1911 to cover the less-well-paid workers and now was expanded to cover everyone. Largely financed by general tax revenues, it provided free hospital, physician, and drug service. It aimed to assure equal medical care for all.

Although the British economy did not suffer extensive wartime damage, it had difficulty regaining the prosperity of the immediate prewar years. During the war, the British had sold off some of their foreign investments. Without this income, they needed to expand exports to pay for a normal level of imports. Labour favored the stick rather than the carrot to achieve this export level. It emphasized austerity—reducing consumption at home—rather than encouraging shifts in the industrial structure to promote production of goods for which there was a growing world demand. This policy, along with a devaluation of the pound sterling from $4.02 to $2.80 in 1949, met the export goal, but the rate of growth of total output in the economy was disappointingly low. It would continue to grow at a lower rate than Western continental Europe in the following decades.

Labour left office when a 4 percent shift in the electorate from 1945 enabled the Conservatives to win a slender majority in 1951. Labour had lost some support by its inability to encourage enough dwelling construction, by its insistence on continuing to regulate consumption several years after the war, and by some disillusionment among its supporters who found that government ownership of major economic enterprises actually changed little in their day-to-day operations. The Conservatives remained in power until 1964, tinkering with the major reforms instituted by Labour but not tearing them down.

This pattern of a spate of reforms increasing government influence on the economy and society, followed by a gradual recovery of power by conservative political elements, also characterized postwar France. There Charles de Gaulle, flamboyant leader of the French Resistance, held the reins of power as the war ended. He accepted, sometimes reluctantly, an expansion of welfare programs and some nationalizations as demanded by the political Left and the Resistance. As his top priority, however, he wished to maintain a government with a strong executive that would allow France to play a major role in world affairs. When de Gaulle concluded that the politicians in Parliament were inclined to return to the prewar game of party politics that he believed had so dangerously weakened the country's resolve in the 1930s, he suddenly resigned as head of the government in January 1946, five months after Churchill left office in England. By this gesture he hoped to awaken his countrymen to the danger but they did not rise to his challenge. They set off no avalanche of demands that he return to power on his own terms. A coalition of the three parties that dominated the

Parliament, Christian Democrats, Socialists, and Communists, governed for another seventeen months and continued the reformist policy, leading to a number of nationalizations and social insurance similar to that in Britain, but also providing for a system of national economic planning.

The constitution these three reformist parties drafted and which the people finally approved by a referendum in November 1946, provided for a Fourth Republic with a dominant Parliament of two houses and a weak executive. It closely resembled the system of the Third Republic so decisively repudiated a year earlier. This paradoxical result came not only from the traditional fears of the French Left which thought it saw the ghosts of Napoleon I or Napoleon III in every powerful executive, but also from the unhappy experience with Marshal Pétain, whose wartime Vichy regime also discredited the strong executive. This move back to traditional politics was reinforced in May 1947, when the Communist ministers were forced out of the French government for failing to follow the policies determined by a majority of their cabinet colleagues. Thereafter coalitions of the center, extending from Socialists through Christian Democrats to conservatives, governed in a series of short-lived cabinets, with no further moves to challenge the capitalist economic system. The Fourth Republic lined up with the United States in the cold war and successfully encouraged national economic growth.

While French military and deportee deaths during the Second World War reached 450,000, this was much smaller than the nearly 1.4 million killed in the First World War. Physical destruction also was less, with the greatest damage done to railways and bridges, not industrial capacity. The chief hurdles to expanding production were repairing the transportation network and finding foreign exchange to pay for imports of raw materials and machinery to raise output from its low level. Most railways, canals, and ports were back in service by 1946. The import problem was met in part by American grants and loans, then Marshall Plan aid from 1948 on, along with a gradual revival of French exports. The government planning commission, founded and headed

by Jean Monnet, encouraged public and private investment in crucial economic sectors such as steel, cement,
and energy production. It successfully promoted a psychology of economic growth among French businessmen,
specifically favoring larger production units and adoption
of more modern technology. By 1947 French industrial
production matched the 1938 level of output and in 1951
surpassed the record year of 1929. Agricultural output
also grew, but more slowly. So France resumed the rapid
economic growth extending back to 1895 that had been
interrupted by the Depression and the Second World War.

Successful in its economic policies, the Fourth Republic
fell over failures in colonial affairs. First it bogged down
in Indochina where its efforts to resume most of its prewar
colonial dominance led to a tragic guerrilla war. Finally
withdrawing in 1954 after a small but humiliating military
defeat at Dien Bien Phu, the regime immediately had to
confront a similar armed uprising in Algeria. The policy of
repression failed to solve the problem in Algeria, as it had
failed in Indochina. Finally, in May 1958, it appeared that
a military coup staged by units of the French army might
overthrow the government in Paris in order to get a regime
even more favorable to a forceful and expensive military
conquest of the Algerian rebels. In this crisis, the frightened deputies swallowed their dislike of Charles de
Gaulle and a majority of the right and center asked him to
become premier. As in earlier national emergencies, the
French called upon a providential man for salvation. De
Gaulle did what was expected of him. While retaining the
loyalty of the army he negotiated with the Algerian opposition. An agreement finally came in 1962. The French
withdrew their forces, Algeria became an independent
state, and most of the European residents of Algeria withdrew to France.

When de Gaulle took control in 1958 he insisted on
receiving power to draft a new constitution for his regime,
the Fifth Republic. This document, overwhelmingly
ratified by the voters at the end of 1958, tilted the balance
of powers in the governmental system toward the president of the republic (de Gaulle) and away from the Parliament. The regime became a compromise between a presidential (the United States model) and a parliamentary (the

Anglo-French model) system. Charles de Gaulle remained president of the republic for seven years after the Algerian settlement in 1962, busying himself with foreign policy initiatives aiming to carve out a major power role for France between the United States and the Soviet Union, and with expanding French military strength including atomic weapons. De Gaulle's successors as president, Georges Pompidou and Valéry Giscard d'Estaing, have maintained the strong presidential political system in France, but until it is tested by a serious crisis we shall not know if this Gaullist legacy can survive.

In Italy, political developments generally paralleled those in France. After the people voted out the monarchy in 1946, the politicians prepared a new constitution which closely resembled that of pre-Mussolini times, with a president replacing the king. As in the French Third and Fourth Republics, it established a dominant Parliament and encouraged a multiparty system. At first, a statesman appeared who could master the system: Alcide de Gasperi, leader of the Christian Democratic party and premier from late 1945 until 1953. Supported by his own party, other center factions, and the nonrevolutionary socialists, de Gasperi put down the challenge of the Communists for power, brought Italy into the Western bloc, encouraged economic recovery with substantial help from foreign aid, became a leader in the European integration movement, and began pouring public funds into an economic development program for the impoverished south. In Italy, industrial nationalization had begun under the Fascists during the Depression when the government took over partial or full ownership of many firms to save them from bankruptcy. A public agency called the Industrial Reconstruction Institute (I. R. I.) managed all these government enterprises and added more in the postwar years. Its expansion owed more to bureaucratic empire building than leftist ideology, as the Communist and Socialist parties devoted more energy to promoting full employment and higher wages than to structural reforms. By the 1950s, the share of the economy held by the I. R. I. and other government agencies exceeded 20 percent. De Gasperi finally fell from power in 1953 and Italy lapsed into the dispiriting practice of government by constantly shifting party coalitions and frequent cabinet crises. The lack of any major foreign or colonial issues allowed the country the luxury of continued do-little governments in the 1950s and 1960s.

When the Second World War ended, Germany seemed devastated. The centers of most of the large cities lay in ruins. Millions of soldiers lay dead. More millions of civilians still lived but competed with millions of refugees for food, clothing, and shelter. Yet, just three years later the Americans and British were operating a massive airlift to protect West Berlin from Communist control, and within a decade of the war, West Germany was fully independent, with the most powerful economy in Western Europe, beginning to rearm, and allied with her former Western enemies. Such a turnabout is one of the most startling episodes of postwar Europe.

Germany was divided into three parts at the end of the war. The easternmost (about one-quarter of the area of 1937 Germany) annexed by Poland, the central section (another quarter) occupied by the Russians, and the west (a little over one-half) under American, British, and French control. Berlin, of course, remained a special case of four-power occupation in the midst of the Russian zone. The central and western occupation zones ultimately became separate independent governments and so one of Hitler's legacies was the end of the unified Germany engineered by Bismarck seventy-five years earlier.

In the West, the occupants encouraged the revival of non-Nazi political activity in 1946 on the local level. Seeing that a self-governing West Germany would reduce their own responsibilities there and bring this part of the country into the emerging anti-Communist bloc, the Americans, British, and French supported the expansion of self-government to the provincial level and then to the entire western zone in 1949 with the creation of the German Federal Republic. The leader of the new Christian Democratic party, Konrad Adenauer, pre-Nazi mayor of Cologne, became the first chancellor (prime minister) of the Federal Republic and held this post for fourteen years, a longer term than Hitler's, he was pleased to note. One reason for Adenauer's long tenure and the relative cabinet stability of his successors is a device in the Federal Republic's Basic Law or constitution that requires the lower parliamentary house to agree upon a new chancellor before voting no confidence in a sitting one. This arrangement, suggested by an American historian, prevents a situation where the two political extremes could unite to oust a chancellor although unwilling to agree on a new policy.

Adenauer's major opposition came from the revived Social Democratic party. West Germany did not go through a wave of Socialist reformism, especially nationalizations, as did Britain and France in the immediate postwar years, for by the time the West Germans could determine their own destinies, the leftist impulse had ebbed in Western Europe. Also, much of the traditional voting strength of the Social Democrats now lay in the Russian zone and their leader, the inflexible Kurt Schumacher, tended to alienate potential recruits to his cause. In fact, the Adenauer government's economic policy reduced direct government activity in the economy and encouraged free enterprise, with extraordinary results.

Observers who visited Germany as the war ended told stories of utter physical disaster. An American newspaperman wrote: "Nothing is left in Berlin. There are no houses, no transportation, no government buildings." Another visitor compared railroad marshalling yards to "children's playhouses the day after Christmas. The industrial barons of the Ruhr presided over a twisted mass of bricks and mortar; for the moment they were junk merchants." Actually, such graphic descriptions were seriously misleading. The bulk of bomb damage in the cities affected their centers, that is commercial establishments and housing, not industry. Myopic journalists did not realize that Germany had more industrial capacity when the war ended than when it began. Postwar dismantling and reparations to the Soviet Union reduced capacity somewhat, but in West Germany this was not extensive. War damage to railways was thorough but as in France and Italy, repairs came quickly. Economic recovery began slowly, however, as millions of people had to adjust to loss of their homes, find new jobs, and cope with very rapid price inflation. A currency reform in the West in June 1948, accompanied by removal of most restrictions on prices, wages, and supplies, sparked a startling expansion of industrial production. From a mid-1948 level only 60 percent as high as 1936, it surpassed that figure in 1950 and achieved another 50 percent increase by early 1953. A variety of factors lay behind this so-called economic miracle. We shall emphasize five of them. As already mentioned, war damage was not as serious as thought. Labor was abundant, by 1948 some 8.5 million refugees had arrived in West Germany and this figure reached 10 million by 1953. Most of them were Germans from Eastern Europe and from the Polish and Russian zones of prewar Germany. Destitute, but usually educated and oftentimes skilled, they worked hard to regain the status and living standards they had lost. Their presence also tended to moderate labor demands for wage increases. This large labor force in West Germany also meant that on a per capita basis, the country's industry advanced at a rate comparable to that of France and Italy. Thirdly, Allied policy toward West Germany played a positive role. It shifted from regulations to hold production down in 1945 to encouragement to increase production by 1947 and then to substantial economic aid. The Marshall Plan and other economic support to West Germany from 1948 through 1954 amounted to nearly $2 billion and helped pay for the import of crucial raw materials. West Germany was well prepared to profit from the world economic boom of the late 1940s and 1950s. Her well developed machinery industry found it easy to export in these years, and had the capacity to expand output. The boom exports of Volkswagens, for example, paid for imports and encouraged further industrial investment. Finally, the Federal Republic's policies turned out to have favored the industrial boom. They depended more on free markets and capitalist incentives than the other major European governments but kept inflationary pressures at bay with tight credit and a balanced budget that limited the growth of the money supply. Such policies caused short-run hardships for the poor and unemployed, but by the late 1950s the country achieved full employment and the West Germans were on the road to affluence.

In Eastern Europe, recovery from the war followed paths

that diverged from the Western pattern, but the ultimate goal of affluence was similar. In the Soviet Union, Stalin returned to the prewar repression of suspected opposition elements, sending millions to forced labor camps, including most of the returning Soviet prisoners of war and repatriated refugees. Artists, writers, even biologists had to toe the party line in their fields. The regime worked vigorously to repair the severe war damage to railways but the desperate need for housing received a lower priority. In 1950 the country exceeded the prewar level of industrial production and it continued its economic expansion guided by a series of Five-Year Plans.

Stalin's fear of opposition seemed to worsen as he aged and in the early 1950s hints that another huge purge was imminent, focusing perhaps on Jews, began to filter out of Moscow. At this juncture, however, Stalin suddenly died in March 1953. After a period of hidden struggles for power, Nikita Khrushchev emerged as the dominant figure in the post-Stalin regime by 1955. As one aspect of Khrushchev's leadership style, he denounced some features of Stalin's rule, especially the extremes to which the purges of the 1930s had led. The new Soviet leader also relaxed the regime's political and ideological conformity. As the Soviet Union began to move away from Stalin's rigid barracks-society in the late 1950s, consumers finally began to receive some of the benefits of industrialization: more housing, clothing, and food. Opposition to the system was still not tolerated but criticism of some of its operational details now became acceptable.

In the Eastern European countries lying between Russia and Germany, there appeared a left-wing reformist trend as the war ended, just as in the West. Coalition governments including Communists came to power, but unlike the Western pattern, the Communists in a few months or a few years took over. Such was the case in Poland, Rumania, Bulgaria, Hungary, and finally Czechoslovakia in 1948. Stalin's decision to encourage Communist regimes here but to hold back the Communist parties in Western Europe from attempts to seize power probably stemmed from two reasons: 1) a Communist attempt at takeover in Eastern Europe faced a small risk of failure as compared to the West; and 2) it would be easier for the Soviets to honor a commitment to defend the Eastern European Communist regimes than Communist governments in the West.

The Communist governments in Eastern Europe tried to carry out agricultural collectivization and rapid industrialization programs on the Soviet model. They succeeded in part but in comparison with countries lying just to the west of the iron curtain, West Germany and Austria, for example, their record was not a good advertisement for centrally managed economies. Yugoslavia became a special case in 1948 when its Communist leader Marshal Tito pulled it out of the Soviet orbit and thereafter followed neutralist policies in foreign affairs. The Yugoslavs tried to decentralize the planning and operation of their economy, using some capitalist-type incentives. The results have been impressive.

Social change in Europe since the Second World War has occurred at a rate faster than ever before. This rapid movement resulted in great part from the sustained economic expansion of the period, although in the Eastern European countries the political change brought by the Communists has had a large social impact. In both West Germany and France for example, industrial output was about 2.4 times larger in 1974 than in 1958. This growing output has led to major shifts in employment. Those engaged in the primary or extractive stage of economic activity—agriculture and mining—fell in numbers, the proportion of those in the secondary sector—manufacturing—rose somewhat, while the share of the people engaged in the tertiary sector—services—gradually climbed and before long will surpass those in manufacturing.

Table One: Percentage Distribution of the Labor Force			
	Primary	Secondary	Tertiary
France 1954	28.2	37.1	34.7
France 1973	12.2	39.3	48.5
W. Germany 1950	24.7	42.9	32.5
W. Germany 1973	7.5	49.5	43.0
Italy 1954	39.9	32.8	27.3
Italy 1973	17.4	44.0	38.6

Such changes in the nature of employment lay behind leading social trends such as the massive movement of European farm workers to the city, the increasing urbanization of the continent, and the tendency of manual workers to move into the property-owning middle class. The increasing wealth produced by the growing economies allowed rising standards of living for people engaged in all sectors. It allowed a mass consumption society to emerge in Western Europe and to appear on the horizon for Eastern Europe as well.

As farm workers left the countryside for urban jobs in manufacturing or the services, the least productive rural land went out of cultivation. The remaining farmers tended to increase the size of their holdings which made them more suitable for mechanization and more efficient use. The number of independent farms in Belgium, for example, has declined by 4 percent a year in recent times. In Poland, where strong peasant opposition reversed agricultural collectivization, and in other Eastern European countries the result was similar, with thousands of peasants finding city jobs. Agricultural output rose despite this shrinking labor force. Machines, fertilizers, improved seeds, and better livestock breeding raised output per man to keep pace. Such improved productivity has brought more income per farm family which helped pay for these improvements and also brought some of the amenities of twentieth century urban life to the farms—pure water, electrical appliances, and automobiles. The transition in agriculture to highly specialized and mechanized farming did not go smoothly. Governments in Western Europe often responded to rural complaints by providing cheap credit, price supports, protective tariffs, and other subsidies to agriculture to keep incomes high and steady.

Many of the new employees in manufacturing also came from immigrant labor, Caribbean blacks to Britain, North Africans and Spaniards to France, Turks and Yugoslavs to West Germany. Drawn by high wages to perform dirty or boring jobs relinquished by local people, these immigrants have remained proletarians but have little political influence because they rarely participate in the political system.

The era of mass consumption in which the bulk of people in a country find it possible to live in comfortable homes, eat as much as they like, and buy durable goods such as automobiles and electrical household appliances, began shortly before the First World War in the United States and appeared in Britain in the later 1930s. It hit Western Europe with full force in the 1950s and 1960s. The spread of TV sets and cars exemplifies this new society of consumers living well above the level of poverty or subsistence.

Table Two: Mass Consumption				
	TVs per 1,000 people		Autos per 1,000 people	
	1960	1973	1960	1973
Bulgaria	0.6	160	—	—
Czechoslovakia	58	234	30	97
France	41	237	110	265
West Germany	83	298	90	260
Spain	8	164	10	100
Britain	211	309	110	240
United States	310	523	340	475

Another aspect of mass consumption is the boom in tourism for all classes. With time available from shorter work weeks and especially the multiweek vacations, and with transportation by efficient railway service, by their own cars, or by cheap airline fares, all Europe sometimes seems to be on the move during the summer, going to Spanish or Bulgarian beaches, Swiss mountains, Greek islands, or British palaces. In the 1970s, they began coming to see American skyscrapers and the Grand Canyon. The growing wealth and leisure also made the fortune of spectator sports. The current boom in these activities began in a small way in the late nineteenth century but now attracts crowds larger than those in America in a number of sports, especially soccer.

The mass consumption society did not mean only fun and games, of course. It also provided the wealth to pay for a broad system of social welfare. Building on their own prewar arrangements and on the British example, all the European countries expanded their welfare systems, usually to encompass medical care, unemployment and old age insurance, and family allowances. The Soviet Union and some other Communist countries do not have unemployment programs and the USSR's family allowance system is one of the least generous.

Europe's growing wealth provided more opportunities for education. Illiteracy among the young has just about vanished, and much larger proportions of young people completed secondary schooling than in the 1930s. In the 1960s, students began pouring into the universities, seeing in them the route to high status occupations. The proportion of young people aged 20-24 enrolled in higher education in Western Europe rose from about 4 percent in 1950 to 11 percent by 1965. It appeared that Europe was moving away from elite university training to mass higher education. But the universities, encrusted with centuries of tradition, found themselves unready for this flood of new students. In the late 1960s these young people, craving excitement and looking for a cause, collided with the gray universities and their dry, highly specialized, and aloof professors. After a year or two of turmoil, the student movement collapsed and almost everyone went back to trying to adapt the students and the universities to each other.

Intellectual currents in Western Europe after the Second World War followed a cycle whose phases paralleled politics. In the late 1940s and the 1950s one observes a decline in ideological commitment and a withdrawal from politics. This trend then reversed in the 1960s with a new radicalism that peaked in the years 1967-70, but then declined in fervor.

When the war ended, fascism had no following in Europe. It had lost; its ideas had led to a very destructive war and genocide. The Communist ideology hung on somewhat longer in the West, partly because its exemplar, the Soviet Union, was a victorious power, and partly because some intellectuals continued to believe that at its core were positive goals, unlike the essential destructiveness of the Nazis. Revelations of Stalin's brutal purges and concentration camps added to critical discussions of Communist practice as found in such books as *Animal Farm* (1946) by George Orwell and *The God that Failed* (1949) by Richard Crossman and sharply weakened its appeal to intellectuals. To fill the gap left by what was called "the end of ideology," some intellectuals moved into the study of power—who has it, how to get it, and how to keep it. Others found a new intellectual fashion attractive: existentialism—a philosophical attitude that developed in Paris as the war ended. Generated out of obscure German philosophy and the experience of the war, existentialism as expounded by writers such as Jean P. Sartre and Albert Camus found the world to be absurd, without purpose. Man is free, condemned to be free, and must create his own values, must find himself in his own choices and actions. Sartre himself chose communism, believing its claims to redeem the wretched of the earth, while Camus, who wrote *The Plague* (1947) and *The Fall* (1946), chose individualist humanism, continuing to mistrust organized political movements. The vogue of existentialism faded in the 1950s as Europe settled down to enjoy the fruits of political stability and economic affluence. Life did not appear quite so absurd after all.

In the fine arts of literature, music, and painting, Western Europe continued the tendencies begun earlier in the century—especially a lust for new forms of expression. While perhaps gratifying to the artists themselves and a small circle of critics, these forms often made it harder for others to determine the artist's meaning and so repelled much of the educated public. Potential consumers of the fine arts retreated to television and as a result the gulf between the artists and the public continued to widen. Yet the Soviet writers Boris Pasternak, *Doctor Zhivago* (1958), and Alexander Solzhenitsyn, *Cancer Ward* (1966) and *The First Circle* (1968), found wide audiences with powerful although rather old-fashioned novels about important events. They showed that talented writers still could achieve literary and public success with the old forms. The films seemed to have a more powerful impact than most of the other arts, from the neo-realism of the Italian classics of the postwar years, i.e., *Shoeshine* and *Bicycle Thief*, to the philosophical and poetic studies of Ingmar Bergman, i.e., *The Seventh Seal* and *Wild Strawberries*. Italy and Sweden excelled in architecture, especially with the bold structures of Pier Luigi Nervi.

171

In the 1960s, European intellectuals began to come back to a more radical political stance. Perhaps this stemmed in part from a new generation, too young to have experienced the Depression and the Second World War and the disillusionment with politics that followed. Seeking excitement by challenging the existing order, the young intellectuals in Western Europe now found models not in Soviet communism, largely discredited by its brutality and its bureaucracy, but in Third World revolutionaries such as Fidel Castro and Mao Tse-tung, made glamorous by distance and a lack of direct knowledge. In the names of leaders such as these and with huge student crowds mobilized over poor study and social conditions in the overcrowded universities, radical intellectuals made a considerable stir. They came close to toppling President de Gaulle from power in France in 1968 when young blue and white collar workers mounted parallel movements to protest their lack of individual power and identity in large industrial and commercial establishments. Although failing to win major political triumphs, the radical movement did democratize universities slightly, in some countries liberalize divorce and abortion laws, and began to focus attention on environmental concerns. The movement emphasized imagination and spontaneity, but little of lasting importance has yet come of it in the arts; no major paintings, books, plays, or philosophical treatises to stir the souls of younger generations. Soured by failure, a few of the radical intellectuals turned to murderous terrorism in the 1970s, especially in West Germany and Italy.

Considering political developments in recent years, we can see how the social changes discussed earlier have had an influence on politics. The rising living standards enjoyed by most manual workers in Western Europe forced Socialist and Communist politicians to rethink their ideology and tactics. If workers began to live better in a capitalist system, if more and more of them acquired property, no longer considered themselves proletarians, and adopted middle class attitudes, would the old slogans of class struggle, proletarian revolution, and nationalization of industry still galvanize wide support? The West German Social Democrats thought not, for in 1959 they revised their party platform to abandon class struggle and revolution in order to uphold values rooted in "Christian ethics, humanism, and classic philosophy." This updating seemed effective, for in 1966 the Social Democrats won a share in power when they joined the Christian Democrats in a coalition government and then in 1969 their charismatic leader Willy Brandt became chancellor, replaced in 1974 by another Socialist, the brilliant economist Helmut Schmidt.

In Britain too, the Labour party came to power under the leadership of Harold Wilson (1964-70, 1974-76), followed by James Callaghan in 1976. As in West Germany, the British Labour party in fact accepted a capitalist economic system seasoned with a large dose of social welfare to answer the grievances of the less well-off. In France, the existence of a large and vigorous Communist party alongside the Socialists split the left-wing vote and enabled the right to retain power after de Gaulle's departure from office in 1969. The two left-wing parties tried to overcome this disadvantage by forging a common program and co-operating in elections. This tactic came very close to success in the presidential election of 1974 when the conservative Giscard d'Estaing won by only a razor-thin margin over the Communist-Socialist candidate. Enough suspicions remained of Communist intentions and of this party's close ties to Moscow to deny the left victory at this point, and in 1977 the coalition began to break down. In Italy, the Communists also followed a conciliatory policy in the 1960s and 1970s. Gaining political control of several regions and major cities through electoral victories over demoralized and corrupt non-Communist factions, they managed these local governments efficiently. In national politics, the Communists hewed to a line somewhat independent of the Soviet Union, claiming to be Euro-Communists rather than Moscow Communists. Their efforts to broaden their constituency by downplaying traditional Marxist slogans and by offering themselves as a nonrevolutionary party capable of operating the inept Italian bureaucracy with firmness and vigor brought them close to power by the late 1970s.

As the economic systems in Western Europe drowned "the Revolution" with a flood of consumer goods, the political left gradually accommodated itself to capitalism.

As Arthur Schlesinger, Jr. has observed, modernization seems to carry nations not toward Marx, but away from Marx. As this was occurring, one of the political left's bugbears, the Franco regime in Spain, reappeared on the scene and effected a reconciliation with Europe. After his victory in the Civil War in 1939, Franco had isolated his country, first to avoid entanglement in the Second World War, and then to limit potential foreign support to the left opposition. Franco never allowed the Falange (Fascist) movement in Spain to dominate his regime and after the war it lost more and more influence. In the 1950s and 1960s, the United States extended military and economic aid to Spain in return for military bases. In similar fashion, West European countries gradually restored normal relations with Spain, especially after 1959 when the Franco government sharply reduced its controls on the economy and began to encourage foreign trade. Soon the Spanish discovered the domestic gold mine of tourism which provided crucial foreign exchange for the rapidly expanding economy. Franco had declared Spain a monarchy again and upon his death in 1975 the grandson of the last pre-Republic king, Juan Carlos, ascended the throne. In a surprisingly peaceful transition, the new constitutional monarchy speeded political liberalization despite sporadic terrorism. The Spanish have demonstrated more political maturity since the demise of the old dictator than most observers ever expected.

In Eastern Europe, and especially the Soviet Union in the 1960s and 1970s, the Communist parties became bastions of conservatism at home, fighting determinedly to prevent political or intellectual liberalization. A desperate fear of change lay behind the Soviet ousting of the mercurial Khrushchev from power in 1964 and the deportation of Solzhenitsyn in 1974. Leonid Brezhnev and Aleksei Kosygin, gray and unimaginative bureaucrats, replaced Khrushchev. The Soviets also refused to let the Communist parties in Eastern European countries move very far from the orthodox line, invading Hungary in 1956 and Czechoslovakia in 1968 when they believed that liberalization had allowed an authentic opposition to surface. The stubborn efforts in these countries to gain some freedom from the Soviet embrace illustrated how liberalism and nationalism continued to attract Europeans. The Catholic church was a leader in keeping these sentiments alive in Eastern Europe, a point recognized once again when the College of Cardinals elected the Polish Cardinal Karol Wojtyla as Pope in 1978.

Despite the Europeans' infatuation with their new affluence, the old ideas of liberalism and nationalism still seem to hold the basic loyalties in Europe. Whether nationalism will be so strong as to prevent the Europeans from uniting to protect their liberalism remains an open question.

Suggested Readings

Works that treat several countries of Europe in the post-Second World War period include Stanley Rothman, *European Society and Politics* (1970), Andrew Shonfield, *Modern Capitalism: The Changing Balance of Public and Private Power* (1969), and M. M. Postan, *An Economic History of Western Europe, 1945-1964* (1967). Michel Crozier, *The Bureaucratic Phenomenon* (1964) is a brilliant study of this issue, with emphasis on the French case. Two outstanding political leaders can be approached in Richard Hiscocks, *The Adenauer Era* (1966), and Brian Crozier, *De Gaulle* (1973). Political matters in these countries are examined in A. Heidenheimer and D. P. Kommers, *The Governments of Germany* (4th ed., 1975), and Philip Williams, *Crisis and Compromise: Politics in the Fourth Republic* (1964). John Ardagh, *The New French Revolution* (1969), presents fascinating accounts of French social change, while Samuel Beer, *British Politics in the Collectivist Age* (1965), and Anthony Sampson, *The New Anatomy of Britain* (1973), describe British politics and society. For Italy, consult Norman Kogan, *A Political History of Postwar Italy* (1966), and for Spain, Stanley Payne, *Franco's Spain* (1967), a concise account. Eastern Europe is treated in Zbigniew Brzezinski, *The Soviet Bloc, Unity and Conflict* (revised, 1967); Adam Ulam, *Stalin: The Man and His Era* (1973); Hedrick Smith, *The Russians* (1976), a fascinating account by a first-rate journalist; and H. Gordon Skilling, *Czechoslovakia's Interrupted Revolution* (1976).

Bomb damage in Hiroshima, Japan. October 14, 1945. *(Courtesy of the National Archives)*

CHAPTER 9

European Search for Security in the Nuclear Age

M. B. Lucas

European supremacy, which had characterized the history of Western civilization since the Middle Ages, finally disappeared in 1945. This supremacy was greatly shaken by World War I, but European power sustained itself due to a number of complex factors. The most important of these were the political situation in Europe, especially in Eastern Europe, the reluctance of the United States to assume leadership in the Western world, and the fact that the colonial empires continued to provide the necessary cheap raw materials for European economic survival. This last factor was especially important. Europe's dependence on non-European sources for food and raw materials which developed during the nineteenth century grew even greater in the twentieth century. When the colonial empires began to disappear after 1945 and European influence began to wane, these economic links were either disrupted or severed. The result was a need to cooperate within the sphere of Europe that overshadowed traditional great power rivalries. Like it or not, for survival in the modern industrial world, Europe had to put aside economic nationalism in order to provide the basics of life.

The Western European nations also found it necessary to reevaluate their military positions within a new world power structure after 1945. No longer did England, France, and Germany control the balance of power. The once mighty British navy was struggling to remain a second-rate naval power, the French army had not recovered from the carnage of World War I, much less the debacle of 1940, and the mighty German military machine had been destroyed by the Allies. As the bipolar structure of world power became increasingly apparent to everyone, it also became obvious to the European nations, both East and West, that without the help and protection of their principals (the Soviet Union or the United States), they could not survive militarily. In the developing cold war, Europe was in the middle.

As the European nations sought to regain a sense of normalcy after the war, it became a necessity for governments to change their political orientation. In Eastern Europe, the client states of the Soviet Union naturally became Communist and began to provide increased social services for their peoples. At the same time, the Western European states, "remaining free," followed the lead of the Scandinavian countries and moved in a similar direction toward a welfare system.

Along with these significant changes, however, the European nations both East and West felt a sense of loss and insecurity with the passage of their leadership role in the Western world. Much of the history and culture of the post-1945 period in Europe has reflected this sense of *malaise* or vague feelings of dissatisfaction, disappointment, and disillusionment. This is reflected in the individual European states' quest for domestic stability and "social" security which characterizes much of the political history of the postwar period.

Nothing has affected the European community as much as the development of the bipolar structure of world power and the resultant cold war which dominated international relations during the 1950s and early 1960s. Forced by the realities of the emergence of the atomic bomb, Western Europe became dependent on the United States and the North Atlantic Treaty Organization (NATO) for protection, while the Eastern European countries have become the satellites of the Soviet Union. Each confrontation in the cold war made the Europeans realize anew their impotence. They had become the pawns in the battle for world domination, or at least it seemed that way to them!

As a result of World War II, military power from the Atlantic to the Soviet border was either destroyed as in the case of Germany, Austria, Italy, and Poland, or severely diminished as in the case of France and England. It was obvious to even the casual observer that without United States aid, Western Europe would not be able to withstand a determined Soviet expansionist policy. Soviet plans for domination of Eastern Europe were already being realized before the end of World War II. Poland, Bulgaria, Albania, Rumania, and Hungary to a certain extent fell under Russian domination as the Red Army moved eastward against the Nazis. The confrontation between the United States and Russia which commenced at the Yalta Conference continued at the Potsdam Conference. By 1948, after the Communist coup d'état in Czechoslovakia and the confrontation of East and West in Greece, United States resistance to Russian assertiveness began to harden. Each action taken by one side caused a similar escalation by the other, and Europe seemed to be left out of the decision-making process. Winston Churchill described the bipolar world that was emerging, divided by an "iron curtain," in a famous speech at Fulton, Missouri, in 1946:

> A shadow has fallen upon the scenes so lately lighted by the Allied victory. Nobody knows what Soviet Russia and its Communist international organization intends to do in the immediate future, or what are the limits, if any, to their expansive and proselytizing tendencies.
> ... From Stettin in the Baltic to Trieste in the Adriatic, an iron curtain has descended across the continent.

With the proclamation of the Truman Doctrine and the announcement of the Marshall Plan in 1947, the United States established the basis for the military unity and economic protection of Western Europe. The first test of the American commitment to Europe came with the Berlin blockade. The success of the United States and the Western European Allies in stopping the Communists in Berlin was followed by the signing of the Brussels Pact which established the North Atlantic Treaty Organization in

179

April 1949. Russia countered by intensifying its control over the Balkans and eventually organizing the Warsaw Pact in May 1955, as a reaction to West German entrance into NATO. By 1949, the situation had stabilized in Europe.

The question has recently been raised as to whether the Soviets really desired to extend their control into Western Europe. Some revisionist historians like Gabriel Kolko and William A. Williams believe that the Soviet actions were a response to a United States attempt to use its economic and military power as a means to achieve global supremacy. Their contention that the Soviets only wanted to secure bases in Eastern Europe, however, appears weakened in view of the Russian actions in Turkey and Iran as well as in Berlin. Whatever the real motives of the Soviets, the Western leaders perceived them as expansionists and countered accordingly.

Once the bipolar world developed, Western European security fell under the nuclear umbrella of the United States. To demonstrate the United States commitment to Western Europe, thousands of American troops were stationed there. In many ways, one could say that the American presence in Europe was and remains more or less that of a hostage which guarantees that in case of war the United States nuclear force will be used. That is certainly not as reassuring to the average European as some Americans seem to think, especially after the focus of the cold war moved from Europe to the Far East. To be sacrificed to the American commitment on the other side of the world bothered European leadership. General Charles de Gaulle first indicated this when in 1960 he withdrew France from NATO and established his *Force de Frappe,* a nuclear capability and delivery system. De Gaulle was not sure that the United States would risk New York City, Chicago, and Los Angeles to save Paris. With its own force, France would have a greater say in the determination of her own future. Although West Germany, Britain, and the smaller countries in NATO remained steadfast allies, evidence exists that their confidence in the United States' judgment and strength has been somewhat shaken by Vietnam and the internal problems that the United States has experienced in the 1960s and 1970s.

Despite these misgivings, the Western European states have been forced to accept the present status even though it is clear that the strength of NATO cannot match that of the Soviets and their allies. In fact, some observers believe that without nuclear war, NATO forces could only hold out from two to four weeks. The latest comparison of NATO and Warsaw Pact strength made by the International Institute for Strategic Studies in London places the Warsaw Pact ahead in all categories except nuclear weapons—945,000 to 630,000 combat troops; 20,500 to 7,000 tanks; 4,025 to 2,350 aircraft; and over 10,000 pieces of artillery to 2,700. Since 1973 there has been a buildup in Soviet strength which has not been matched by NATO. At the same time, the Western Europeans have been unwilling to make up for the withdrawal of some of the American troops and thus must rely even more heavily on the American nuclear umbrella. The Russians seem to have accepted the risk of Western European nuclear defense policy since their latest tanks and armored personnel carriers provide for protection against radioactive fallout, thus enabling them to pass through areas devastated by atomic weapons. These developments may or may not be negated by the building and eventual deployment of neutron weapons.

Strategically, Western Europe still remains one of the most important areas in the world. It is an area as vital to the security of the United States as Eastern Europe is to the security of the Soviet Union. It is an area that will bear the full brunt of any confrontation between the United States and the USSR.

The Europeans are well aware of this. They know that their survival could be decided by the two major powers without any consultation with them, and that they could be destroyed over issues that have nothing to do with them. Because of this, there has been an intense European interest in the relationships between the United States and Russia as well as the United States commitments to other powers. Every nuance in United States-USSR relations is carefully assessed and evaluated with regard to European survival. Since 1970 there has been a tendency to downplay the cold war in Europe despite events like the building of the Berlin Wall and the invasion of Czechoslovakia.

At the same time the American or Russian influence over their respective allies seems to have declined somewhat. Yet the reality of the balance of terror is still with every European.

A major contributing factor toward the European search for security was its loss in control of the economic destiny of the Western world. World War I dealt a blow to the European economic establishment from which it never recovered. As early as 1920, the United States began to outproduce Europe, and by 1955 produced about twice as much as the European nations.

The devastation of World War II left the Western European economy in ruins. Europe proved unable to provide even the necessities of life for its people. In response to the economic and political problems created by this devastation, the United States began the Marshall Plan in July 1947. The only Eastern European nation to show an interest in the Marshall Plan was Czechoslovakia, but under pressure from the Soviet Union its leaders eventually rejected participation. During the period of the Marshall Plan, Great Britain received $3.176 billion in aid while France got $2.306 billion, Italy $1.474 billion, West Germany (not originally included) $1.385 billion, the Netherlands $1.079 billion, and Greece and Austria over $500 million each. This enormous investment enabled the Western European nations to begin the process of economic recovery. Although few economists expected the rapid economic growth begun under the Marshall Plan to continue beyond a short period of direct aid, Western European recovery continued well into the 1960s. There were none of the cyclical fluctuations that were typical of the interwar years. For example, West Germany experienced an annual growth in its Gross National Product (GNP) of 8.4% between 1949 and 1954, 6.6% between 1954 and 1959, and 7.6% between 1960 and 1963. Although not as spectacular as Germany, France also made significant progress with a 4.8% increase in its GNP between 1949 and 1954, a 4.1% increase between 1954 and 1959, and a 4.7% increase between 1960 and 1963. Because of certain internal problems, Great Britain's GNP increase was more modest, but steady—2.7% from 1949 to 1954, 2.3% from 1954 to 1959, and 2.5% from 1959 to 1963.

The Marshall Plan alone could not have brought about the recovery of Western Europe. A multitude of other factors were involved, not the least of which was the establishment of the Common Market. Because of nationalism and traditional trade rivalries, the creation of an extranational body to promote European economic development was very difficult. The first step was the establishment in 1948 of the Organization for European Economic Cooperation (OEEC); the United States had asked for an European organization to take charge of allocating the funds of the Marshall Plan. But then the major powers involved dragged their feet until June 1948, when the United States representative, Averell Harriman, announced to the OEEC Council that it must henceforth take charge of the allocation of Marshall Plan aid.

The reluctance on the part of the Western European nations to band together earlier was partially due to their pessimistic expectations concerning the program, their lack of experience in handling economic problems in a unified manner, and the hope on the part of some, especially the British, that they would be able to get more by dealing directly with the United States. However, the success of the OEEC in distributing funds and promoting trade among its members (trade across members' borders doubled between 1948 and 1955) convinced most of the European leaders of the value of economic cooperation. It should be noted that the OEEC was an international rather than a supranational organization; none of the participants sacrificed national sovereignty.

The next development toward European economic cooperation came in a May 1948, Congress of Europe attended by 750 delegates, among whom were some of Europe's leading statesmen—Churchill, Robert Schuman, Léon Blum, and Paul-Henri Spaak. Although a proposal for the political and economic unification of Europe failed, the Council of Europe, a permanent European assembly designed to encourage cooperation, was established.

Great Britain led the resistance against European integration because of a feeling that she was not really part of Europe and that her interests would be better served by acting as a middleman between Europe and the United

States. Also, Britain feared that her position in the British Commonwealth would be endangered in such an arrangement. This problem remained one of the major stumbling blocks for Britain in considering the Common Market later. As a result of this opposition, the Council of Europe served in an advisory capacity only. The first president of the Council, Paul-Henri Spaak, resigned his office in 1951, attacking those who thwarted the establishment of a United Europe with these words: "If a quarter of the energy spent here in saying no, were used to say yes to something positive, we should not be in the state we are in today."

There were factors at work, however, that continued to favor some kind of supranational cooperation in Europe. The 1948 Communist coup in Czechoslovakia, the Berlin blockade, the explosion of the Soviet Union's first atomic bomb in 1949, and the outbreak of the Korean War in 1950 which began a twenty-year United States preoccupation with Asia led many of the European leaders to see that a larger European community was a necessity. The United States encouraged this view, believing that it would make Western Europe a stronger partner in the cold war.

Surprisingly, France took the initiative and under the leadership of Jean Monnet and Robert Schuman produced a workable plan for European economic integration that proposed the combining of the coal and steel resources of Europe. After almost two years of negotiations, France, Germany, Italy, and the Benelux countries (Belgium, Holland, and Luxembourg) signed the agreement establishing the European Coal and Steel Community (ECSC). Great Britain refused to join. In addition to the reasons discussed above, many of the British Labour party leaders saw the ECSC and other such organizations as conspiracies on the part of big business to destroy the national labor movements. The ECSC, however, quickly revealed the advantage of unity. ECSC production increased twice as fast between 1950 and 1955 as production in Great Britain. Although the ECSC encouraged the overproduction of steel, losing some support from the industrialists, its overall success caused many former opponents to become supporters of further European unification.

Political and diplomatic events also contributed to a

growing realization that Europe must seek further economic integration. Nasser's nationalization of the Suez Canal, the failure of British and French attempts to force the return of the canal to its shareholders, the cutting off of oil imports to France in the winter of 1956-57, and the refusal of the United States to help Britain stabilize the pound sterling all showed Europe's relative weaknesses.

Thus, when the Benelux countries began negotiations for the further integration of Europe's economy, France gave its support. Proposals for a common tariff among ECSC members, originally suggested in 1955, were finally realized in the 1957 Rome Treaty with the creation of the European Economic Community (EEC) or Common Market. The member nations—France, West Germany, Italy, and the Benelux countries—established a goal of eliminating customs barriers within ten years, thus creating an economic unit that could compete with the United States.

The Common Market attempted to balance traditional national economic interests and international economic integration by creating an elaborate organization. Authority was distributed among four bodies: the Council of Ministers, an elected Commission, a Court of Justice which would settle disputes among members, and an European Parliament. De Gaulle's restrictions on the power of the Common Market and the emergence of unforeseen difficulties in the 1960s and early 1970s, however, severely curtailed the powers of the Common Market and the hopes of an integrated European economy.

Britain did not join the Common Market, forming instead the European Free Trade Association (EFTA) in 1960, a much looser organization consisting of Great Britain, Austria, Denmark, Norway, Portugal, Sweden, and Switzerland. The success of the Common Market, Britain's chronic economic problems, and the attempts of President John F. Kennedy to bring Europe and the United States closer together in order to avoid a tariff war between America and the Common Market forced Britain to reconsider joining. Between 1963 and 1972, attempts on the part of Britain to join the Common Market were frustrated by British demands and de Gaulle's intransigence. Finally, the obstacles were cleared and Britain, along with Ireland and Denmark became members in 1972. British integration into the Common Market was slow, however, because of the failure of their government to cooperate completely. For example, Britain continued to demand that some Commonwealth products receive preferential treatment, that the British contributions to the Common Market budget be reduced, and that several other rules and regulations be changed. British imposition of import controls over some goods from Common Market countries in 1974 and her reluctance to share North Sea oil have continued to add to dissatisfaction.

In fact, although the overall production of the Common Market remains impressive, economic integration among its members remains a problem. During the 1973 oil embargo each country went its own way, and since 1975 financial problems have caused Italy, Britain, and France especially, to act independently in many trade situations. At the same time, the mutual reliance among members (61 percent of their manufactured goods were sold within the community in 1968) convinced many of the advantages of continuing the system. Even the British public seems to have decided that continued participation is a good idea. In a national referendum in 1975, the British voters approved membership in the Common Market by a two to one margin. The future of the Common Market appears to depend on the ability of its leadership, the continued growth of interdependence as each member specializes in certain areas (like Italy with its refrigerators and wine), and the need to provide a common solution to the economic and financial problems facing the Western world today.

With the memories of the interwar years and World War II imprinted on their minds, most Europeans continue to have paramount concern about political stability. Out of the multiplicity of issues facing each national government, certain common problems can be isolated: the growth of social welfare programs, the primacy of economic issues, and the desire to maintain stability. The European nations have dealt with these issues in a variety of ways since 1945, though some similarities can be seen in both methods of attacking the problems and degrees of success.

Germany suffered more from the effect of World War II

than any of the other major countries. Divided into zones of occupation by the Allies, her former leaders being tried at Nuremberg for war crimes, her economy crippled, and most of her cities in ruin, it was obvious that her reconstruction process would require greater efforts than that necessitated by her defeat in World War I. As the cold war developed, Allied cooperation broke down and Germany was realistically divided into two segments—West Germany controlled by the Allies, and East Germany, a satellite of the Soviet Union. This became a political fact when the German Federal Republic (West Germany) was formed in May 1949, with Bonn as its capital. Berlin, the former capital, remained a divided city within the Russian sphere of influence with only a single road linking it to the West. West Berlin's vulnerability was graphically demonstrated by the Russian blockade which lasted from July 24, 1948, to September 30, 1949, during which the Western Allies were forced to supply the city from the air with 277,264 flights.

On September 15, 1949, Konrad Adenauer, a Christian Democrat, was elected chancellor of West Germany. Concentrating on two major policies, economic recovery and the political acceptance of West Germany into the Allied camp, Adenauer turned West Germany from an occupied country into a valued ally. Following a policy similar to that of Gustav Stresemann after World War I, Adenauer sought help and concessions from the West in return for German fulfillment of commitments to the Allies. He eventually placed West Germany completely on the side of the Allies, even to the point of rejecting a 1954 Soviet offer to reunify Germany in return for neutrality. The admission of West Germany into the Common Market and NATO, and her inclusion in the Marshall Plan testify to the success of Adenauer's policies.

Since the end of the Adenauer era in the early 1960s, political and economic developments have been generally decided on the foundations laid down by Adenauer. Although Germany has experienced some terrorist activity from the Left—notably the Baader-Meinhof gang—and though a small right-wing movement gnaws at the German conscience, political and economic stability have continued. By the 1970s, Germany was once again the strongest nation in Western Europe and the most important member of NATO.

More than any of the other European nations, West Germany reflects the effect of economics on politics. What is generally called the German "economic miracle" was essential to West German political stability. Since the early 1950s, the West German economy has grown rapidly and Germans consider it the most vital issue today. Production continues unabated as a new model Volkswagen has proved to be as popular as the older "beetle." And even the energy crisis has not shaken the value of the new German mark. Of all the major Western countries, West Germany seems to have coped more successfully with the economic problems of the late 1960s and 1970s. West Germany's future is promising.

France, on the other hand, has suffered from both political and financial instability in the postwar period. General Charles de Gaulle, leader of the Free French during the war, foresaw and attempted to correct these problems, as well as many others that stemmed from the old Third French Republic, by urging the French people to adopt a constitution that provided for a stronger executive. The Constitutional Assembly, however, dominated by parties of the Left, continued one of the weaknesses of the Third Republic by placing most authority in the legislature. Convinced that such a government would foster instability, de Gaulle opposed the constitution. When a second constitution contained some of the same flaws, de Gaulle, convinced that France would one day recall him to power, resigned in disgust. Thus, the Fourth French Republic began its very short and unsuccessful existence.

As financial and colonial problems intensified, French governments fell with regularity and rapidity. Even successes in colonial policy were not enough to guarantee political stability. For example, Premier Pierre Mendès-France ended French involvement in Indochina and granted autonomy to Tunisia in 1954, but fell from office when he failed to change his Radical party's economic policies. Nor was the economic recovery of France enough to ensure longevity in leadership. Part of the problem was France's loss of power and prestige and the inability of most Frenchmen to come to terms with their nation's diminished role in world affairs. The failures in World War II, the large-scale collaboration with the Nazis, the loss of Indochina in 1954, the failure of the Anglo-French intervention in Egypt in 1956, the independence of Tunisia and Morocco in 1956, and the overshadowing power of the United States in European affairs all contributed to this feeling. Many Frenchmen decided that France needed a "Man on Horseback" to lead her to greatness again.

The split over Algeria in 1956 gave de Gaulle his chance to return to power. Against Algerian independence, he seemed to provide at least a vestige of the old French *gloire* while the Fourth French Republic was unable to even provide coherent policy. With the help of the army, he took over France in 1958 and created the Fifth French Republic, which provided for a more stable system of government through a stronger president. Much to the dismay of his supporters, he granted Algeria independence two years later, and then defeated a Secret Army Organization (OAS) attempt to overthrow him, despite its widespread terrorist activities.

Even before the resolution of the Algerian situation, de Gaulle began an attempt to weaken the influence of the United States in Europe. His program was to take French forces out of NATO and to develop his own defense capability. That policy, combined with the success of the Common Market, an upsurge in the French economy, and de Gaulle's own personal charisma, greatly increased French influence in Europe and the world generally.

However, several deep-seated political and economic problems remained unsolved, and in May 1968, a general strike swept through France, causing some alarm regarding the durability of de Gaulle's regime. Although the fall elections gave him an even larger majority, de Gaulle resigned in 1969 when the French electorate failed to approve a constitutional change he advocated.

Since the departure of de Gaulle, much of France's influence in international affairs has declined. In recent years, greater efforts to solve some of the outstanding social problems have been made, but with the French economy lagging further behind that of West Germany's, the Gaullist legacy seems to be fading. Although the elections of 1978 did not give the Left a majority, its strength indicates the government's need to confront and solve nagging economic and social problems.

Great Britain also found her position of power and greatness slipping. In 1945, the British people stunned the world by electing a Labour government and forcing their great wartime leader, Winston Churchill, out of office. Between 1945 and 1951 the Labour-controlled Parliament created a welfare state and began dismantling the British empire. The government became responsible for not only the political, but also the economic security of its citizens. Most of the economy became either government owned or controlled. As a result, every Englishman is taken care of by the government from the "womb to the tomb."

Churchill, returning to power in 1951, made only minor adjustments in the new system such as the reduction of income taxes and the return of some industries to private ownership in order to stimulate the economy. Economic and financial problems, however, continued to plague the Conservatives, even after the retirement of Churchill in 1955. The rejection of long-term planning, wildcat strikes, the reduction of capital investment, and poor industrial management reduced the efficiency and productivity of British industry, causing instability of the pound sterling and increased competition from abroad. The British share of world trade declined from 21.3 percent in 1951 to 19 percent in 1956 and dropped even lower in the 1960s.

Although the welfare state has provided security for the average Englishman, it has not created the utopia that its advocates had promised. The loss of British power and prestige, the end of the British Empire, the desperate economic problems caused by foreign competition in traditional British markets, the high price of oil, the antiquated British industrial system, and the lack of discipline in the labor force have taken their toll. Many have put their hopes on the North Sea oil fields which will be in full production by the mid-1980s, and the British entrance into the Common Market. So far, however, indications are that neither of these will provide permanent solutions.

Italy was a defeated nation after World War II, but, although the scene of severe fighting, did not suffer as much physical destruction as Germany. The two most important developments in postwar Italy have been the impact of the cold war and economic improvement. Due to the growing tension of the cold war, the United States pressured the Italians to drive the Communist party out of the government in 1947. That action, along with increased economic development, helped provide Italy with one of its most politically stable periods.

However, starting in 1953 and continuing through 1978, there has been a leftward trend in Italian politics. This was the result of decreasing cold war tensions, rapid economic growth, the moderating position taken by the Italian Communist party leadership, and papal acceptance of the welfare state. Italian efforts to provide more welfare measures, coupled with a booming economy in the 1950s and 1960s, provided Italians with a semblance of political and economic security. Overpopulation and unemployment problems were eased by the large-scale use of Italian workers in West Germany, an arrangement which also provided Italy with much needed foreign exchange. As a result of minimum unemployment, labor union membership in Italy for the first time since before World War II has been electing moderate leaders, a definite indicator of a better standard of living.

However, the high inflation of the late 1960s, the increase in the price of oil, and competition from the Japanese and others have caused the Italians to look for more reforms or at least some answers to problems that the government seems unable to solve. Strikes, industrial kidnappings, widespread political terrorism such as the kidnapping and execution of Aldo Moro, and governmental paralysis seem to have caused the workers once again to look to the Left for solutions to their problems. For Italy, the future remains uncertain.

The Scandinavian states, on the other hand, are very stable and should remain that way in the foreseeable future. The Norwegian Labor party, the Swedish Social Democrats, and the Danish Social Democrats have been in power since the interwar years. A political split in the Labor party in Norway in 1965 resulted in a center coalition cabinet. An economic slowdown in Denmark in the mid-1960s, together with an increase in taxes, caused the Social Democrats to give way to a center coalition. In Sweden, the voters elected a non-Socialist government in 1976 for the first time since World War I. None of these political changes, however, seriously affected the welfare states that had been established before World War II. Denmark, Norway, and Sweden are more involved in social welfare programs than any other European countries. The success of their programs depends on continued economic growth, which has slowed some since 1965, and on public popularity, which continues to run high. Since the war, indices of quality of life which include such things as literacy, life expectancy, and the standard of living have placed these countries at or near the top in the world. Most Scandinavians seem to feel that their social welfare programs are the basis of their superior quality of life. These programs serve as models for many other European countries.

In Spain and Portugal, clerical-Fascist governments have ruled during most of the postwar period. Under these systems, the political power is allied with the Catholic church, each supporting the other. In effect, the church becomes a means of social and political control. General Francisco Franco, who had ruled in Spain since 1939 after a bloody civil war, was able to consolidate his regime to the extent of naming his successor, King Don Juan Carlos, who came to power in 1975. Antonio de Oliveira Salazar, the dictator of Portugal, was not quite as successful, and Portugal has been unstable since his death. The possibility of democratic governments on the Iberian peninsula, however, appears greater than at any time since World War II.

The Benelux countries—Belgium, Holland, and Luxembourg—have followed policies similar to those of the Scandinavian countries, but with less success. Internal divisions over language, exacerbated by slow economic growth in Belgium, have caused some seemingly insoluble problems for that government, while rapid economic development in the Netherlands has successfully kept the multiplicity of political parties there at a manageable level.

The study of European security in the postwar period reveals three basic trends. First, from 1945 to the mid-1950s the cold war dominated the scene. Secondly, from the mid to the late 1960s, economic cooperation along with the concerted efforts of most Western European nations predominated to provide more social services for their citizens. If the powers could no longer determine world policy or control vast colonial empires, which only France attempted, they could at least provide a better life for their citizens. Following the lead of the Scandinavian countries, social welfare programs became an ever-increasing portion of their budgets while they depended on the United States for military protection. Finally, since the late 1960s, economic problems and the resultant political instability have caused many governments either to curtail social programs or increase political controls. With the current problems of increased inflation, the high cost of energy, and the apparent buildup of Soviet strength in Eastern Europe, some of the emphasis on social programs will probably decrease.

Already, social programs are being slowed down or even cut back. In Sweden, the electorate demanded maintaining the status quo on social welfare programs in recent elections, while Britain and Italy suffer chronic fiscal problems due to the fact that their economies cannot keep pace with the increasing costs of government. Rising expectations have caused workers in the lesser-developed European countries like Spain and Italy to seek jobs in other countries, mainly West Germany; while many in the domestic work force refuse to take lower paying, low prestige, service jobs. For example, England, with a very low unemployment rate, has had to import Indians, West Indians, and Pakistanis to run the subways, sweep the streets, and do other menial tasks. There is now a permanent force of migrant workers in Europe.

The failure of these welfare programs in some states like Italy along with domestic political problems in others like Belgium and West Germany have resulted in increased terrorism which in turn has caused a tightening of domestic security, the centralization of state power, and the loss of some liberties. Good examples are the French struggle with the OAS, the British fight with the Irish Republican Army (IRA), and the attempts of Italy and Spain to cope with urban terrorists. Where this might lead and what political developments will follow is difficult to forecast.

193

However, if current trends continue, increased state police control will probably result.

There has also been a great deal of speculation about the development of Eurocommunism. Since the decline in economic growth in the late 1960s, the power of the Communists in Italy, France, and Portugal has grown as have left-wing parties in other states. This is probably another example of traditional European reactions to economic problems more than a genuine desire to embrace Communist ideology. The enormous strength of the Communists in Italy, combined with the recent governmental failures, could cause grave concerns for future United States policy in Europe since Italy provides the main base for the United States Sixth Fleet.

Although Europe has declined in power and influence in world affairs since 1945, the average citizen is better off than ever before. Europe is once again a powerful economic and cultural influence in the world, but at the same time the growth of terrorism, the expansion of centralizing trends in government, and the present energy crisis are challenges that the European nations will have to face in the future. Their success or failure will have a great impact on the United States and the world.

Suggested Readings

Two of the best general surveys of Europe since World War II are Carl G. Gustavson, *Europe in the World Community Since 1939* (1971) and Richard Mayne, *The Recovery of Europe, 1945-1973* (1973). C. E. Black and E. C. Helmreich, *Twentieth Century Europe: A History* (1972) presents a complete picture of European affairs since 1945. Helpful for an understanding of the European economic recovery are David Landes, *The Unbound Prometheus* (1970), A. Maddison, *Economic Growth in the West* (1964) and U. W. Kitzinger, *The Politics and Economics of European Integration* (1963). Two of the best studies of the Common Market are Stephen Holt, *The Common Market: The Conflict of Theory and Practice* (1967), and Louis Lister, *Europe's Coal and Steel Community: An Experiment in Economic Union* (1960). Ronald N. Strumberg, *After Everything: Western Intellectual*

History Since 1945 (1975) is an excellent survey of the main themes of Western thought since World War II.

Postwar British history is covered in Francis Boyd, *British Politics in Transition, 1945-1963* (1964) and Alfred F. Havighurst, *Twentieth Century Britain* (2nd ed., 1966), while Maurice Bruce, *The Coming of the Welfare State* (1961) provides a solid survey of the growth of the social services programs. Philip Williams, *Crisis and Compromise: Politics in the Fourth Republic* (1964) is an excellent survey of the problems of postwar France, and Dorothy Pickles, *The Fifth French Republic: Institutions and Politics* (3rd ed., 1966) provides an excellent introduction to the de Gaulle government. David Childs, *From Schumacher to Brandt: The Story of German Socialism, 1945-1965* (1966) and Richard Hiscocks, *The Adenauer Era* (1966) are indispensible for an understanding of postwar Germany.

Norman Kogan, *A Political History of Postwar Italy* (1966) is a valuable introduction. Although an older work, Frederic Fleisher, *Sweden: The Welfare State* (1956) still provides one of the best studies of the Swedish welfare state. Stanley G. Payne, *Franco's Spain* (1967), Hugh Key, *Salazar and Modern Portugal* (1970), and Arend Lijphart, *The Politics of Accommodation: Pluralism and Democracy in the Netherlands* (1968) are useful introductions to some of the smaller countries in Western Europe.

President Achmed Sukarno of Indonesia welcomes four hundred delegates from twenty-nine "Third World" nations at the Bandung Conference, held April 1955. *(Wide World Photos)*

CHAPTER 10

The Collapse of the European Empires

William J. Miller

The fall of the European empires after World War II derived from many remote antecedents. Among these were the American Revolution, the Latin American wars of independence, the Sepoy Mutiny in India, and the Chinese Revolution of 1911-12. This collapse or "decolonization" stemmed more immediately from colonial nationalism, Western liberal ideals, the influx of Marxism, the two world wars, and the anticolonialism of the United States and Soviet Russia. Each power confronted separation in its own peculiar way. Undoubtedly, the British adapted best to colonial liberation by their grant of self-rule and eventual dominion status to several colonies in the late nineteenth and early twentieth centuries. These actions culminated in the establishment of the British Commonwealth of Nations in 1931 and in the creation of the "multiracial Commonwealth" after India's independence in 1947. France adjusted much less successfully, however, because she failed to "assimilate" her overseas possessions completely into the administration of the mother country herself, a tactic followed generally by the Portuguese as well. Italy surrendered her "beggar's empire" as a defeated nation after World War II, while the

Dutch and Belgians lost their holdings rather abruptly, to a considerable extent by reason of anachronistic administrations. The First World War began colonial separation, the Second accelerated it, while the post-1945 years witnessed actual imperial demise.

This essay poses the following questions: What elements in the colonial process itself prepared the way for decolonization? What role did Soviet and American anticolonialism in World War II play in decolonization? Why was India central to post-1945 separation? Was it the force of nationalism from the subject peoples themselves, or more a weakening of the Western will that liquidated the European empires? Lastly, what significant mistakes were made with decolonization?

The "Age of Imperialism" (1870-1914) is often associated with economic exploitation, testifying to the durability of the views of John A. Hobson, the British liberal economist, and V. I. Lenin, the Soviet leader, who closely identified capitalism and imperialism. Most scholars agree today, however, that ideology (especially the competitive drive of Social Darwinism), national power, and the actions of those on the spot (in the "peripheral" or colonial area themselves) have more or less equal weight with the economic factor. British professors John A. Gallagher and Ronald Robinson term this period the "formal empire," in which Britain sought political domination of colonial areas to create a sizable free trade area, secure from the protectionist powers. Actually, the erection of the empire was a confession of British vulnerability in face of competition with Germany and the United States who directly challenged her economic domination and world position. In contrast, the preceding era (the earlier years of the Victorian period) saw "informal empire," in which Britain virtually monopolized overseas commerce without the burden of colonial rule. After the exploration of the Congo by American newsman Henry M. Stanley (1874-77) revealed the wealth of Central Africa, the British seizure of Egypt in 1882 started the "scramble" for that continent, peacefully partitioned by the Berlin Conference of 1884-85. Then, after Russia commenced building the Trans-Siberian Railway after 1891, the powers shifted their attention to East Asia, threatening the partition of

China until halted by American sponsorship of the "open door," guaranteeing equal access to Chinese ports.

The climax of Western imperialism was reached by 1890-1905, when the backlash by the "subject peoples" saw the Italian defeat at Adowa in 1896, Britain's trauma of the Boer War in 1899-1902, and the amazing Japanese defeat of Russia by 1905. The South African struggle halted British expansion, spurred Hobson's criticisms, and forced England's ententes with France in 1904 and Russia in 1907. By this time, the British empire consisted of "settlement colonies," dominated by white peoples in various stages of self-rule, such as Canada, Australia, and New Zealand, along with "tropical colonies" in Africa and Southeast Asia with native majorities. Australia and New Zealand had received "dominion status" by 1907, the year this designation was first used, granting them complete autonomy. This move away from the mother country stemmed greatly from their fear of Japanese expansion, echoed dramatically at the Imperial Conference of 1897. The Pacific dominions, therefore, veered more and more toward their own national defenses, while moving away from the empire's concerns, refusing to accept the mother country's assurances from the Anglo-Japanese Alliance of 1902. Tropical areas, in contrast, such as India, Malaya, and some African regions, ruled by officials appointed by the Colonial Office, were considered incapable of self-rule. France distinguished her "vielles colonies" (Algeria, the Antilles, and Réunion, departments of France herself) from her later-acquired West African and Indo-Chinese territories, governed by the Colonial Ministry. The former were "citizens," while the latter were designated as "subjects," although all stood in various stages of evolution to becoming Frenchmen themselves.

The First World War totally reversed the tide of imperialism. Europe lay mortally weakened. The passing of the world's financial capital from London to New York signaled the demise of the old "Eurocentric world." Oswald Spengler's *Decline of the West* (1918) warned of the rise of the Oriental races. Liberal ideology from the seeming triumph of democracy served to discredit the empires. President Woodrow Wilson's Fourteen Points, although referring primarily to the oppressed of Eastern Europe, ostensibly promised national self-determination to all subject peoples. Britain pledged eventual self-rule to India in 1919 by the Montagu-Chelmsford Reforms, the first of the nonwhite colonies to receive this, while France made political concessions to the Moslems of Algeria. A new era of "responsible rule" attempted to establish benevolent administration over the subject peoples. The "mandate system" that resulted, created the institution of "trusteeship" under the League of Nations, which established self-rule as the ultimate goal for the former colonies of the German and Ottoman empires. Now, the major powers could no longer treat their colonies as mere booty; instead, international surveillance established a new spirit of paternalism.

This policy brought about "indirect rule," which placed control of local administration in native hands as part of a policy of colonial education in self-government. During the interwar period, a native ruling elite arose, drawn from the upper classes, mostly in the rural areas. Educated in European universities, they imbibed liberal and often Marxist ideals. Margery Perham, the Laborite historian who lived for many years in East Africa, praised the colonial administration of these times. Lord Frederick Lugard's regime in Nigeria earned special commendation. Perham's book, *Colonial Sequence, 1930-1949* (1967), eulogized British rule as representative of the World War I transition from exploitation to patronization of colonial peoples. Some of the native elite later became spokesmen for independence, but since they did not derive from the common people, they never espoused extensive social reform. Instead, in the popular view, they became identified with the old established societies. Thus, in the post-World War II era of decolonization, they tended to yield the leadership of colonial nationalism to more radical elements, drawn usually from the urban proletariat.

Despite the general atmosphere of paternalism, "indirect rule" in many ways prepared the decline of colonization, especially in Southern Africa and Southeast Asia. Development of industry, mining, and agriculture stimulated commerce and the growth of cities without appreciably raising living standards for the great majority. Within urban environs, there developed a new proletarian class with its attendant social problems. This soon joined with the growing working classes on the farms and in the mines to agitate for social change. Grievances derived from racial inequality, forcible troop recruitment, confiscation of native property, and economic subservience to the mother country. Colonial administration represented perpetuation of the old social status quo. New nationalist leaders, drawn from the cities, especially from the liberally inclined university-educated elements, assumed the leadership of a rapidly developing demand for autonomy and/or political independence. Thus, paradoxically, progressive methods of colonization helped conceive decolonization itself.

Another product of World War I, international communism, played its part as well. Young bourgeois intellectuals from the colonial areas—Chou En-lai, Liu Shao-chi, and Li Ta-chao of China, Ho Chi Minh of Indochina, Mohandas K. Gandhi of India, and Jomo Kenyatta and Kwame Nkrumah of Africa—imbibed Marxism in the West or in the Soviet Union itself. V. I. Lenin hosted the "Congress of the Peoples of the East" at Baku in 1920, where he proclaimed a popular crusade against Western imperialism to assembled delegates from the oppressed of Asia. His offer of Soviet military and technological advisers was accepted notably by China's Sun Yat-sen, Mustafa Kemal of Turkey, Shah Riza Khan Pahlavi of Persia, the Wafd party of Egypt, and later Morocco's Abd'-el-Krim'. Sun proudly proclaimed in 1923, "We no longer look to the West. Our faces are turned to Russia." But Soviet attempts to capture the subject peoples failed when Sun's soldier-successor, Chiang Kai-shek, purged Soviet advisers from the Chinese Nationalist party in 1927 to prevent a Communist coup. Two years later, Mustafa Kemal also broke with the Soviets, as moderate groups, often supported by the West, retained control in most colonial areas. Temporarily, the USSR now turned away from international communism to concentrate on its own First Five-Year Plan in 1928. Nevertheless, the attraction of Marxism to the intellectual classes of the underdeveloped world could not be denied. As a significant example, the movement to the Left away from Confucianism and Western liberalism in Chinese universities had helped establish the Chinese Communist party (CCP) in 1921.

Britain responded to the mounting intensity of colonial nationalism by creating the British Commonwealth of Nations in 1931. A rather loose, federal-type of structure, it was bound together by common allegiance to the Crown. One of its founders, General Jan Christiaan Smuts of South Africa, described the Commonwealth as a "procession," consisting of "a large variety of communities at a number of different stages in their advance towards complete self-government." The dominion Parliaments claimed equality with the body at Westminster, with the tropical colonies in various degrees of subservience. Although the dominions reasserted their allegiance to Britain, tied to the mother country by their racial affiliations, the tropical colonies did not develop an equal affinity despite Christianity and British political institutions. Where civilizations had been long established, such as in China, India, or Moslem North Africa, nationalism had flamed with the appearance of the first Westerners in the nineteenth century. Elsewhere, the reaction was long delayed, as with sub-Sahara Africa. There burgeoning populations slowly created land hunger as a social aggravation, while native religious revivals sharpened racial antagonisms against Westerners. Europeans, on the other hand, tended to disregard the nationalism in these underdeveloped areas, because so often the tropical colonies were the artificial creations of some local administrator. Yet these political entities often cut across tribal lines, thereby straining nationalism all the more. Thus, once again colonization prepared its own antidote. The West had shaped the world to its image and therefore aroused its nationalism—"the bitterest enemy of imperialism and perversely its finest fruit," in the words of American historian Rupert Emerson.

Should Britain grant self-government and perhaps dominion-status to her Afro-Asian tropical colonies? This question generated much heat in the interwar period, with India the focus. Although she advanced closer to "responsible rule" by another "Government of India Act" in 1935, she represented Britain's greatest colonial problem and soon became a model for the tropical colonies. There were many British statesmen who opposed this trend for India. Winston S. Churchill, former First Lord of the Admiralty, led a group of "die-hards," who feared the effect of India's separation on both the security of the empire and debt-ridden Britain. He was supported principally by former Conservative Prime Minister Austen Chamberlain, Lords Salisbury and Birkenhead, and the former High Commissioner for Egypt, Lord Lloyd, all members of Churchill's "India Defence League." Others, like Lord George Curzon, viceroy of India from 1898-1905, positioned themselves even to the right of Churchill, urging forceful repression of "agitators."

Other Britons presented another opinion, reflecting their country's exhaustion from the war and its "overextension" in addition to a sincere humanitarianism. Lord Irwin (Halifax), viceroy of India from 1926 to 1931, spoke boldly in support of that country's dominion status. Anti-imperialists like Geoffrey Dawson, editor of the *Times*, and Philip Kerr (later Lord Lothian and ambassador to the United States)of *The Round Table*, argued for the political education of colonials for the eventual creation of "coloured dominions" in a new "multiracial Commonwealth." "The desire for self-government is essentially healthy," Kerr wrote in 1925. These opinions slowly gained ascendancy.

As Britain moved through the 1930s, the country was ceasing "to believe" in the empire, in the words of historian A. J. P. Taylor. The changing moral climate of the depression, Marxist criticism, and the steady liberalization of colonial policies pushed things along. By 1939, most Britons reluctantly admitted that virtually all overseas possessions were entitled to eventual self-rule, even as they nostalgically clung to the empire. There could not be one political standard for the West and another for the East, or one for whites and another for nonwhites, as India served to keep alive the question of extending dominion status to the "coloured territories." There seemed to be ample time to bring these changes about in an orderly, constitutional manner. But World War II would shatter this projection by greatly accelerating events.

Like the Napoleonic imperium, which inspired the Latin American wars for independence, the Second World

War demolished the *raison d'être* of European empires like castles of sand. The humiliating fall of France inspired formation of national groups in Indochina and North Africa, where Field Marshall Erwin Rommel's dramatic victories blasted the illusion of Western European superiority. Japan's rapid conquest of Southeast Asia in just five months completed this devastation, especially by the capture of the "invulnerable" fortress of Singapore on February 15, 1942, probably Britain's greatest defeat of the war and "a milestone in the process of decolonization," in the words of historian Rudolf von Albertini. Probably most appalling was the reluctance of the native populations, many of whom welcomed the Japanese as liberators, to defend the British position. A shock wave of self-criticism charged throughout the empire. When the Japanese ravaged Southeast Asia for its oil, tin, and rubber to facilitate a rapid victory, the peoples looked to independence, not a restoration of the European empires. When the war turned against them, the Japanese set up national governments throughout the region. At their departure, the Japanese declared these countries independent, undoubtedly to disrupt the European return.

The war contributed additional factors to future decolonization. Allied idealism, like the "four freedoms" of the Atlantic Charter (August 1941) as well as the principles of the new United Nations' organization promised emancipation of oppressed peoples. Also, contributions by colonial forces to Allied victories, as with the Australians in North Africa, the Canadians on D Day, and Filipinos in the reconquest of their islands, made the continuation of empire seem morally unjustifiable. Her colonials had seen Europe's "soft spots" at firsthand. Military duty overseas, foreign travel, and personal contacts bred new expectations and prompted postwar political activity.

Likewise, Britain's association with her antiimperial allies, the United States and the Soviet Union, jolted the colonial structure. The USSR dedicated itself to the obliteration of Western imperialism, while President Franklin D. Roosevelt, a disciple of Woodrow Wilson, opposed empire on principle. The American executive clashed frequently with the "die-hard" Prime Minister Winston

Churchill on the colonial question. Roosevelt pressured Britain to place her tropical colonies under United Nations trusteeship and to set definite timetables for independence. The continuation of empire posed a greater potential for future war than international communism to the American liberal. Churchill fired back that "he had not become the king's first minister to preside over the liquidation of the British Empire," late in 1942. A product of the Victorian period, Churchill viewed the empire as essential to world stability and World War II as another of those once-a-century British struggles (since the age of Philip II) to preserve the balance of power. However, the world tour of former presidential candidate Wendell L. Willkie after August 26, 1942, placed the United States against the old imperialism, favoring "one world" dedicated to political freedom.

The British and American views clashed in the Far East especially. Roosevelt urged Churchill to return Hong Kong to China to strengthen her situation in the postwar balance of power in East Asia and was especially critical of British policy in India. But the prime minister remained adamant. Lord Malcolm Hailey, former viceroy of India and noted authority on colonial policy, patiently explained to the president's advisers that references to the American Revolution were quite irrelevant to Britain's colonial problems. The home secretary, Herbert Morrison, compared ultimate freedom for the underdeveloped areas to presentation of "a latch key, a bank account, and a shotgun" to a child of ten. In fact, the British regarded American antiimperialism as only a cloak for their own expansion. When the United States seized Japan's Southwest Pacific islands after the war, refusing any international supervision, Britain accused the Americans of creating a new "informal empire" of their own. The American scholar, William Roger Louis, holds that United States and Russian anticolonialism definitely inclined Britain to release her empire, while encouraging colonial nationalists, but that it was "the awareness of changing times" rather than demands from Washington and Moscow that prompted the British to decolonize. Nevertheless, Britain's alliances with the United States and the Soviet Union hobbled the empire. British historian Bernard Porter likens this to entrusting stolen property for safekeeping to a policeman, who is reluctant to return it afterward.

Roosevelt's death in April 1945, and Churchill's defeat the following July placed the fate of the empire in different hands. Clement Attlee, the new Labour prime minister, whose colonial views were a complete departure from Churchill's, adopted United Nations trusteeship as the best way to colonial emancipation. Attlee perceived that Britain no longer could retain the empire on its traditional basis, because the postwar international power alignment had turned against her. Naval strength had built the "formal empire" after 1870, but the advent of air power and the atomic bomb made it impossible to preserve it in the future. The defense of the empire in the recent war had enormously overburdened Britain while disclosing the Mideast and India as its main stress points.

Although the Labour party had not expressly endorsed colonial separation during the interwar period, the anti-imperialist Fabian Colonial Bureau and Socialist League within its ranks now forced it in this direction. As followers of Hobson, the Fabians and the Socialists espoused the economic argument. Favoring their views, Attlee sought to grant immediate dominion status to the mature colonies, India, Burma, and Ceylon, while relinquishing the Palestine mandate, but to require other tropical colonies to undertake long periods of preparation, under Britain's trusteeship, before self-rule could be granted. London would determine the timetables. The Colonial Development and Welfare Act (1945) set aside special funds for medical, educational, and agricultural reforms in those areas. Trusteeship appealed to a cross-section of the parties. Labour accepted it because it promised eventual colonial liberation, while many Conservatives acquiesced because it enabled Britain to retain the empire somewhat longer. But Attlee and his followers could not realize how the passion of colonial nationalism would soon render trusteeship obsolete and its schedules unworkable by compelling British departure before power transitions could be made effectively. This situation often left the former colonies without sufficient education for the responsibilities of freedom.

The period of decolonization after 1945 divides into two

distinct eras. From 1945 to 1950, the powers freed those colonies already on the verge of independence, mostly in South Asia and the Mideast. Then following a pause of six years, another time span from 1956 to 1965 saw decolonization essentially completed largely in Southeast Asia and sub-Sahara Africa.

The pressure of colonial nationalism caused India's separation in August 1947, to proceed much too quickly, leaving her with mountainous social and political problems. The endemic quarrel between Mohandas K. Gandhi's Congress party, demanding immediate independence, and the Moslem League of Mohammed Ali Jinnah, which pressed for separation from a Hindu-dominated India, had torn the interwar period. Churchill long had resisted Indian demands and refused to be intimidated by Gandhi, that "half-naked fakir." The Japanese conquest of Burma, however, forced Churchill to dispatch Sir Stafford Cripps, prominent Labourite, in April 1942, with an offer of dominion status for India. This was refused, with a demand for independence. After the war, the Attlee government tried to mediate between Moslems and Hindus, but soon grew weary of the harangue, much of which accused Britain of insincerity. London suddenly announced in early 1947 that final separation would take place in one and one-half years, and appointed Lord Louis Mountbatten, former commander of the wartime China-Burma-India theater, to oversee the transfer of power. The withdrawal deadline provoked a scramble among India's leaders for position in the new state, aggravating nationalist quarrels and forcing events off schedule. Mountbatten was coerced to grant partition and a revised date for independence (August 15, 1947). Conservative critics charged that the establishment of a departure date, before any final agreement was reached, deprived Britain of all bargaining power. Inflamed nationalism compelled Britain's hasty departure, and separation produced many tragedies, depriving hostile Hindus and Moslems of British mediation, and left a legacy of political and social problems, especially a population growth-rate already out of control. Churchill ranted at this "clattering down of empire," even though Britain's acquiescence retained India and the new Moslem state of Pakistan for the Commonwealth.

India's independence, however, acted as a model for other British tropical colonies, for it admitted the first "coloured dominion" to create the "multiracial Commonwealth." General Smuts, Lord Halifax, and Prime Minister John Curtin of Australia, its principal sponsors, envisioned it as a model of racial cooperation to the rest of the world and a bridge between East and West. Participants enjoyed membership in the "sterling bloc," individual citizenship while in Britain, and common commercial policies. The multiracial Commonwealth helped Britain to prepare psychologically for the period of decolonization to follow, leaving her in a better position than France, the Netherlands, Belgium, or Portugal in this regard. Von Albertini speculates that a Churchill government might not have shown sufficient flexibility for colonial separation that Labour had accepted, although more rapidly than projected. The way to dominion status or self-rule now lay open to the tropical colonies, but the hope of its founders that the multiracial Commonwealth might become a "third force" in the world between the American and Soviet blocs proved ultimately disappointing. Nevertheless, the new organization did provide a cushion for Britain in the departure of her empire by rendering this transition less abrupt.

Burma and Ceylon followed India's example but took different paths to independence. Burma had attained "semi-self-government" by World War II, but the conquering Japanese installed a nationalist government headed by U Aung San, head of the militant "All Burma Students' Union" in the 1930s, dedicated to independence. With reconquest in 1944, the British found this group well-entrenched. Churchill's government refused to deal with it, although Lord Mountbatten urged conciliation. The Burma White Paper of May 1945, promised dominion status but set no date. Although Labour finally admitted U Aung San to the government, failure to accommodate his nationalists fully lost Burma for the Commonwealth when she attained independence in 1948, despite the leader's assassination that year. Ceylon's liberation, on the other hand, represented a model of British constitutional evolution. Because she had not been subjected to Japanese occupation, her moderate native elite administrators remained in power, unlike the Burma situation. Hence, Ceylon opted for Commonwealth membership the same year. But in Burma's case, London succumbed to nationalist pressure and allowed herself to be pushed too quickly once again, leaving Burma with overwhelming social and political difficulties. In addition, Britain wanted to retain colonial goodwill, derived from India's independence.

Many of the mistakes of early decolonization magnified themselves in Britain's surrender of the United Nations mandate over Palestine in June 1948. Departure left hostile Arabs and Israelis deprived of their mediators. Creation of the new Jewish state, the product of the Zionist Movement, the Balfour Declaration of 1917, and Jewish emigration from Nazi Germany, created a hated relic of Western imperialism within a Moslem world. Numerous Palestinian Arabs were deprived of their lands, leaving a Mideastern "running sore" to the rest of mankind. British withdrawal, accomplished in haste so that the parties could solve their own problems, also deprived her of ready access to Mideastern oil, an increasingly intensifying economic problem. However, with Indian, Burman, and Ceylonese independence, and with the erection of the new Israeli state (which foreswore the Commonwealth), the first stage of British decolonization came to an end with the release of those areas that could be held no longer.

Whereas Britain strove for the political evolution of her colonies to eventual self-rule, tied to her through the Commonwealth, France sought a close "assimilation" of her overseas possessions in a "Greater France." Her "vielles colonies," established in the seventeenth and eighteenth centuries, already were departments of France herself with representation in the assembly of the mother country. Herbert Luethy, the Swiss scholar, attributes much of this practice to the French historic absorption of Roman, barbarian, and Nordic elements. The Normans then brought this cultural amalgam to England, southern Italy, and to the Mideast when the Crusader states were established after 1099. French culture had proved its benefit to mankind by the universalism of the Age of Louis XIV, the Enlightenment, and the French Revolution, and her colonies shared in these traditions. Even the "subjects" of the nineteenth-century colonies, West Africa and Indo-china, were gradually becoming Frenchmen themselves in a supranational "Empire of one hundred million." These latter areas had been acquired, however, to redress the power balance against Germany after the war of 1870-1871, as espoused by Premier Jules Ferry, who pointed to the new empire as evidence that France still enjoyed front rank among the nations. An influential minority of French nationalists, with elements of the military and the church, and a few businessmen, backed the empire, but with little popular support. The factors of power and prestige proved the *raison d'être* of the empire, not economics. The colonies supplied the mother country with raw materials, but their few manufactures were kept out by tariff barriers, an old mercantilist practice. Little was done for colonial peoples themselves. French overseas officials measured progress in terms of road building and administration. Advance for the colonial lay primarily in the army, hence the prestige of the Foreign Legion. For the influential minority backing the empire, however, the colonies' role in World War II as the base of French resistance after defeat in Europe proved their value.

When Algerian delegates demanded independence in 1947 from the assembly, the French reaction was disbelief that they wanted actual separation. Surely no one could fail to grasp the benevolence behind "assimilation." Perhaps this view explains the determined French resistance to the liberation of Indochina up to the final disaster at Dien Bien Phu in 1954 and to the independence of Algeria, conceded in 1960. This last overthrew the Fourth Republic and brought General Charles de Gaulle to power with a new colonial policy. "Assimilation" proved an anachronism. It succeeded with the "vielles colonies," but its attempt to absorb millions of Indochinese and West Africans of the later empire would have produced more and more French political paralysis. Decolonization came violently to France, because "assimilation" afforded much less preparation than Britain's multiracial Commonwealth.

Despite the French example, the Dutch proved themselves even more inept for the separation of Indonesia in 1949, despite the war in nearby Indochina and liberation of Burma and Ceylon. Rule by the old East India Company had nurtured a native elite administration since the seventeenth century, stressing economic development, but there was no popular political participation until creation of a representative Volksraad in 1922. Little modernization was achieved under government policy called "light compulsion." Education lagged badly; fully 93 percent of the populace were illiterate in 1941. Oil interests contributed little to needed social services. The Japanese installed a Republic of Indonesia in 1944, composed of radical nationalists headed by Achmed Sukarno. The returning Dutch found this regime well entrenched but would not recognize it until 1947, all the while trying to detach the island of Java. When this effort failed, the Dutch attempted a "police action" in the large cities, actually a disguised military intervention. At this point, the United States intruded to compel another Dutch recognition of native independence a year later, finalized in 1954. Almost total Dutch rigidity in the matter of separation produced a result divorced from their interests, similar to the French experience.

The Americans, adhering to their World War II anticolonial policy, had forced the Dutch from Indonesia and at the same time tried to discourage restoration of the British and French empires in Southeast Asia, freeing the Philippines themselves in 1946. Their antiimperialism, however, presented a dilemma to the Americans, whose European allies were the principal imperial powers. Faced with this dichotomy, the United States was destined to forfeit its somewhat favorable image in the eyes of the emerging nations through its "loss of China," which also canceled what was left of European interests in East Asia.

After the Japanese conquest of Manchuria in 1931, the United States by default assumed defense of the European "treaty ports" and the "open door" in China. Many in Britain especially urged the Americans forward to oppose Japan, while London tried conciliation. Sir Robert Vansittart, chief diplomatic adviser, sought to appease Japan, because Britain could not oppose the Japanese and Nazi Germany together. Neville Chamberlain, chancellor of the exchequer after 1931, led a movement to revive the Anglo-Japanese Alliance. Following Pearl Harbor, the powers officially withdrew their treaty rights in 1943 in agreement with Chiang Kai-shek's Nationalist government, which the Americans supported.

The Communist victory in China by 1949, however, completely drove American and European interests from the Asian mainland, diplomatically isolating the United States and China until President Richard M. Nixon's visit in February 1972, and official United States recognition in January 1979. In the meantime, American support of "military dictatorships," such as Taiwan, South Korea, and South Vietnam on China's frontiers, discredited the American image with many of the former colonial peoples. Professor John K. Fairbank points out that these actions convinced the Chinese to identify the old treaty system with the Americans, grown rich by their following in the wake of nineteenth century British imperial policy. United States participation in the Korean War (1950-53) hardened this conviction of the Chinese, who, thereupon, moved forward as potential leaders of the "Third World," now a popular term for the emerging nations.

Following collapse of Western influence in China, something of a pause ensued for the years 1950-56, representing a hiatus in the progress of decolonization. In this interim, twenty-nine of the emerging states met in conclave, hoping to form a new international bloc that could balance the American and Soviet spheres. President Sukarno hosted the conference at Bandung, Indonesia, April 18-24, 1955. Premier and Foreign Minister Chou En-lai of the People's Republic of China utilized his considerable charm and acumen in an attempt to capture the allegiance of the Third World, but the many divisions prevented any lasting agreements. Resolutions condemned colonialism and the arms race, but no significant pronouncements were forthcoming. An informal cooperation in the United Nations General Assembly resulted, however, soon to be dominated by the emerging nations, while Chou En-lai developed considerable rapport with Asian and African leaders. Subsequent group meetings at Cairo and Belgrade did establish the category of "nonaligned nations," but joint policies could not be concluded. Although devoid of concrete accomplishment, the Bandung Conference did at least represent "the coming of age of the Asian and African states," in the words of President Carlos P. Romulo of the Philippines.

The second era in the devolution of colonial power commenced in 1956, to climax about 1965. Egyptian President Gamal Abdel Nasser's nationalization of the Suez Canal in July 1956, provoked a British-French armed seizure of that waterway. Recalling the lesson of unchecked aggression from the Hitler period, Prime Minister Anthony Eden's action stemmed from pressure by a Conservative segment, which wanted to halt the disintegration of empire to retain some of Britain's overseas interests. Surprisingly, the United States joined the Soviet Union to sponsor a United Nations condemnation of the takeover, forcing Allied withdrawal, and transforming Nasser overnight into a Third World hero and foremost leader of the Arab peoples.

Nasser's action triggered a new period of colonial separation, primarily in sub-Sahara Africa and Southeast Asia. London found colonial administration increasingly difficult in the face of mounting agitation at home and abroad. Also, as parts of the empire fell away, other areas lost their significance. For example, with the elimination of the German threat to the Indian Ocean, Britain's concern for eastern and southern Africa began to wane after World War II. Once India separated in 1947 and the Suez Canal was lost in 1956, her interest in both Africa and Southeast Asia diminished even more. As Professor D. K. Fieldhouse explains it, empires often formed interlocking systems. When some elements were removed, others lost their strategic significance. Lastly, business groups frequently managed to retain some of their economic assets by reaching agreements with the rising states. These interests now looked to the European continent, soon to organize into the Common Market, to make up for what they lost, more or less resigned to the departure of the colonies.

Nasser's defiance, along with the freedoms gained in the northern sections of the continent, inspired independence movements in Southeast Asia and sub-Sahara Africa. Several British colonies in Southeast Asia became the Federation of Malaysia on September 16, 1963, consisting of Malaya, Singapore, Sarawak, and North Borneo with Singapore separating to form its own state in 1965. Following the Japanese conquest of that area in World War II, sub-Sahara Africa assumed a new importance for its cocoa, palm oil, cotton, diamonds, tin, and bauxite. Modernization, however, had produced new industries, growing cities, social mobilization, and a definite political awareness. A West African Students' Union saw birth in Nigeria early in the war, while such Western-educated nationalists as Jomo Kenyatta of Kenya, Hastings Banda of Nyasaland, and Kwame Nkrumah of the Gold Coast organized similar groups, masking often as community leagues, youth movements, and trade unions in the growing urban societies. In Britain, however, the Conservative group that had inspired Eden's seizure of the canal sought to slow devolution of the colonies by strengthening Britain's hold on southern Africa, still economically profitable, in an effort to preserve something of Britain's world position. They also hoped to transform the multiracial Commonwealth into another "informal empire," in which Britain could retain many of her commercial interests, no longer burdened with political administration. Their ambitions collided head on with the program of Nkrumah, especially, who personified the urban, semi-sophisticated nationalist of the West African towns, despised by the British residents as "babu" or "wogs."

Attlee's Labour government administered the Gold Coast under United Nations trusteeship, based largely on Margery Perham's suggested policy of "benevolent paternalism." This called for a painstaking political education in local government, drawing administrators again from the moderate rural tribesmen, hardly representative of majority opinion. Self-government would not be attained until at least the end of the century. Nkrumah protested this policy. When the British arranged elections for a representative assembly in 1948, riots erupted in Accra, and Nkrumah was jailed for his agitation. Surprised at this upheaval, the British summoned Lord Malcolm Hailey, who warned his government to prepare for immediate decolonization in most of sub-Sahara Africa by promoting new educational programs, economic development, and nationalist participation in central government. The year 1948, therefore, saw a major change in British policy. Three years later dominion status was granted and Nkrumah made prime minister over a ruling council. But London's lack of sufficient preparation was evident in face of the collapse of trusteeship. Although the independent state of Ghana emerged in 1957 (with membership in the Commonwealth), making Nkrumah a hero to southern Africa, his country was not ready to stand alone, a recurring theme in decolonization. Monstrous economic problems eventually forced his overthrow by a military coup in 1966. Yet Nkrumah had hurled a thunderbolt into the realm of sub-Sahara Africa.

Tom Mboya of Kenya shouted, "Europeans, scram out of Africa." Seemingly the African's time had come, but that determined group of British Conservative MPs still attempted to salvage something of their interests by promoting white settler groups as centers of ruling power. Their efforts totally failed. The Conservative government of Harold Macmillan and especially Colonial Secretary Iain Macleod overruled their colleagues and began separation. Nigeria emerged independent in 1960, but with a Moslem-Christian question still unresolved, while Uganda was freed the following year. Jomo Kenyatta, leader of the fierce antiwhite Mau Mau tribe, led Kenya to freedom in 1963, while Tanganyika combined with Zanzibar to form Tanzania a year later. Special problems occurred in the case of ascendent white minorities. South Africa's ruling "Afrikaners," descendants of the original Boers, dominated the black majority by the "apartheid" policy of racial segregation. The Commonwealth so criticized South Africa on this issue that she resigned from the organization to become independent in 1961. Rhodesia separated from the new republic of Zambia in 1963 to become independent two years later under Premier Ian Smith, again because of Commonwealth criticism of her racial policies. She symbolized a final stronghold for those last imperialist Conservatives. Thus, Britain was "hustled and harried" out of sub-Sahara Africa and Southeast Asia in the 1960s but generously supplied technical and other advisers, when the new states later found themselves unprepared for the problems of independence.

France separated easily from the rest of her African possessions in total contrast to her experiences in Indochina and Algeria. French West Africa and French Equatorial Africa dissolved into Senegal, Cameroon, Togo, Ivory Coast, Gabon, and others, while Madagascar became the Malagasy Republic between 1958 and 1960. The Belgian Congo, on the other hand, presented another example of freedom gained too soon. Despite a native standard of living higher than most of her neighbors and a commendable economic development, the Congo barred the professions to blacks. Nationalists like Patrice Lumumba and Joseph Kasavubu pressured for independence, forcing a sudden Belgian withdrawal in 1960. Civil war tore the land for the next five years as natives quarreled over political issues and the inclusion of the industrial province of Katanga. United Nations intervention and return of Belgian advisers helped restore order, achieved under the military regime of Colonel Joseph Mobutu, who adopted the name Zaïre for the new state.

By 1965, Portugal was left with the largest overseas empire, a return to the situation of the sixteenth century. Mozambique and Angola represented large holdings in Southern Africa, relics of the slave trade, along with Macao on the China coast, a holdover from the opium traffic. Somewhat like France, she permitted her European colonials and those of mixed blood to become citizens of Portugal herself as "assimilados." Native peoples, however, were barred until 1954. As the modern world's oldest colonizer, the Portuguese sought primarily to impregnate less fortunate races with the "blessings" of Western Christian civilization. Their administrative corruption and constant financial difficulties, however, frequently made the colonies the subject of German and British partition schemes in the late nineteenth century. Portuguese administrators were amazingly unprepared for decolonization after World War II, calculating they were somehow immune to nationalist eruptions around them. When Antonio Salazar's government was overthrown in 1974, the new military government granted independence to Angola, Mozambique, the islands of São Tomé and Príncipe and the Cape Verde Islands. They offered Macao to China but were refused in 1977. Angola's independence immediately invited a Cuban invasion, under Russian sponsorship, soon answered by the influx of American and Chinese advisers. Angola threatened to become another Belgian Congo and an arena for great power competition as her price for independence without sufficient preparation.

Although a phenomenon still in progress, decolonization witnessed completion generally by the mid-1970s, leaving Europe politically what she was geographically—only a peninsula on the great Eurasian continent. Today Britain retains only Hong Kong "east of Suez," besides Gibraltar, and a few scattered islands throughout the world, totaling less than a million inhabitants. France holds the islands of Martinique, St. Pierre, and Miquelon; Belgium and the Netherlands have lost their empires, while Portugal keeps principally Macao. K. M. Panikkar, the Indian scholar, stresses that decolonization reflected the ephemeral superiority of sea power vis-à-vis the great land masses of Asia and Africa, whose people were resentful especially against the subordination to which they were subjected by the West.

Therefore, by way of summary and in answer to the five questions posed at the beginning of this essay, many aspects of colonization prepared for separation, especially the processes of modernization: growth of industry, mining, commerce, and modern cities, producing social mobilization and an urban proletariat. As Rupert Emerson put it, "Imperialism forged the tools with which its victims could pry it loose." From the new working class sprang the Western-educated native intellectual, who soon became the spokesman for colonial nationalism. He fed upon much urban and rural discontent, roused by land seizure, forcible conscription, racial discrimination, and economic subordination.

Also, we have observed that American (and Soviet) anticolonialism during World War II lessened Britain's determination to retain her empire while encouraging colonial nationalists, but her realization that the empire's time had come proved more significant. Professor von Albertini tells us that Roosevelt's agreement at Yalta to exclude the British tropical colonies from trusteeship tended to solve that issue with Churchill, sealed by the former's death and the latter's electoral defeat in 1945. The Labour party's acquiescence in decolonization was actually more decisive than opposition from Washington or Moscow.

India's independence in 1947 proved decisive to colonial separation, because it opened the Commonwealth to the tropical colonies. Her entrance, as the first "colored dominion," gave that organization a "multiracial" character. Like Canada for the settlement colonies, India became a model for the tropical areas. Thus, Britain created her "fourth empire," after the commercial and colonial empire of the "Age of Discovery" which terminated in the American Revolution, to be succeeded by the "informal empire" based on world commercial supremacy, and finally the "formal empire" after 1870 which territorially expanded to an area equal to the continental United States.

True, the multiracial Commonwealth did cushion Britain for the trauma of decolonization, but it proved only a thin disguise for the wholesale loss of the empire. Once the colonies had separated, the extent of British economic decline since 1870 became more apparent, because only an outdated, shopworn industrial machine remained, long shielded by the empire. As Bernard Porter expresses it, the empire had acted as a wrapping around a naked and sick body. From that point Britain turned to economic cooperation with the European continent. On the other hand, the new Commonwealth failed as a substitute for empire, for there was little real unity. Too much time was wasted castigating the mother country for past "exploitation," and the multiracial Commonwealth never produced that international "third force" to balance the American and Soviet spheres.

Colonial nationalism probably proved a greater factor in imperial devolution than Western acquiescence, although these components are like opposite sides of the coin. American historian Raymond F. Betts acknowledges the decisive role of both causes, but decides in favor of colonial nationalism, whose fury demolished opposition. The West beheld the French bloodlettings in Indochina and Algeria as prime examples of the economic and moral strain that European resistance to this floodtide would have caused for the former colonial powers.

Mistakes abounded during decolonization. Most significant, however, was the Western failure to prepare adequately for separation, although Europeans could not have remained longer in face of national resistance. Once leaders obtained freedom, like true revolutionaries, they had no clear idea of what was to follow. Often they invited Western advisers to return, giving rise to the charge of "neo-colonialism," what the British liberal and anti-colonialist Fenner Brockway defines as "the persistence of imperialist penetration despite achievement of self-government." The Communist world castigated American policy particularly with this charge, especially during the Vietnam War, along with United States support of West Germany, Israel, and Japan, as well as patronage of NATO, foreign aid, and the Peace Corps. Britain's creation of Malaysia in 1963, Belgium's support of Tshombe's Katanga succession, and French intervention in Gabon were European targets, as well as such figures as King Hussein of Jordan, President Chiang Ching-kuo of Taiwan, and President Park Chung Hee of South Korea. Yet the great economic disparity of the developed and underdeveloped countries makes Western assistance mandatory for the former colonials. No capable Third World leader seeks a return to his nation's past; participation in the modern world makes this impossible. An era of "international philanthropy" is required as East and West need each other, but old antagonisms die hard. However, the new policy enunciated by Deputy Premier Teng Hsiao-p'ing of the People's Republic of China in 1978 to turn openly to the industrial countries for technological assistance may signal the beginning of a change in Third World attitudes. Should this be so, perhaps we may yet see Emerson's projection borne out: that imperialism may be regarded in the future less for oppression and more "as the instrument by which the spiritual, scientific, and material revolution which began in Western Europe with the Renaissance was spread to the rest of the world."

Suggested Readings

Decolonization is still in progress in the late 1970s and the literature on it, although burgeoning, is somewhat tentative. For essential background, see J. A. Hobson, *Imperialism: A Study* (1902) and V. I. Lenin, *Imperialism: The Highest Stage of Capitalism* (1916). Likewise, Joseph A. Schumpeter's assault on the economic interpretation,

Imperialism and Social Classes (1951) should be consulted, as well as William L. Langer, *The Diplomacy of Imperialism* (1960). D. K. Fieldhouse has challenged Hobson, Lenin, and their followers in *The Theory of Capitalist Imperialism* (1967), and *The Colonial Empires* (1966). The classic article by Ronald E. Robinson and John A. Gallagher, "The Imperialism of Free Trade," which attacked the traditional periodization of the Age of Imperialism by showing the expansionist continuity between Britain's "informal" and "formal" empires, is in *Economic History Review*, 2nd series, vol. VI, no. 1 (1953), pp. 1-15. William Roger Louis, the American scholar, edits a cross-section of historical opinion on this Robinson and Gallagher controversy in his compendium *Imperialism* (1976). The student should also see Harrison M. Wright (ed.), *The New Imperialism: Analysis of Late Nineteenth Century Expansion*, (2nd ed. 1976) and Raymond F. Betts (ed.), *The "Scramble" for Africa: Causes and Dimensions of Empire* (1966), in the D. C. Heath "Problems" Series, as well as Betts' essay *Europe Overseas* (1968).

Decolonization really begins with World War I, and Dame Margery Perham gives a favorable view of "indirect rule" in Africa during the interwar period in *Colonial Sequence, 1930-1949* (1967). Herbert Luethy presents a fascinating interpretation of French colonialism in *France Against Herself* (1955). Also see K. M. Panikkar, *Asia and Western Dominance* (1969), which skillfully describes the effects of separation.

On the World War II era, see William Roger Louis, *Imperialism at Bay: The United States and the Decolonization of the British Empire, 1941-1945* (1978).

For the period after 1945, which witnesses actual colonial separation, see Rudolf von Albertini, *Decolonization: The Administration and Future of the Colonies, 1919-1960* (1971), and Rupert Emerson, *From Empire to Nation* (1960). Fenner Brockway presents a liberal view in *The Colonial Revolution* (1973), while I. Robert Sinai's stimulating *The Challenge of Modernization* is valuable from another perspective. Hugh Tinker, *Ballot Box and Bayonet* (1964) is a brief, but useful work on the emerging Asian nations, while John K. Fairbank describes the effects of American contacts on a resurgent China in *Chinese-*

American Interactions: A Historical Summary (1975). Bernard Porter's popular work *The Lion's Share: A Short History of British Imperialism, 1850-1970* (1975) is good on the causes and effects of British decline. A. P. Thornton, *Imperialism in the Twentieth Century* (1978) is an extended essay on the whole subject.

Finally, Tony Smith edits another volume in the D. C. Heath "Problems" Series: *The End of European Empire: Decolonization After World War II* (1975), a useful compilation of historical opinions on the subject.

Foreign workers neighborhood in Marseilles. The graffitti reads: "Immigrant workers all to the demonstration. . . ."
(Philip Chiviges Naylor)

CONCLUSION

Europe in the 1970s and Beyond

Thomas E. Hachey

European society entered the 1970s with a profound feeling of uncertainty about the future. Indeed, what appeared to be at stake was not the primacy or even the prominence of European culture but rather its very survival. Since the times of the Renaissance, the commercial revolution, the rise of nation-states and the age of exploration and colonization, Europe's cultural and economic hegemony throughout the world both endured and expanded. The industrial revolution of the late eighteenth and nineteenth centuries would have assured European global dominance for another substantial period had it not been for several intangible but no less powerful contemporaneous phenomena, most notably nationalism and, later, socialism. In 1914, however, European imperialistic ambitions and nationalistic rivalries which had heretofore clashed at remote distances in colonial theatres now spilled across homeland frontiers and convulsed the continent in a horrendous and costly war. Few realized at the time that this conflict had unleashed forces which would lead directly to the imminent decline of the European world order, and to the corresponding succession of such non-European powers as the United States, Japan, and the Soviet Union to positions of new prominence and influence in the world. What World War I had begun, the Second World War would complete and, despite the Marshall Plan and a phenomenal economic recovery in the years that followed, Europe's preeminence was certainly eclipsed in an age of superpowers and her future was clouded at best.

It was not so much a feeling of despair as it was a sense of urgency which obsessed most Europeans as they warily embarked upon the closing decades of the twentieth century. Earlier maps and referents regarding state, society, and economy were no longer viable nor pertinent in this perplexing age of transition. Western industrial societies were propelled into an era of multinational corporations, politico-economic cartels and unprecedented social upheavals further complicated by the influx of foreign laborers. Not surprisingly, government leadership often proved unequal to the new challenges as statesmen felt themselves left suddenly without guideposts or compasses on journeys whose way stations and destinations were no longer familiar. And change was as complex as it was profound. No single event could satisfactorily account for the radical alterations in what had been the reasonably familiar patterns of European life. True, the massive consequences of the energy crisis had had a pervasive and sobering effect, but the mounting spirit of anxiety in Europe had begun even before that shattering experience. While the prosperity of the 1960s could indulge the luxury of youth assuming a stance of alienation from a system which both subsidized and cushioned those same righteous rebels against financial shock, the 1970s could not. Economic realities compelled young and old alike to recognize the absurdity of thundering against the materialism of a consumer society when the very survival of society had become more than merely a rhetorical question. Prosperity could no longer be taken for granted as the backdrop against which to enact the drama of protest. The impotence of the state in its desperate attempt to defeat "stagflation," particularly the effort to control food and fuel prices, cast an ominous pall over the plans and expectations of most Europeans.

Meanwhile, as confidence in governmental institutions was steadily eroded, there were predictable experiments with, or expressions for, alternatives which were sometimes rational and, occasionally, radical. Disillusionment with the "system" manifested itself in attacks against schools and government-run social services, the very institutions once considered vital to all schemes for social reform, while a high premium was then placed upon what were essentially market instruments, such as vouchers for "free" schools and a negative income tax. Big government became as much the object of contempt and suspicion as big business, as evidenced in the mounting attack on centralization. Paradoxically, at the very time when statesmen from the nine member European Economic Community (Common Market) were seeking to eradicate obstacles to a pan-European economic entity which might possibly serve as a precursor to a trans-national political body, the doctrine of separatism was spreading among restive elements of the continent's population. Demands for Welsh and Scottish home rule resounded at Westminster, and kindred voices were raised amongst the Flemings and Walloons in Belgium. Bretons demonstrated in France and, in Spain, Catalans conducted strikes while Basques resorted to outright terrorism. Still more fearsome secessionist activity appeared to loom in the future of Yugoslavia where an enforced confederation threatened to dissolve upon the passing from power of a venerated octogenarian leader, Josip Broz (Tito). Political devolution constituted the very antithesis of every supranationalist ideal since Woodrow Wilson's cherished League of Nations. Yet, it was becoming a desirable alternative for people who were frustrated by their inability to influence decisions of impersonal and remote administrations on issues affecting the quality of life.

More violent forms of protest were in evidence from Portugal to Scandinavia as students, socialists, and various groups of political agitators took to the streets where their confrontation tactics guaranteed them media exposure and notoriety if nothing else. For this new generation the old categories of "Left" and "Right" often were rendered irrelevant. The most common and least privileged of the people were generally conservative, while the upper-middle bourgeois class was frequently quite radical. During the 1968 riots in Paris, for example, it was the workers and the Communists who defended the Gaullist state against the inflamed and economically privileged student protesters. Similarly, in the United States that same year, laborers fought pitched battles with "radical chic" revolutionary types from the affluent suburbs over such incidents as the desecration of an American flag. New theorists of the Left soon despaired by changing the antirevolutionary tenor of the working class, just as Karl Marx earlier had been disgusted by the essential conservatism of the peasant, and an elitist revolutionary role was substituted for class action. In such circumstances, it is hardly surprising that a virulent strain of political extremism should have suddenly surfaced in European society.

Anarchism was not a new phenomenon on the continent and, except for a heroic interlude during the time of the Spanish Civil War, it had seemed to have run its course in the era immediately preceding World War I. But the anarchist way of life and thought erupted once more on the European scene with frightening intensity during the late 1960s, as well as in the decade that followed. The contemporary anarchist groups included men and women, usually in their twenties or thirties, who were often university-educated people from affluent upper middle class families. What these anarchists shared in common with their kindred spirits of an earlier age was an emphasis of spontaneity, a doctrinaire insistence on "purity" of motive, and absolute distinctions between ideological good and evil. Whether it was the Baader-Meinhof gang executing a businessman after the West German government refused to capitulate to ultimatums, or the Red Brigades levying the same penalty upon a former Italian head of state when the authorities ignored demands to release imprisoned Brigade comrades, the contemporary anarchists did not argue the merits of their position: they proclaimed them. And it seemed of little importance to the modern anarchist whether "the people," in whose name the acts of terrorism were often undertaken, approved or even understood the alleged motives for such behavior.

Value orientation and beliefs comprise another area in which the assumptions and structures of European industrial societies have recently shifted. Universities first felt the shock waves as student populations, far larger and more diverse than ever before, challenged traditional practices and agitated, often violently, for change. Throughout Western and Central Europe in the early seventies, student militancy was on the rise, typified by such demands as expanded curricula and power sharing in university administrations. And nearly everywhere the official response to the revolts followed a common pattern: an initial period of dismay and shock, followed by concessions to the more moderate student demands. In West Germany, where individual states rather than the national government financed and supervised higher education, the situation understandably differed widely from place to place. Some universities remained comparatively calm throughout the crisis years while others, notably the Free University of Berlin, became almost completely politicized and dominated by radical elements. Elsewhere in Europe, the intensity of the student movement reflected the contrasting pace of changing values or mores within different societal institutions. In France, for instance, family life had been apparently democratized far more rapidly than the values that underlay the behavior and expectations of teachers, and perhaps for that very reason the *lycées* and universities in that country promptly became new arenas of political conflict.

Indicative also of the spirit of the times was the women's movement which developed in most of Europe less rapidly than in America during the seventies. But, again, the nature of the protest, which most often took the form of seeking progressive legislation in the areas of sexuality and the family life, varied considerably across the continent. Sexual permissiveness and equality in Scandinavia actually went further than in the United States, while in Spain more traditional and conservative attitudes endured. Between these northern and southern geographical and moral extremes there existed a variety of gradations; and among the Catholic populations of Latin Europe, restraint characterized the tone of reform. Nevertheless, on sexual matters the Roman Catholic Church seemed no longer to maintain a monolithic stance. Although Pope Paul VI unconditionally opposed any change on the subject of contraception, as did his two immediate successors

227

in 1978, many of the clergy expressed ambivalence or openly adopted more flexible positions. Contraception, of course, constituted a less inflammatory issue than did abortion; and it was over the latter controversy that a major battle developed in France during 1971. Several hundred of that nation's outstanding women in the arts, literature, theater, and the cinema lent their support to a campaign against France's antiquated legislation on abortion. The law, which dated back to 1920 and reflected the national concern over the declining birth rate in the aftermath of the First World War, made it a criminal act to perform or to undergo all such operations. The trial of a French teenage girl who was prosecuted under that same law in 1972 aroused the ire and indignation of women liberationists, intellectuals, and leaders of the medical profession alike. Only after the election of a new president, Valéry Giscard d'Estaing, the appointment of two women cabinet members, and many months of protracted and acrimonious debate did the National Assembly, in 1974, finally pass a bill legalizing abortion during the first ten weeks of pregnancy.

Not even the most theocentric societies were immune to the winds of change which swept Europe in the 1970s. The Catholic and conservative Republic of Ireland not only retained laws against contraception and abortion, but also against divorce. Clerical influence in politics had long been customary in Ireland but by the seventies both church and state were a trifle embarrassed by the "special position" accorded the Roman Catholic Church under the 1937 Irish Constitution. The bishops, as well as the Dáil Éireann leadership, at least exhibited a consciousness of the need to shed the reactionary image of a clerical state when both supported the removal from the Constitution of the partisan clause pertaining to the Church, although the effect may have been merely cosmetic. Meanwhile, in Italy, reformers succeeded in passing an extraordinarily cautious law in 1970 which allowed for the possibility of divorce after a five-year waiting period. But the Christian Democratic party and the Catholic hierarchy perceived even that procedure as entirely unacceptable and the issue was ultimately decided in a referendum held in May 1974. The Italian voters proved less traditional than their church and political leaders and defeated the move to repeal the divorce law by a majority of 60 percent. Indeed, to a certain degree, the acceptance of divorce in Italy and of contraception and abortion in many other European societies signaled the final triumph of the old doctrine of individual rights. And it is a measure of the complexity of the times that this should have happened at a period when, under the combined pressures of environmental and resource problems, many were coming to believe that individual choices would have to be more constrained than ever before for the sake of collective survival.

Cutting across these shifts in mass attitudes were other factors which underscored the intrinsic relationship between changing values and beliefs on the one hand and commitments or loyalties to institutions of governance on the other. In France, for example, the rising levels of protest by marginal economic groups cannot be sufficiently explained without an appreciation of how the shift from a parliamentary to a presidential regime promoted new avenues of collaboration between certain interest groups and the bureaucracy. These new avenues diminished the role of the parties and of other interest groups. Not unnaturally, groups that found themselves suddenly excluded from the bargaining and representation system comprised, in turn, new and major sources of unrest. Similar realignments of parties and interest groups, owing to a wide variety of reasons, were apparent in Scandinavia where the electorate's enthusiasm for the social welfare state became more muted in the 1970s, and also in Britain where nationalization over a period of a generation had altered many of that society's pluralistic components.

Still another dimension to the socio-political strains and pressures of the decade was the plight of foreign workers throughout Western and Central Europe. By 1974, the number of aliens working in the nine nations of the recently expanded Common Market was more than double what it had been a decade earlier. Counting families, their number approximated ten million people. The greatest concentrations were in France, where nearly two million foreigners constituted 8 percent of the total working force, and Germany, where two and a half million people similarly represented 8 percent. Outside the EEC, Switzerland, with about a million foreigners, contained the highest proportion of aliens of any European country. The chief source of immigration to France was Moslem North Africa, from which came a million or more people from the same Arab countries which Paris had once governed in colonial days. Portuguese, Italians, and Spanish, in that order, also comprised a substantive part of France's alien labor force. In Germany, another Moslem people, the Turks, were most numerous, followed closely by the Italians. Problems of social adjustment in circumstances such as these doubtlessly were inevitable, especially since non-Europeans accounted for so large a percentage of the immigrant workers. The strangeness of language, religion, custom, and manner incited fear and aroused hostility amongst the native European populations. As in England, where immigrants by the tens of thousands from the former Asian and African colonies of the British Empire sought a new life for themselves and their families, the alien worker throughout continental Europe did the hard labor and held the menial jobs that the native-born scorned. And nearly everywhere, they occupied substandard housing in miserable industrial age ghettos.

What was at best an uncongenial situation for the foreign laborer was exacerbated by the economic recession of the mid-1970s. The prosperity of the sixties had nearly removed anxieties over unemployment from the public consciousness, but the severity of the economic situation in the seventies changed peoples' once optimistic attitude and outlook. It was perhaps only natural that country after country should try to close its doors to further arrivals while also seeking the deportation of those illegal immigrants who lacked work permits. In late 1973, five of the Common Market countries declared a general ban on immigration by non-Community citizens and, a year later, Switzerland held a referendum to determine whether half of the aliens already in that country should be compelled to leave. The referendum was defeated, largely because of the efforts of opponents who advanced humanitarian reasons and the pragmatic consideration of the indispensability of the foreign workers to the national economy. But such referenda, successful or otherwise, portended an uncertain future for the immigrant laborer.

In much the same way as the previously noted realignments of constituencies and pressure groups had posed problems of adjustment for different governments and interests, the alien represented, however unwittingly, an element of change within the work force. And that fact earned for him the dislike, if not the outright hostility, of the labor union leadership. The latter were soon to realize that for European unions the old incentives, sanctions, and other forms of control operated far less effectively as more and more of their clients were foreign laborers with only temporary links to the society in which they worked. This circumstance placed yet another strain upon the restive European working class during a decade in which economies struggled to overcome the alternating blows of recession and inflation.

In this era of changing values and beliefs, religion continued to be an important dimension in the lives of millions in Europe but, on the continent that was the historical home of Western Christendom, the general attitude toward faith was destined to change in the aftermath of the Second World War. The secularization of European life had progressed incrementally for more than two centuries, during which time religion had shifted from the center to the periphery of social concern. Functions once performed by the church were assumed by secular agencies, but that was essentially an institutional change which did not necessarily denote a decline in belief. Indeed, individuals in the nineteenth and twentieth centuries perhaps have been more personally "religious" than those in the eighteenth, as the practice of faith in modern times ceased to be a matter of universal custom and has become instead a conscious and private choice. There were, as ever, scientific positivists, or philosophical atheists like Jean-Paul Sartre, who continued after 1945 to insist upon the irrationality of religion. They were in turn followed by antireligious or irreligious fads, such as the "God is dead" cult of the sixties, or the believers in *homo novus*, the "new man" concept, perhaps best symbolized in the early seventies by French critic Jean-François Revel's book, *Without Marx or Jesus*. Until the 1960s, however, churchmen were more likely to be influenced by such current but essentially traditional religious thinkers such as the

Catholic writer Gabriel Marcel or the Jewish sage Martin Buber. European Protestant circles were still dominated by followers of Karl Barth's dialectical theology, while the teachings of Reinhold Niebuhr and Paul Tillich exerted a kindred influence over divinity schools in the United States. Then, suddenly and unexpectedly, clergymen and laity alike felt the shock waves of reform and change which were reverberating through other societal institutions.

A sense of both crisis and opportunity pervaded Christian churches as quasireligious communes and cults proliferated on the fringes of the youth culture in the 1960s, whose members expressed manifest spiritual yearnings and sought religious gratification in various forms of occultism. Clergymen were at first uncertain over how to respond to such radically new conditions but after brief periods of hesitation many of them did embrace "modernism" and the "religion of relevance." Eager evangelicals from the Anglican, Roman Catholic, Methodist, and scores of other Christian churches, promptly substituted the mantle of ecumenicism for that of sectarianism, as they embarked upon their common quest for peace and universal justice. The religious militancy in evidence throughout much of the Western world in the 1960s and early 1970s became particularly prominent in South America. Argentina's professedly revolutionary *Movimiento de los Sacerdotes para el terces Mundo* was estimated in the early 1970s to number as much as a fourth of the clergy among its supporters. Brazil contained a similarly large and active segment of revolutionary priests, including an archbishop, all of whom preached a message of hate and rebellion against the Yankee capitalist and other foreign imperialists. In Europe, Protestant theologians modified traditional Christian doctrines to the extent that they very nearly became indistinguishable from such ideological beliefs as socialism. And progressive Dutch and German Catholic theologians assailed so many tenets of Rome's teachings that in May 1972, the Vatican weekly, *L'Osservatore della Domenica,* complained that these attacks were often "graver and more offensive than even Protestant authors would dare to make."

Indeed, the Church of Rome was still attempting in the

late 1970s to put the brake on a spirit of religious liberalism and reform which the church itself had partly initiated a decade and a half earlier. It was Pope John XXIII's extraordinary 1963 encyclical on liberal thought and social action in the church, and the Vatican Council which opened under that same pontiff in 1962, which initially moved the church toward its self-proclaimed goal of *aggiornamento*, or "renewal," and institutional reform. Elsewhere, some American blacks were converting to Islam while some European youths aspired to Buddhism. Arnold Toynbee, author of the monumental work, *The Study of History*, (1954) led many in supposing that out of the mingling of cultures and disintegration of Western civilization would come a global faith which would include elements of all the major world religions. But in fact, as Roland Stromberg has pointed out in *After Everything* (1975), the trend was toward more diversity and less unity than ever before, with a strong preference being exhibited for individualized religious or ideological styles. It soon became apparent that even the revolution of expectations inspired by Vatican II was far less substantive than supposed. The leadership of the Roman church became more international and masses in the vernacular were authorized. Yet, efforts to go much further, to give national or regional church councils autonomous authority, for example, or to abandon the celibacy of the priesthood, have been firmly resisted by Pope John's immediate successors, Pope Paul VI, and Popes John Paul I and John Paul II. Hence, even while demonstrating impressive adaptability, the church, like other Western institutions, tended to slow the process of change, carefully weaving the new into the old social fabric.

In an age which saw the erosion of institutional authority, even communism, the "official" secular religion which supplanted Christianity in Russia in 1917, and in much of Central and Eastern Europe after 1945, felt the restless and relentless clamor for change. The Russian Communist party pursued an intensive policy of repression against those same forces of change, especially before the death of Stalin in 1953 when the crudest of party bureaucrats served as overseers of the arts. With Nikita Khrushchev's assumption to power in the Soviet Union, a new cultural and intellectual climate appeared to be emerging from the emptiness of the Stalinist era. In 1956, at the very time that revolts against the Communist state were occurring in Poland and Hungary, Vladimir Dudintsev published *Not by Bread Alone* which argued that Russian writers should be free of ideological restraint, while also attacking bureaucracy in state and party. The limits of Soviet toleration, even under Khrushchev, however, were made dramatically apparent when the 1958 English-language edition of Boris Pasternak's *Doctor Zhivago* brought its author international fame and a Nobel Prize for literature. While Pasternak was not forbidden to travel to Stockholm to accept the prize, it was clear that to have done so would have resulted in his permanent exile. Pasternak declined the award since, as he explained in a letter to Khrushchev, to live in exile abroad was quite unthinkable. The author died in early 1960 and, for a time, the cultural "thaw" and the spirit of dissent in Russia seemed to have perished with him.

But the social ferment of the sixties and seventies transcended even the iron curtain and new voices of protest echoed from the Communist heartland. Ironically, it was Nikita Khrushchev who inadvertently assisted the rise to prominence of Russia's most notable literary rebel, Alexander Solzhenitsyn. Khrushchev authorized the publication of Solzhenitsyn's *One Day in the Life of Ivan Denisovich* in 1962 as part of the Kremlin's effort to discredit Josef Stalin. But Solzhenitsyn continued his eloquent indictments of Stalinist terrorism even after the fall of Khrushchev in 1964, although his books *The Cancer Ward* (1966) and *The First Circle* (1968) had to be smuggled out of Russia and published abroad. At home, these works were secretly circulated among the Soviet intelligentsia. When, in 1970, like Pasternak before him, Solzhenitsyn learned that he had been awarded the Nobel Prize for literature, he too declined to journey to Sweden and accept the award for fear of being exiled. Unlike Pasternak, however, he acknowledged the honor by issuing a public and condemnatory attack on the lack of free expression in his own country. His final rupture with the Soviet regime came at the end of 1973 with the publication in Paris of

The Gulag Archipelago, a documentary history of the horrendous labor camps of the Stalinist era which far exceeded Khrushchev's earlier exposé. Alexander Solzhenitsyn soon became for many, both in and outside Russia, the very symbol of resistance to the Soviet leaders who were, afterall, the heirs of Stalin. The sheer volume of his accomplished literary production won him a world reputation, and he was compared to Tolstoy—whom he admired and sought to imitate. In early 1974, as he doubtlessly had anticipated, Solzhenitsyn was arrested and sent into exile aboard an airplane bound for West Germany. Even the Kremlin, which had not hesitated in 1966 to order the trial and imprisonment of Andrey Sinyavsky and Yuly Daniel for far less provocation, was not inclined to jeopardize East-West detente in 1974 by the rash treatment of the leading dissenter against the Soviet system.

Perhaps even more noteworthy for Europe were the schisms which began to appear during this era of change in the seemingly once monolithic Communist movement. Communist Yugoslavia had defied Stalin after the Second World War by adopting a "road to socialism" independent of Moscow. Albania became the next European heretic in the 1960s and joined with Communist China in condemning the Soviet Union for pursuing policies of reconciliation with the West and thus betraying the "have nots" of the world. Khrushchev was toppled from power in October 1964, when he began preparations for a world congress of Communist parties intended to be the instrument which would expel the Chinese for ideological treason. The more cautious party leaders, both in Russia and in her European satellite nations, feared the divisive consequences of such an expulsion. But nonetheless, the alienation between Moscow and Peking intensified in the years that followed, while in European Communist circles the worst fears of Khrushchev's successors were about to be realized.

In January 1968, Communist party leader Alexander Dubček began a process of liberalization in Czechoslovakia which took that country farther and faster along the path of liberal reform than any Soviet satellite had traveled in the entire post-Stalin period. After the Dubček government failed to respond to admonitions from Moscow, Russian troops and soldiers from four other Warsaw Pact nations occupied Czechoslovakia in a swift and bloodless move on August 21, which led to the dismantling of the Prague reform movement. Soviet party secretary Leonid Brezhnev later declared, in a speech delivered that November in Warsaw, that the invasion was justified on the grounds that when socialism was threatened in one country, other socialist nations were similarly imperiled and thus had an obligation to respond accordingly. That rationale, which soon became known as the "Brezhnev Doctrine," was promptly challenged not only by Western Communist parties but also by still another assertive satellite nation, namely Rumania. Eastern Europe, from Warsaw to Bucharest, once Moscow's indisputable ideological preserve, began by the 1970s to respond to long dormant elements of unrest which brought the region closer into tandem with the more sweeping changes underway on the rest of the continent.

If the homogeneity of the Communist parties in Eastern Europe seemed, by the seventies, to be mildly contaminated by varying degrees of revisionism, the mood of their ideological comrades in Western Europe was often openly defiant of Moscow's wishes. Western Communist parties, anxious to win political respectability within their native countries, publicly challenged Moscow's prosecution of Soviet historian Pyotr Yakir, just as they later protested the harrassment of Soviet physicist Andrei Sakharov and his fellow dissenters. For its part, the Kremlin denounced the independent posture of the Western parties as a "betrayal" of Marxist principles. What soon became known in the West as Eurocommunism may have caused the Russian party leadership at least as much concern as the greater latitude some of the satellite nations were seeking in the management of their own affairs. The Communist party in France toyed with the prospect of joining a Socialist coalition in order to participate in that country's governance, while in Italy the role of the Communist party was sufficiently consequential in national elections to make participation in the ruling Christian Democratic coalition government all but inevitable in the none too distant future. Yet, much as Russia might genuinely resent the independent tone of these Western parties, and publicly condemn the abandonment of revolutionary principles in favor of parliamentary tactics, the Kremlin perhaps did not find these developments entirely uncongenial. There was for Moscow, if nothing else, the satisfaction of knowing that the imminence of Communist ministers in Western European cabinet governments was causing intense concern over problems of secrecy and security in Washington and in other NATO capitals. The swift undercurrents of change, afterall, were having an impact upon the political landscape of the West as well.

Public attitudes toward both domestic politics and foreign policy at the beginning of the 1970s were destined to alter traditional power structures and ideological mindsets of the preceding decades in Western Europe. In West Germany, for example, the cold war polemics of the Konrad Adenauer era were replaced by the policies of *Ostpolitik*. This quest for increased contact with the Communist governments of Eastern Europe followed the October 1969, election of Willy Brandt as Germany's first Social Democratic chancellor in nearly forty years. After negotiating a treaty with the Soviet Union which renounced the use of force in questions of European security, Brandt did what Adenauer had adamantly refused to do; he recognized the border along the Oder and Neisse rivers as the actual Polish-German boundary in his effort to normalize relations with Communist Poland. He also championed Britain's bid for admission into the Common Market and revalued the mark at a higher and more realistic rate which more accurately reflected Germany's true financial strength against the devalued British and French currencies. By 1973, however, inflation and unemployment, together with seemingly meager dividends yielded by the policy of *Ostpolitik*, contributed to a decline in Brandt's popularity. The discovery of a spy in his immediate entourage only a year later toppled him, but not the Social Democratic party, from power, and Helmut Schmidt succeeded to the party leadership and to the chancellorship. A tough-minded pragmatist, Schmidt doubtlessly reflected the new mood of caution and reduced expectations which typified the majority sentiment in West Germany toward either domestic or foreign issues. In the uncertain seventies, Europe's most affluent society had opted for a policy of playing it safe.

Elsewhere in Western Europe, the political outlook appeared no brighter. Following the death of French President Georges Pompidou in 1974, the Gaullist party remained the largest in the National Assembly but could offer no leader of real stature. Consequently, Valéry Giscard d'Estaing, the charismatic presidential candidate of the Independents, defeated the Gaullist and other candidates in the first round of a national election and then edged Socialist François Mitterrand by a margin of less than 2 percent of the popular vote in the subsequent run-off election. Giscard d'Estaing's political allies defeated his leftist opponents in the 1978 elections in which the Communists who polled 20 percent of the vote actually lost ground. The Left's defeat, however, was attributable not so much to the French president's popularity as it was to the rivalry and eventual alienation that developed between the Socialist and Communist parties in France. But victory at the polls did not resolve the country's worsening economic situation, and the inflation of the mid and late 1970s led to ever-rising prices and unemployment. Giscard d'Estaing was of course handicapped as a non-Gaullist working within the constitutional pattern of the Fifth Republic that had been devised for the needs of Charles de Gaulle himself. And like de Gaulle, Giscard d'Estaing retained his country's independent nuclear deterrent which, by the late seventies, amounted to little more than an expensive prestige gadget. Indeed, the French president issued a statement on November 21, 1978, which reflected the Americanophobic theme which was once a hallmark of speeches delivered by the late Charles de Gaulle. In it Giscard d'Estaing warned his fellow Common Market members that they must not be allowed to fall under the "excessive influence" of the United States. He further remarked, and this was the more noteworthy statement, that he would like to see the European Economic Community develop into a confederacy "in which no member state can impose its will on any other member." The French president's plaintive proposal was in itself a tacit admission that when it came to the really substantive issues of Common Market policy,

France might try harder but she remained a poor second in influence to West Germany owing to that nation's possession of Europe's strongest economy.

Across the Channel, the London government was struggling with even more somber financial problems. Britain, which a short time ago had been second only to the United States among advanced industrial nations, had fallen to next to last—just ahead of Italy. The June 1970, election of Edward Heath as prime minister, and the forty-three seat margin (330 vs. 287) in the House of Commons which the Conservatives won over Labour, showed that the voters were unhappy with the "stop-go" financial policies of the previous decade which had curtailed investment at home whenever a foreign balance-of-payments deficit threatened. Heath did successfully manage Britain's entry into the Common Market, the wisdom of which many of his countrymen questioned, but he proved unable to stem the tide of inflation with his scheme of mandatory limits on wages. The coal miners took advantage of the oil embargo and world fuel crises by striking for increased pay in the autumn of 1973. Confident that the country was behind him, Prime Minister Heath called an unscheduled election in February 1974. The results were not what the Conservatives had hoped, but neither were they conclusive. Labour emerged five seats ahead of the Conservatives, but still seventeen seats short of a majority and thus dependent upon the Liberals and militant Scot and Welsh "home rule" parties. Harold Wilson became prime minister once again but rampant inflation, bitter intraparty feuds among Labour leaders, and the failure of Britain's North Sea oil venture to provide a "quick solution" for the country's economic ills, led to his voluntary retirement from the premiership in 1976.

There was of course the potential for change in Britain when Queen Elizabeth II, in November 1978, opened what had to be the last session of the parliamentary body then in office. Under the statute requiring a general election at least once every five years, the British electorate was to be polled no later than October 1979. James Callaghan, who had succeeded Harold Wilson as prime minister and Labour party leader, chose the spring of 1979 to make his bid for reelection. Margaret Thatcher had already deposed

Edward Heath as Conservative party leader in 1975 and her fellow Tories held a respectable 281 seats in Commons to the Labour party's 312, which meant that Labour remained in power only with the help of the Liberals (13 seats) and other independent parties. Neither of the two major parties appeared to have any solution for the sectarian strife in Northern Ireland, the causes of which, in part, could be traced back to the Reformation. Some Tories did, however, support the Labour Government's scheme to hold referendums, in March of 1979, on the issue of local assemblies for Scotland and Wales as the first step toward devolution. But perhaps the most divisive issue remained the state of the economy. Prime Minister Callaghan pledged to carry on with his voluntary wage restraints, under which unions would limit demands for wage increases to a maximum of 5 percent. That stand was fiercely opposed by the eleven million-member Trades Union Congress and was also attacked by Callaghan's own Labour party at its annual meeting at Blackspool in October 1978. Conservative leader Margaret Thatcher condemned, as expected, Callaghan's "rigid pay policies" and called instead for "responsible" collective bargaining. Despite the acrimony, however, a sizable percentage of the British electorate appeared reasonably satisfied with Labour's success in reducing the 1978 annual rate of inflation to 8 percent. The fact that that figure could be viewed by so many as acceptable, at least when compared with the exorbitant inflationary rate of a few years earlier, suggests a notable adjustment in the national temper. Perhaps as Bernard Nossiter reasons in his book, *Britain: A Future That Works,* the United Kingdom is content with a legacy of less and harbors no ambition to keep up with the Jones's, or the Germans.

Any judgment on British complacency would be premature at this writing, however, for paralyzing strikes in the 1980s could cripple the economy and radically alter public opinion. Even as Callaghan's party, in early 1979, was repudiating his 5 percent pay-hike formula, workers in the public sector, from teachers to trash men, were vowing to push for raises of up to 40 percent. Voters perhaps reflected a national sense of apprehension over these developments when, in early May 1979, they gave Margaret Thatcher and her Conservative party a clear majority in the House of Commons.

Similar pulsations of popular unrest could be detected from the Baltic to the Adriatic during the late seventies as dissatisfaction with the management of the welfare state developed in Scandinavia while pro-communist and anti-Turkish demonstrations reverberated through Italy and Greece respectively. Additionally, European economies were rendered a staggering blow, as were western economies generally, by the OPEC nations' quantum jump in oil prices during late June 1979. That Europe and the West was moving toward the entrance of a new age was fast becoming, rightly or wrongly, a widely accepted belief. But on the subject of what lay beyond the threshold of that entry there was no consensus whatever and the speculations of experts varied between the extremes of cautious optimism and hopeless pessimism.

Prophets of doom were not novel to the 1970s. Oswald Spengler, in his 1918 publication, *The Decline of the West*, had prophesied the imminent demise of Western civilization. Ortega y Gasset's brilliant 1930 essay, *The Revolt of the Masses*, conveyed a somewhat similar theme of European decline from lack of creative leadership. Paul Valery's 1924 essay on the European malaise, entitled *The Intellectual Crisis*, and T. S. Eliot's even more famous 1922 poem, *The Waste Land*, are in this same spirit. Aldous Huxley, *Brave New World* and George Orwell, *1984* (1949) are two of the more popular antiutopian novels which, in the thirties and forties, predicted the perpetual imprisonment of man by the banalities of technology in a totalitarian world. Succeeding decades witnessed the growth of existentialism and other philosophies of despair. It was, therefore, in harmony with a time-honored tradition that Robert Heilbroner published in 1974 a book entitled *An Inquiry into the Human Prospect*. Heilbroner concluded that the only long-term solution to the world's troubles lay in the abandonment of "the lethal techniques, the uncongenial life-ways, and the dangerous mentality of industrial civilization itself." Meanwhile, he foresaw a grim struggle for survival, accompanied by a resort to authoritarian governments and consequent curtailment of political and intellectual freedom.

It is, however, somewhat precipitous to write the obituary of the Western or, indeed, the European age. Over the last hundred or more years, Western society has tended to address many of its social needs on the assumption of ever-expanding prosperity, and on the premise of continued global dominance. Neither proposition is guaranteed to survive even this century. Non-Western societies are more likely in the future to resemble the West in ideology, social organization, and technology, thereby ushering in an age of unprecedented and unimagined possibilities. There will, of course, continue to be those voices of pessimism which warn of impending apocalypse. But in the light of historical experience, the stronger probability is that Western man, once he has comprehended the full implications of the changed or changing circumstances, will seek instinctively to adjust to them.

In any event, the oldest of Europe's ideologies is alive and well. Liberalism, which Ortega y Gasset once called "the noblest cry that had ever resounded on the planet," has shown new signs of vitality in the 1970s. It inspired the return to freedom in Greece, and gave new life to Portugal and Spain after the deaths of Salazar and Franco. Everywhere, whether in the cafes of Prague or on the streets of Moscow, one can sense that a powerful aspiration toward freedom remains. The survival of this spirit is perhaps more crucial than whatever shifts in goals and priorities or restructuring of institutions the contemporary crisis may ultimately require. Indeed, the nation state which so facilitated the transition from an agrarian to an industrial and urban economy may very well be an anachronism in the twenty-first century. Moreover, existing economic institutions may already be obsolete since industrial capitalism is not significantly closer today than it was fifty years ago to meeting basic human needs in an age of abundance. The essential problem of the technological era has not been one of sufficient production but rather one of adequate distribution. Whatever solutions the future may offer in resolving such anomalies and inequities, it seems not unreasonable that such answers will derive from and contribute to what is already a rich and varied Western tradition.

Suggested Readings

In place of footnotes, the following titles comprise the major references for this essay as well as additional suggested studies. The reader is advised to consult Suzanne Berger et al., "New Perspectives for the Study of Western Europe," in Social Science Research Council *Items*, Vol. 29, No. 3 (September 1975) for an imaginative disquisition on future directions in the study of European history. H. Stuart Hughes, *Contemporary Europe: A History* (1976) provides what is perhaps the most authoritative and readable general text on the subject while Roland Stromberg, *After Everything: Western Intellectual History Since 1945* (1975) is an eloquent and insightful analysis of contemporary European culture. An excellent presentation of revolutionary extremism is afforded by Frantz Fanon, *The Wretched of the Earth* (tr. 1966) while Christopher Booker, *The Neophiliacs*, offers an instructive commentary on the fragmentation of culture and the need for reintegration. Especially recommended from the ever-growing body of literature pertaining to future trends are R. Buckminster Fuller, *Utopia or Oblivion: The Prospects for Humanity* (1966) and Judith Shklar, *After Utopia: The Decline of Political Faith* (1957). Readers interested in the combined theme of anarchy and student unrest will find an engaging study in David Martin, ed., *Anarchy and Culture: The Problem of the Contemporary University* (1969); and for a representative work on revolutionary extremism, see Daniel Cohn-Bendit, *Obsolete Communism: A Left-Wing Alternative* (1968). A worthy sequel to Jose Ortega y Gasset, *The Revolt of the Masses* (1930) is Michael D. Biddis, *The Age of the Masses* (1977) which ranges widely over the fields of natural science, philosophical and religious thought, and social and political ideas. Lastly, for an entertaining collection of essays on the variety of modernisms generic to contemporary society, see Irving Howe, *The Decline of the New* (1970).

2187

D
443
E86   European traditions
in the twentieth
century

DATE			
OCT 0 7 1986			